India Studies in Business and Economics

The Indian economy is considered to be one of the fastest growing economies of the world with India amongst the most important G-20 economies. Ever since the Indian economy made its presence felt on the global platform, the research community is now even more interested in studying and analyzing what India has to offer. This series aims to bring forth the latest studies and research about India from the areas of economics, business, and management science. The titles featured in this series will present rigorous empirical research, often accompanied by policy recommendations, evoke and evaluate various aspects of the economy and the business and management landscape in India, with a special focus on India's relationship with the world in terms of business and trade.

More information about this series at http://www.springer.com/series/11234

Sony Pellissery · Benjamin Davy
Harvey M. Jacobs
Editors

Land Policies in India

Promises, Practices and Challenges

Springer

Editors
Sony Pellissery
National Law School of India University
Bengaluru, Karnataka
India

Benjamin Davy
TU Dortmund University
Dortmund
Germany

Harvey M. Jacobs
Department of Urban and Regional Planning
University of Wisconsin-Madison
Madison, WI
USA

ISSN 2198-0012 ISSN 2198-0020 (electronic)
India Studies in Business and Economics
ISBN 978-981-10-4207-2 ISBN 978-981-10-4208-9 (eBook)
DOI 10.1007/978-981-10-4208-9

Library of Congress Control Number: 2017937287

Printed on acid-free paper

This Springer imprint is published by Springer Nature
The registered company is Springer Nature Singapore Pte Ltd.
The registered company address is: 152 Beach Road, #21-01/04 Gateway East, Singapore 189721, Singapore

Foreword

Planning matters. Law matters. Property matters. These three simple messages inspire the growing PLPR community to examine the difficult relationships between public and private interests in the use of land.

This text introduces the home web page for the International Academic Association on Planning, Law, and Property Rights (PLPR, see plpr-association.org). Initial steps toward an academic association took form almost 20 years ago under the leadership of several interdisciplinarily inclined scholars, most notably Profs. Rachelle Alterman (Israel Institute of Technology), Willem Salet (University of Amsterdam) and Ben Davy (TU Dortmund University), through the creation of a track session at the Association of European Schools of Planning (AESOP) 1999 annual conference in Bergen.

These and other scholars then met at the 2006 World Congress of Planning Schools in Mexico City under the leadership of Rachelle Alterman and laid out a charter for the new PLPR. The association was formally established through an inaugural symposium in Amsterdam in 2007. It has since held annual conferences in 10 different counties (as of this writing), including European and North American locations, and it has enjoyed leadership representing 11 different countries, including European, North American, Australian, Asian, and Southwest Asian nationalities. It has also sponsored several regional conferences, and it regularly administers a PLPR track at the annual AESOP conferences.

The genesis of PLPR as an academic association was prompted by the need to fill a multi-dimensional—both multi-national and multidisciplinary—niche that had not yet been filled. PLPR began through and has maintained strong ties with AESOP, which is itself multi-national, but it has always been broader, pulling in scholars from North America, Australia, and Asia who do not regularly participate in AESOP events. Equally, if not more importantly, from its inception it has also been deeply interdisciplinary, residing at the intersection of scholarly work on planning, law, and property rights.

Planning, law, and (private) property rights necessarily implicate each other in any established system that involves an interplay between governmental and market institutions—which is to say virtually everywhere, especially in systems that engage capitalist economies dependent on well-developed and protected rights to private real property. Yet these three interconnected institutions are typically contemplated separately for ease of understanding and practice. Planners tend to focus especially on governmental planning, lawyers tend to focus especially on the legal mechanisms used to implement plans, and real estate economists tend to focus especially on the role of property rights in land markets (which are necessarily publically planned to some degree, even if conventionally thought of as free-market systems).

Scholars in each of these disciplines are of course mindful of the concepts and institutional considerations encompassed by the others, but the complexities and nuances presented by each make comprehensive study of the others especially daunting. Even so, the world is increasingly interconnected, and news of institutional arrangements, practices, and outcomes in one setting travels readily to others. In such a world, the need to more intelligently understand the interactions between planning, law, and property rights, especially within national, cultural, and spatial context, is all the more compelling.

PLPR was established to create a forum for bringing together and nurturing such deeply multi-national and interdisciplinary study. Its members include not only academics (and some practitioners) who are experts in their particular discipline but who also have real interest in better understanding more fully the nuances and implications of the others (as well as some members formally trained in multiple disciplines, e.g., planning and law, economics and planning). In addition to nurturing graduate students with this interdisciplinary bent, the association's core functions include the provision of a peer group of scholars and the promotion of cross-national and comparative perspectives on scholarly work at the intersection of planning, law, and property rights. As noted, PLPR does this primarily through the organisation of regular annual conferences, as well as by sponsoring more focused, regional conferences.

In addition to soliciting conference papers by individual authors (or collaborating authors) that address explicitly topics encompassing some combination of planning, law, and property rights, there are at least three ways to promote scholarly cross-national, comparative perspectives on the interplay between those domains. One is to facilitate the work of several authors who undertake a focused, in-depth comparative study of several distinct systems along two or more of those domains (see, e.g., Norton and Bieri 2014). Another is to facilitate the work of a larger number of authors who conduct a broader study on a larger collection of nationalities but do so on a more focused aspect of planning, law, and property rights, such as expropriation (see, e.g., Alterman 2010), or from a higher altitude perspective. The third is to facilitate the work of a larger group of authors from one or more countries who evaluate a single country in greater depth, doing so on a broad array of topics related to planning, law, and property rights as experienced by that country or relative to the experiences of other countries more generally. The work presented by this book is an exemplar of this third approach.

Several challenges confront multi-national, interdisciplinary study, including especially language problems—using the same words to mean very different things, or different words to mean the same thing; conceptual challenges that arise in attempting to transfer ideas generated in one national setting that are likely to morph as applied in a different setting; and conceptual biases that appear as scholars most familiar with the issues and concerns confronting their own national and cultural backgrounds attempt to characterize and evaluate the issues and concerns confronting those of another, or as scholars native to the country that is the object of study attempt to analyse and convey the issues and concerns of that country to scholars from others. One way to counter these inherent challenges is to facilitate face-to-face presentation and dialogue in a forum that allows collaborators to present their work, seek clarification, challenge assumptions, and altogether more fully comprehend the arguments and assessments of their colleagues. The work presented by this book, again, is an exemplar of such an effort.

As described more fully in Preface, this book presents a selection of papers drawn from presentations made at the first South Asian Regional Conference held by PLPR in September 2015 at the National Law School of India University, Bengaluru. Focusing on pressing policy challenges confronting India today, it brings to bear ideas, analyses, and insights that that can only come through cross-national, comparative work. These papers speak to a broad array of topics implicating planning, law, and property rights in India, given challenges confronting India that are unique to India and others that are more universal, including the social context of real property rights (focusing especially on the role of human rights and jurisprudence in grappling with contentious claims); concepts and debates related to land as commons; concepts and debates related to land markets; issues related to the public acquisition, use, and disposition of private land; and debates over the relationships between private property rights and public welfare imperatives (especially housing and environment).

This work represents an exciting addition to the scholarship that has been fostered by the establishment of PLPR, and it moves PLPR further toward its promise of facilitating and nurturing truly multi-national and interdisciplinary work at the intersection of planning, law, and property rights. I am delighted to recommend this compilation of compelling papers to you the reader.

Sincerely,

January 2017

Richard K. Norton
Professor and Chair
Urban and Regional Planning Program
University of Michigan, USA
President
International Academic Association on Planning, Law, and Property Rights

References

Alterman R (2010) Takings international: a comparative perspective on land use regulations and compensation rights. American Bar Association, Chicago

Norton RK, Bieri DS (2014) Planning, law, and property rights: a US-European cross-national contemplation. Int Plan Stud 19(3–4):379–397

Preface

India has 304 million hectares of land and approximately 256 million households (Census of 2011). From the point view of planning, law and property rights, three factors are important when attempting to establish a relationship between the land and people. First, the Indian subcontinent has 15 agro-climatic zones with quite varying physical attributes prevailing in those zones. The value of the land, and potential use of land, is thus hugely different throughout the country, and affects the occupations people can adopt. Second, India is a federal union where socio-political organisation of the Indian republic is through 29 states and seven union territories. This division is not primarily based on agro-climatic aspects, but rather based on language and culture. Therefore, within one regional state, more than one agro-climatic region is often found. These regional states were governed by local kings prior to colonisation of the country. Thus, customs and rules (both pertaining to property and otherwise) that prevailed in each of these regions are longstanding and continued in the post colonisation and post-independence era. These regional states make laws and policies pertaining to the governance of land. Third, India is a hierarchical society with social groups at the bottom of hierarchy having limited access to land. Most of the landless population (about 30%) and people who hold less than one hectare of land (about 50%) belong to lower caste and indigenous communities. Yet these people have special rights which are constitutionally protected. These three factors present a complex scenario for land policies in the subcontinent.

The papers included in this volume are based on presentations made at the First South Asian Regional Conference of the International Association on Planning, Law and Property Rights (PLPR) held during 1–3 September 2015 at National Law School of India University, Bengaluru. Commencing with an inaugural symposium in 2007 and one annual international conference each year, PLPR has developed into a leading venue for an academic exchange between spatial planners, land use lawyers, architects, surveyors, and urban and regional sociologists.[1] The regional

[1]For more information, please visit http://plpr-association.org/.

conference was funded by *Deutsche Forschungsgemeinschaft* (German Research Foundation), as closing conference of the FLOOR[2] subgroup on socio-ecological land policy. During the conference, 45 papers were presented. Papers that underwent a successful review process after the conference are included in this volume. The editors of the volume are fully cognizant that comprehensiveness of land policy scholarship is not present in this volume; no single volume could accomplish this. However, the papers included in the volume represent current strands of research in the domain and point out some of the emerging areas where empirical research is required. In the remainder of this preface, we provide a brief introduction to each of the papers included in this volume to facilitate readers' curiosity as they tread into the complex maze of Indian land policy issues.

Ever since the adoption of the Constitution in 1950, the question of land has been contentious. Though property rights were recognised as a fundamental right in the Constitution, through major court battles (between powerful landlords and the state that wanted to ensure distribution of land to landless population), this changed since the aims of land distribution could not be achieved when a liberalist interpretation of the fundamental right to land existed. The first two chapters of the volume relate to this question of the social content of property rights and legal routes to realise the social rights through land policies Chapter "Human Dignity and Property in Land—A Human Rights Approach" by Benjamin Davy asserts that some property rights have been recognised as human rights to respect and promote the inherent dignity of each human being. He examines the relevant human rights documents sponsored by the United Nations and points out why recognising property as human right is critical to the realisation of other socio-economic rights. Chapter "Evolution of Property Rights in India" by Madhumita Mitra examines the evolution of property rights through legal battles in Indian courts and resultant jurisprudence that has emerged in independent India.

Chapters "Postcolonial Evolution of Water Rights in India and the United States" and "Conflicting Interests and Intelligible Utilisation of Common Property Resources: A Study of a Tropical Wetland in South India" deal with the question of the commons. In Chapter "Postcolonial Evolution of Water Rights in India and the United States", Jesse Richardson shows how path dependency of policies is created through post-colonial structures. He takes the case of water rights in India and USA to empirically argue this case. Christabell in Chapter "Conflicting Interests and Intelligible Utilisation of Common Property Resources: A Study of a Tropical Wetland in South India" presents an alternative story. She examines the policies and programmes of a South Indian state towards wetlands and examines in detail the case of a lake. She points out how conflicts arise among multiple stakeholders over the use of common property resources. Both marginal communities and environmental values lose in this game.

[2]FLOOR is an acronym for Financial Assistance, Land Policy, and Global Social Rights. Publications and working papers of the FLOOR research group are available at www.floorgroup.de.

Chapter "Land Transfer Tax Policy Regime and Its Influence on Property Markets: Analysing the Land Transfer Tax Policy of Kerala in the Last Decade" by Nirmal Roy deals with the complex question of land markets. He takes the case of the state of Kerala and examines how changes to lax tax structure affects land prices and thus land markets. One of the major losses for the exchequer of the Indian state from land market is that people report nominal value for land in any transaction, while major chunks are exchanged between parties in non-taxable cash form (black money). In this context, this chapter examines the impact of lowering taxes for facilitating land markets. The study concludes that after a short spell of impact on land market through taxation changes, the status-quo is generally maintained.

During the period surrounding the conference, one of the intensely debated public policy issues was that of land acquisition. Chapters "Development or Disaster? Land Acquisition and Dispossession in the Mining Belts and Coastal Zones of Rural Odisha, India" and "The "Public Purpose" That Is Not Inclusive" deal with the question on land acquisition. Land acquisition laws formulated in 1894 by the British colonial regime are not viable for providing land for the development of industries. Though over 60% of labour force gains their livelihood from agriculture and allied activities, the agricultural sector contributed only 15% of GDP. Thus, policy imagination is focused on increasing the productivity of land by easing the land acquisition process and making such acquired land available for industrial investment. Chapter "Development or Disaster? Land Acquisition and Dispossession in the Mining Belts and Coastal Zones of Rural Odisha, India" challenges this view and argues how land acquisition for industries may be leading to displacement in mineral-rich regions. Chapter "The "Public Purpose" That Is Not Inclusive" explores this issue by addressing the assumption of 'public purpose' that is behind the land acquisition. In India, as in many countries, state power is weakened by social forces and private aims are advanced in the name of public purposes.

One of the biggest challenges that Indian land policy is due to tremendous urbanisation. This issue is the subject matter of Chapters "The Cyclical Interaction of Institutional Constraints to Formal Affordable Housing Market in Raipur, India" and "City in Crossfire—The Environment Versus Development Debate in Navi Mumbai". Farmers, particularly small famers, are leaving the land, and seeking livelihood opportunities in cities. The urban centric growth model has encouraged this trend. According to the census of 2001, there were 384 cities with a population of 100,000 or above (Class I Urban Agglomerations). The census of 2011 reported that the number of such cities had increased to 468. If we consider small towns (urban agglomerations that do not have the population size of 100 thousand) they total 53 million or 43%, of India's population. The gush of migration to urban areas has brought new pressures on housing, infrastructure and traffic. Chapter "The Cyclical Interaction of Institutional Constraints to Formal Affordable Housing Market in Raipur, India" by Aparna Vedula and Sarika Bodhankar deals with the dilemma of protecting the environment in contrast to the efficient building of infrastructure. The question of mangrove protection and discharge of industrial effluents into the water bodies creates problem for sustainable planning; this has lessons for other cities in India. As the paper shows, the planned city of Navi Mumbai reduced the congestion and provided better housing. Yet, are these houses affordable? In the context of bourgeoning property values in urban areas, this is a complicated question. Padmini Ram takes up this question in Chapter "City in Crossfire—The Environment Versus Development Debate in Navi Mumbai". She draws on her doctoral work based on the city of Raipur in the state of Chhattisgarh. She argues that as the housing demand increased, the state first privatised the housing sector which then led to inequities forcing the state to revamp its Housing Board. Within three years of public intervention, sufficient stock of affordable housing for the city was created.

As pointed out in the beginning of this preface, one challenge to land policy in India is the huge differences among regions and states on the one hand, and the differences between stated policies and actual practices. Chapter "Property Regimes in India: A Study of Political Determinants of Structural Factors" by Deepa Kailasam Iyer makes an attempt to understand the driving forces behind the variations among states. She points out how dominant social groups and occupational categories in particular states shape the land policies in those states.

The final chapter by two of the editors aims to connect the global discourses on land policies with the challenges faced by policy makers in India. Some of the challenges are not unique to India, for instance the global trend toward urbanisation and thus the importance of urban property issues and planning, or the need to have land records system for facilitating transactions. India has plenty to learn from global experiences on such issues. On the other hand, some of the issues such as how land inequality is created through historical social structures are unique, and the answers for them will need to come from within the country.

Bengaluru, India	Sony Pellissery
Dortmund, Germany	Benjamin Davy
Madison, USA	Harvey M. Jacobs

Contents

About the Editors

Sony Pellissery is Professor at the National Law School of India University, Bengaluru. After his doctoral studies at Oxford, UK he served as Associate Professor at the Institute of Rural Management, Anand for five years. He is involved in developing a Master's Programme in Public Policy at the National Law School of India University, Bengaluru. He is the recipient of Prof. G. Ram Reddy Social Scientist Award—2015.

Benjamin Davy is Professor of Land Policy, Land Management and Municipal Geo-information at the School of Spatial Planning, TU Dortmund University, Germany. He is essay editor of *Planning Theory* and member of the editorial boards of the *Journal of the American Planning Association*, *Planning Theory and Practice*, and *The Public Sector*. From 2010 to 2016, he was the Vice President and President of the International Academic Association on Planning, Law, and Property Rights. Ben Davy's areas of research include property theory, land policy, planning theory, and real estate evaluation.

Harvey M. Jacobs is affiliated to the University of Wisconsin-Madison, USA, where he holds a joint appointment as Professor in the Department of Urban and Regional Planning and the Gaylord Nelson Institute for Environmental Studies. He is also a Visiting Professor at Radboud University Nijmegen, Netherlands, and is a 2008 recipient of the L'Ordre des Palmes Académiques, awarded by the French Government. Professor Jacobs' academic specialty is the social and legal aspects of land policy, with a particular focus on property rights. Professor Jacobs has been invited to give lectures on his research and consult on aspects of his work in countries around the world, including in Africa, Asia, the Caribbean, Europe, and throughout North America.

Human Dignity and Property in Land—A Human Rights Approach

Benjamin Davy

Abbreviation of human rights documents

1975 Helsinki Final Act	Final act of the Conference of Security and Co-Operation in Europe
CEDAW	Convention on the Elimination of All Forms of Discrimination Against Women
CRC	Convention on the Rights of the Child
CRPD	Convention on the Rights of Persons with Disabilities
ECHR	(European) Convention for the Protection of Human Rights and Fundamental Freedoms
ECHR_P1	(First) Protocol to the Convention for the Protection of Human Rights and Fundamental Freedoms
ICCPR	International Covenant on Civil and Political Rights
ICERD	International Convention on the Elimination of All Forms of Racial Discrimination
ICESCR	International Covenant on Economic, Social and Cultural Rights
ICRAM	International Convention in the Protection of the Rights of All Migrant Workers and Members of Their Families
UDHR	Universal Declaration of Human Rights

The Supreme Court of India, in interpreting the right to life under Article 21 of the Constitution of India (1949), used a broad definition which linked life, human dignity, and minimal property: 'We think that the right to life includes the right to live with human dignity and all that goes along with it, namely, the bare necessaries of life such as adequate nutrition, clothing and shelter ...' (Justice Bhagawati in Francis Coralie v. Union Territory of Delhi, AIR 1981 SC 746). *The 2007* Global Report on Human Settlements *quotes this and other cases decided by*

B. Davy (✉)
TU Dortmund University, Dortmund, Germany
e-mail: benjamin.davy@udo.edu

S. Pellissery et al. (eds.), *Land Policies in India*, India Studies in Business and Economics, DOI 10.1007/978-981-10-4208-9_1

the Supreme Court of India to assert that '[h]ousing rights in India are an extraordinary example of practice departing sharply from law' (UN Habitat 2007: 158). The assertion is even more surprising because India belongs to a group of countries that reject the protection of property as a constitutional right. Land rights are a contentious issue everywhere, but in India, in 1955, the right to property as one of the fundamental rights (Article 36 of the Constitution of India) was repealed in order to facilitate nation-wide land reforms (Shea 1956: 1). The drastic measure, UN Habitat seems to think, has not been sufficient. Several chapters in this book deal with the evolution of property rights (Chap. 2), land acquisition (Chaps. 6 and 7), or housing in India (Chaps. 8 and 9). Chapter 1 introduces these chapters, yet not from an Indian perspective, but from the perspective of UN-sponsored human rights law and of political philosophy.

1 The World of Things and Citizenship of the World

We enter the world of things in different ways. Some want to read their names above the entrance of high-end real estate; others claim a marginal space from the commons to read their morning paper (Fig. 1). Perhaps we can appreciate that a person, who displays her name on her own tower or enjoys the funnies, feels to be a better person. However, we may also be disgusted by watching someone being obscenely self-centered or having to live rough. Access to the world of things does not merely define our status in the ownership society, but also speaks to our sense of decency or shame. Our sense of decency or shame is the link between human dignity and private property.

Figure 1 illustrates what Oxfam reports regularly claim: a connection between wealth and poverty that causes a vast and growing gap between the very rich and the poor (Hardoon 2017). But what constitutes the connection? Surely, there is not direct connection between a real estate tycoon in Manhattan and a homeless man in

Fig. 1 Access to the world of things © 2008 and 2015 Benjamin Davy (Fifth Avenue, New York City; Dublin, Ireland)

Dublin. Already Adam Smith, however, asserted an indirect connection between wealth and poverty: 'Wherever there is great property there is great inequality. For one very rich man there must be at least five hundred poor, and the affluence of the few supposes the indigence of the many' (Smith 1776: 408). Over the centuries, a variety of explanations for the gap between the wealthy and the poor have been offered. Without claiming that this is the only possible explanation, this chapter asserts that the connection between wealth and poverty is rooted in a broad and widespread misunderstanding of property rights. According to this misunderstanding, private property is an absolute right to exclude anybody but the owner from the use of things, with no or little intrinsic limitation, and this right is protected only if a person already owns property.

Unless private property—in particular, property in land—is understood as a manifestation of human dignity, a perversion of property rights ensues which contributes to a widening gap between the wealthy and the poor. In order to make this point, the chapter takes a human rights approach. The examination of private property as a human right is a rather universal way to think about access to the world of things. For one, it is a good way to understand what is 'human' about property rights (as opposed to property as an instrument of exclusion, wealth, capital accumulation, exploitation). However, private property is conceivably the least probable case of claiming that all human rights derive from human dignity (see, e.g., Preamble and Article 1 of the Universal Declaration of Human Rights—UDHR). In the remainder of the chapter, I shall demonstrate through legal analysis that property relations under UN-sponsored human rights law are quite different from most systems of constitutional property and common or private law. I shall test this result from the perspective of political philosophy and the concept of human dignity. As it will turn out, the human right to property is not an absolute right of owners to have access to the world of things and to exclude everybody else. Rather, property as a human right is a polyrational institution that accounts for vulnerability and need. Property as a human right humanizes the access to the world of things and the distribution of wealth and poverty.

What is the advantage of considering property as a human right (and not as a right under constitutional and common or private law)? Like human dignity and private property, 'human rights' also are a contested concept. Friedrich August von Hayek blamed the framers of the Universal Declaration 'to play an irresponsible game with the concept of "right" which could result only in destroying the respect for it:' 'The conception of a "universal right" which assures to the peasant, to the Eskimo, and presumably to the Abominable Snowman, "periodic holidays with pay" shows the absurdity of the whole thing' (von Hayek 1976: 105). Von Hayek neglected the ideational quality of human rights. The authors of human rights negotiated agreements between the global and the local, the grand and the tiny, and they produced a compelling narrative by putting aside much of their local knowledge, parochial preferences, and ignorance of the world. This is particularly true for UN-sponsored human rights (U. Davy 2013 and 2014b; Henkin 1979; Morsink 1999). The human rights discourse is the most suitable forum of debating access to the world of things in different countries and jurisdictions. The strength of this discourse surely is not its clarity and rigorous application of logic: The 'human rights vocabulary … is riddled with contradictions that would not stand up to logical scrutiny for a minute' (Kennedy 2002: 106). Human rights are inherently ambiguous: Human rights are what we enjoy when we feel safe and content, and what we direly need when we feel hopeless and destitute. The 'ambivalent porosity' of human rights is 'their secret strength' (Kennedy 2002: 106). But this is not a fresh insight. Clarifying human rights has always been a difficult task. In preparation of a draft for the Universal Declaration, a UN-sponsored symposium asked eminent scholars for their opinion on the true nature of human rights. One of the most remarkable (and skeptical) responses came from Mahatma Gandhi: 'I learnt from my illiterate but wise mother that all rights to be deserved and preserved came from duty well done. Thus the very right to live accrues to us only when we do the duty of citizenship of the world. From this one fundamental statement, perhaps it is easy enough to define the duties of Man and Woman and correlate every right to some corresponding duty to be first performed. Every other right can be shown to be a usurpation hardly worth fighting for' (UNESCO 1948: 3).

Presumably, no other human right but property deserves Gandhi's skeptical assessment more. Can property be a human right at all or must property be considered a mere commodity (Joireman and Brown 2013)? In natural law discourses on human rights, property occupies a prominent position (e.g., Locke 1698) and has been considered essential for individual liberty (Levy 1988; Schlatter and Richard 1951: 151–161): 'What our generation has forgotten is that the system of private property is the most important guaranty of freedom …' (von Hayek 1944: 136). The right to property often is associated with ownership, wealth, access to the world of things, the distribution of goods, and command over resources. Above all, property is associated with the proprietor's power to exclude others. A popular expression of the Western property paradigm defines 'property' as 'that sole and despotic dominion which one man claims and exercises over the external things of the world, in total exclusion of the right of any other individual in the universe' (Blackstone 1766: 2 [Book II, Chapter 1]). Blackstonian property fully contradicts Mahatma Gandhi's concept of human rights deriving from the idea 'that all rights to be deserved and preserved came from duty well done' (UNESCO 1948: 3). Blackstone does not ask any landowner to fulfill a 'duty of citizenship of the world' prior to confirming her 'sole and despotic dominion.' Surely, the Western property paradigm has not been completely blind to the correlation of rights and duties. The notion of property as duty-related right, as a source of social obligations, is well established in some jurisdictions and among property scholars (Alexander 2009; Ankersen and Ruppert 2006a; Davy 2012; Mirow 2010; Ondetti 2016; Singer 2000; Singer and Beermann 1993; van der Walt 1999, 2005, 2009; van der Walt and Viljoen 2015). Too often, however, social obligations are conceived of as a collateral duty of the proprietor. To Gandhi, the fulfilling of the duties associated with property is, in fact, a necessary condition without which property merely is a kind of 'usurpation'.

With good reasons, Mahatma Gandhi (and others) has been suspicious of human rights as duty-free entitlements. Consider, for example, the following 'human rights' case. In 2008, the United Kingdom nationalized Northern Rock, a bank and mortgage lender owning about £ 24 million as a result of bailout measures financed by the Bank of England. The shareholders were informed that the company had no residual value and therefore no compensation would be payable. Eventually, the case reached the European Court of Human Rights, and the applicants claimed that the government had breached its obligations under Article 1 of the (First) Protocol to the Convention for the Protection of Human Rights and Fundamental Freedoms (ECHR_P1). Article 1 ECHR_P1 protects the right to possession. Case law and academic discourse agree that possession, in this context, means property (Allen 2010; Ovey and White 2006: 345–375; Ploeger and Groetelaers 2007). The applicants in the Northern Rock case claimed a violation of their human right to property because the United Kingdom had nationalized the ailing bank without paying adequate compensation to the company's shareholders. The court asserted that compensation can help restore a fair balance between the interests of a bank's private owners and the public interest in protecting the financial sector in the United Kingdom. The court declared the application inadmissible, however, finding that 'it was entirely legitimate for the State authorities to decide that, had the Northern Rock shareholders been permitted to benefit from the value which had been created and maintained only through the provision of State support, this would encourage the managers and shareholders of other banks to seek and rely on similar support, to the detriment of the United Kingdom economy' (European Court of Human Rights, 10 July, 2012, Dennis Grainger et al. v. United Kingdom, Application no. 34940/10, para. 42). The financial crisis, which had started in 2007 with the default on subprime loans in California, surely has changed the way in which many people think about economic liberty, private property, the invisible hand of the markets, or restraints on government interventions. The change remained critically superficial, however. How else is it possible that the European Court of Human Rights even considers whether one of the major players in the collapse of the mortgage market has been violated in its *human* right to property? The language of Article 1 ECHR_P1 explicitly pertains to 'legal persons', but surely this cannot mean that all follies of the financial sector are protected by human rights as the legitimate use of private property.

The purpose of this chapter is to examine property in land as a human right. Property as a human right, the chapter asserts, is not merely a repetition of the absolute individual right to exclude others, as glorified by Blackstone. Property as a human right rather exemplifies the bond that connects all human rights to human dignity. The connection reaches beyond the concept of social obligations as an inherent component of a human right to property. Property in land must be considered as a human right with an emphasis on the human. Such emphasis helps focus our attention on marginal property, minimal property, informal ownership, vulnerable individuals and groups, or social welfare. Such emphasis does not exclude wealthy women and men from the protection by a human right to property, but it shifts the meaning of property from absolute ownership to everybody's freedom of some access to the world of things. From the perspective of legal positivism, I shall demonstrate that property as a human right is quite different from constitutional property or property in common or private law. From the perspective of political philosophy, I shall demonstrate as to how human dignity helps in the establishing, providing, and restricting of property rights.

2 Property and Human Rights Law

2.1 The Golden Rule of Property as a Human Right

Property rights—especially private property that enables land uses restricted to one landowner—pose many riddles to human rights discourse (Allen 2007 and 2010; Chigara 2004; Howard-Hassmann 2013; Jacobs 2013: S90–S92; Krause 2001; Krause and Alfredsson 1999; Ovey and White 2006: 345–375; Ploeger and Groetelaers 2007; Sprankling 2014; van Banning 2002; van Genugten and Perez-Bustillo 2001). Is property as a universal human right identical with property in common or private law? Or with constitutional property? Does the government have a positive duty to provide deprived women, men, or children with some property? The discourse on the human right to land smartly goes beyond the Western property paradigm (De Schutter 2010; OHCHR 2014; Sprankling 2014: 130–132; van Banning 2002: 323–336), but that leaves open the question about the scope and meaning of property as a universal human right. With regard to property as a human right, Brian Simpson thinks that the Universal Declaration captures four 'basic underlying ideas': (1) recognition of property, (2) basic minimum of property for everyone, (3) regulatory limits to property, and (4) no taking of property without compensation (Simpson 2001: 757). Although Simpson's account moves beyond the Western property paradigm, it still does not capture the entirety of what UN-sponsored human rights have to say about property relations.

From the perspective of legal positivism, property as a human right is the bundle of all human rights that deal with property relations. Obviously, several human rights can be enjoyed only if simultaneously some access to land is granted: 'Land-related issues present a number of urgent challenges to human rights, given that land is an essential element for the realization of many of them' (OHCHR 2014, para. 72). Nobody can join a peaceful assembly (Article 21 ICCPR) without gathering with others in a space suitable for articulating political opinions. Nobody can raise a family (Article 13 ICESCR) in outer space. A bundle of human rights, however, is connected even more closely to property relations. An appropriate label for this bundle is the golden rule of property as a human right (Davy 2012: 164–167): Property relations comply with human rights, if

- no one is held in slavery or servitude (Article 4 UDHR; Article 8 ICCPR),
- marriage is entered into only with the free and full consent of the intending spouses (Article 16, para. 2, UDHR; Article 23, para. 3, ICCPR),

- the government respects everyone's right to own private property (Article 17 UDHR and several conventions, e.g., Article 5 ICERD; Articles 15 and 16 CEDAW; Article 15 ICRAM; Article 12 CRPD),
- the government protects everyone's right to work (Article 23, para. 1, UDHR; Article 6 ICESCR), and
- the government fulfills everyone's right to an adequate standard of living (Article 25 UDHR; Article 11 ICESCR).

A legal positivist asks what the law actually says, not what would be a desirable content of law (Kelsen 1960). With respect to UN-sponsored human rights law, a legal positivist inquires into which human rights are binding law and what is their meaning. Legal positivism keeps the analysis of property free from 'imagination … and affections' (Blackstone 1766: 2 [Book II, Chapter 1]). A certain amount of 'purity' of legal analysis is helpful if, as in the case of property law, the literature is inundated by presupposed ideas. On the one hand, property literature often equates 'property' with the Western paradigm of private property (Allen 2007; Epstein 1985; Honoré 1961: 107; Penner 2000; Posner 2007; Schlatter 1951). On the other hand, property literature on the global South highlights idiosyncrasies such as informality (Perlman 2010; Roy 2005; Roy and AlSayad 2004) or traditional and communal property systems (Godden and Tehan 2010; Ankersen and Ruppert 2006b). An analysis of property and UN-sponsored human rights law, informed by legal positivism, suffers less from regional or local imagination and affections. After all, UN-sponsored human rights law presents a generally accepted frame of reference to all considerations on property, ownership, possession, tenure, and similar rights in statutory law, case law, and literature (Alfredsson and Eide 1999; Clayton and Tomlinson 2000; Eide 2001a and 2001b; Eide et al. 2001; Henkin 1979; Kälin and Künzli 2009; Kälin et al. 2004; Ovey and White 2006; Simpson 2001; Sprankling 2014; Tomuschat 2008; van Banning 2002). Property as a human right often is different from what constitutional law (van der Walt 1999) or common/private law consider as property. For example, the European Court of Human Rights (ECtHR) extends the protection of property (Article 1 ECHR_P1) to social assistance (ECtHR, Gaygusuz v. Austria, 16 September 1996) or the 'proprietary interest' of slum dwellers in their informal housing (ECtHR Grand Chamber, Öneryıldız v. Turkey, 30 November 2004).

The law and everyday practice often seriously diverge, just as UN Habitat (2007: 158) deplores with regard to housing rights in India. Using legal positivism as a method by no means implies ignorance of the frailty of human rights. In many countries, human rights are violated and their protection is critically ineffective. Nevertheless, UN-sponsored human rights are a suitable framework for a comparative analysis of property. The members of the international community have drafted and successfully ratified several human rights policy and law documents dealing with property relations (Davy 2012: 164–176; Dehaibi 2015; Howard-Hassmann 2013; Joireman and Brown 2013). These documents represent a surprising consensus on property relations (the golden rule), a consensus that the predominant literature on property has yet to appreciate (but see, e.g., Dolidze

2016; Sprankling 2014; van Banning 2002). Surely, it must be interesting what the UN-sponsored human rights have to say about property, and how widespread they have been accepted through the ratification by States Parties.

The sources of UN-sponsored law are based on a document that, without being binding law itself, has deeply influenced the concept and perception of human rights: the Universal Declaration of Human Rights (UDHR, Resolution 217 A [III]). On December 10, 1948, the United Nations General Assembly adopted an International Bill of Human Rights (Alfredsson and Eide 1999; Kälin et al. 2004; Kälin and Künzli 2009: 13–14; Morsink 1999; Tomuschat 2008: 22–24). The main text of this document is the UDHR. Legally, the Declaration is not a binding international law treaty, but 'merely a statement of ideals' (Simpson 2001: 756). Yet, it was adopted by the General Assembly and has inspired a continuous discourse on human rights as well as numerous international treaties. The international community did not stop with the declaration of human rights, but produced a number of international human rights treaties. The first two international treaties transforming the Universal Declaration into binding law were based on General Assembly resolution 2200A (XXI) of 16 December 1966: the International Covenant on Civil and Political Rights (ICCPR; entry into force 23 March 1976), and the International Covenant on Economic, Social and Cultural Rights (ICESCR; entry into force 3 January 1976). Membership to both covenants is widespread, yet with notable exceptions. The two maps in Fig. 2 show the large community of States Parties as well as the human rights laggards.

Several international treaties ('conventions') on human rights elaborate the concept of the Universal Declaration and the two covenants. These treaties affirm the golden rule of property as a human right with respect to anti-discrimination. Since international treaties only apply to signatories, and membership fluctuates, the various property clauses are not universally, but multilaterally, binding law. Still, these property clauses reflect the ideas and values accepted in the global discourse on human rights.

Table 1 demonstrates that attention for the elements of the golden rule of property is distributed unevenly among the human rights documents. The Universal Declaration and most conventions cover all or most elements. The two covenants, however, divide up between them their attention for property relations. The reason for the division is the classification of a right as civil, political, economic, social, or cultural. The drafters of the covenants classified the prohibition of slavery and forced marriages as civil rights and put the right not to be owned into the ICCPR. The drafters of the covenants classified the right to work and the right to an adequate standard of living as economic and social rights and added these rights to the ICESCR. The right to own property (Article 17 UDHR), however, never was translated into binding treaty law (Kälin and Künzli 2009: 431; Krause and Alfredsson 1999: 365–366; Sprankling 2014: 9–11 and 203). The right to own property can be considered a civil or political right as well as an economic, social, or cultural right (Davy 2012: 170). Obviously, property comprises political aspects (e.g., ownership of social media), but also touches on civil rights (e.g., property and family law). Property also relates to economic rights (e.g., ownership of the means

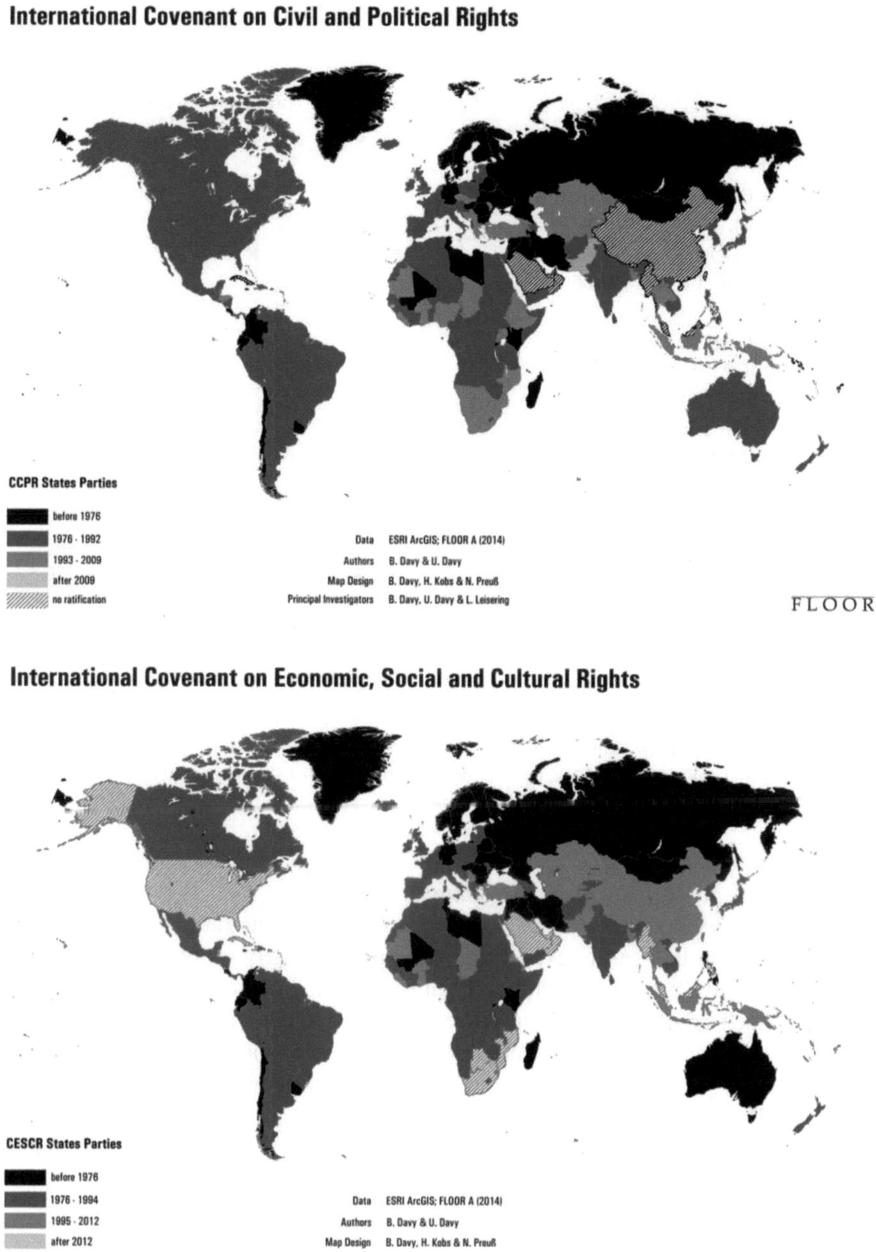

Fig. 2 ICCPR and ICESCR—membership status (as of 2016) © 2017 floor project

Table 1 Property-related provisions in UN-sponsored human rights documents

Name of document	No slavery	No forced marriage	Right to own property	Right to work	Adequate standard of living
Universal Declaration of Human Rights, 1948 (UDHR)	✓	✓	✓	✓	✓
International Covenant on Civil and Political Rights, 1966 (ICCPR)	✓	✓	✖	✖	✖
International Covenant on Economic, Social and Cultural Rights, 1966 (ICESCR)	✖	✖	✖	✓	✓
International Convention on the Elimination of All Forms of Racial Discrimination, 1966 (ICERD)	✖	✓	✓	✓	✓
Convention on the Elimination of All Forms of Discrimination Against Women, 1979 (CEDAW)	✖	✓	✓	✓	✓
United Nations Convention on the Rights of the Child, 1989 (CRC)	✓	✖	✖	✓	✓
International Convention in the Protection of the Rights of All Migrant Workers and Members of Their Families, 1990 (ICRAM)	✓	✖	✓	✓	✖
Convention on the Rights of Persons with Disabilities, 2006 (CRPD)	✓	✓	✓	✓	✓

✓ = the document includes this element of the golden rule of property
✖ = the document does not include this element of the golden rule of property

of production), social rights (e.g., the right to housing or food), or cultural rights (e.g., property in an ancient burial ground). Property, in fact, is polyrational, and human rights discourses help better understand the various rationalities associated with property. In this sense, even if the attempt to identify property as political or civil or economic or social or cultural right is futile, it still can inspire discourses on property. Each covenant would have been suitable for including the right to own property. The Commission on Human Rights, before abandoning the proposal of a right to property, regarded property in the context of economic, social, or cultural rights (CHR 1954: para. 40–71).

2.2 *Property Relations in UN-Sponsored Human Rights Law*

The golden rule of property integrates a variety of human rights pertaining to property relations. The right to own property (Article 17 UDHR) is the most obvious such right. But international law actually created property as a human right from a different angle: Human rights emphasize that not all can be owned as property. The abolition of slavery, servitude, and compulsory labor, and the prohibition of forced marriages are the two prongs of the right not to be owned. The first element of the golden rule of property as a human right (Davy 2012: 164–167) is the *abolition of slavery*, embedded in the Slavery Convention (1926) and Article 8 ICCPR. As 'no one shall be held in slavery,' human rights law prohibits the commodification of women and men. No one must be treated like a commodity that can be sold and bought in a marketplace. Slavery, servitude, and forced labor turn women and men into things that someone else can own. Although slavery also can affect the freedom of expression or the right to health, it is most closely related to property. According to Article 1, para. 1, Slavery Convention (1926), slavery 'is the status or condition of a person over whom any or all of the powers attaching to the right of ownership are exercised.' The motives for the abolition of slavery—ranging from humanism to the protection of England's commerce from the competition by former colonies—are obscure (Tomuschat 2008: 14). Yet, the abolition of slavery was one of the first steps in the development of universal human rights (Kälin and Künzli 2009: 420–421). In 1815, the delegates to the Congress of Vienna banned slave trading. In 1926, the international community adopted as *ius cogens* that over no person the right to ownership be exercised (Article 1 and 2 of the Slavery Convention). Article 8 ICCPR abolishes slavery, servitude, and compulsory labor. Still, slavery persists today (Shahinian 2009 and 2010) in the form of bonded labor, forced labor, domestic labor, and sex trafficking. Although property and slavery have been tied together in history, property literature only rarely mentions the connection. At least, Henry George and the land reform movement have been aware of the similarity between property in land and slavery (see, in more detail, Davy 2012: 166–167).

The second element of the golden rule of property as a human right (Davy 2012: 164–167) is the *prohibition of forced marriages*. Article 1 (c) of the Supplementary Convention on the Abolition of Slavery, the Slave Trade, and Institutions and Practices Similar to Slavery (1957) declared forced marriage as a 'practice similar to slavery.' Article 23, para. 3, ICCPR states that 'no marriage shall be entered into without the free and full consent of the intending spouses.' A forced marriage—or conjugal slavery—is a crime against humanity (Frulli 2008). In some countries, forced marriages are not seen as similar to slavery or bonded labor. The prohibition of forced marriage draws from the idea that the commodification of familial relationships violates human dignity. No women must be owned or traded by her father, husband, guardian, or anybody else.

The *right to own property* is the third element of the golden rule of property as a human right. It is less known, however, that the human right to own property is binding law only with regard to particularly vulnerable humans (Davy 2012: 174–176; Jacobs 2013: S91–S92; Sprankling 2014: 207–209). Under Article 17 UDHR, governments have to protect property rights:

1. Everyone has the right to own property alone as well as in association with others.
2. No one shall be arbitrarily deprived of his property.

The property clause of Article 17 UDHR covers the proprietary relations that many legal systems offer for the protection of private and common property (Davy 2012: 167–168; Jacobs 2013: S90–S91; Kälin and Künzli 2009: 431–439; Krause and Alfredsson 1999: 364; Krause 2001; Morsink 1999: 139–156). A government infringes the human right to own property by taking arbitrarily the land owned by an individual alone or in association with others. Article 17 UDHR was only in part transformed into universal human rights (e.g., Article 5 ICERD; Articles 15 and 16 CEDAW; Article 15 ICRAM; Article 12 CRPD). Article 17 UDHR also has been adopted by regional human rights law (e.g., Article 1 ECHR_P1; Article 21 of the American Convention on Human Rights; Article 14 of the African Charter on Human and People's Rights; Article 17 of the Charter of Fundamental Rights of the European Union). Sprankling (2014: 204–206) concludes from the widespread regional recognition of property that, after all, the right to own property is a universal human right. The conclusion is unconvincing; the acceptance by regional treaties of the right to own property rather indicates that only a regionally fragmented agreement on property could be achieved. The legally binding human rights treaties that protect the right to own property (and are potentially effective worldwide) focus on the property relations of vulnerable individuals and non-discrimination (Davy 2012: 174–176):

- The International Convention on the Elimination of All Forms of Racial Discrimination, 1966 (ICERD), puts States Parties under the obligation to prohibit and to eliminate and to guarantee the right of everyone, without distinction as to race, color, or national or ethnic origin, to equality before the law, notably in the enjoyment of the right to own property alone as well as in association with others and the right to housing (Article 5 [d] v and [e] iii ICERD).
- Under the Convention on the Elimination of All Forms of Discrimination Against Women, 1979 (CEDAW), each State Party shall take all appropriate measures to eliminate discrimination against women in rural areas in order to ensure, on a basis of equality of men and women, that they participate in and benefit from rural development. States Parties shall ensure to women in rural areas equal treatment in land and agrarian reform as well as in land resettlement schemes (Article 14, para. 2 [g] CEDAW). The States Parties shall give women equal rights to conclude contracts and to administer property and shall treat them equally in all stages of procedure in courts and tribunals (Article 15, para. 2, CEDAW). In particular, States Parties shall ensure, on a basis of equality of men and women, the same rights for both spouses in respect of the ownership, acquisition, management, administration, enjoyment, and disposition of property, whether free of charge or for a valuable consideration (Article 16, para. 1 [h] CEDAW).
- Article 15 of the International Convention in the Protection of the Rights of All Migrant Workers and Members of Their Families, 1990 (ICRAM), contains a property clause in favor of migrant workers: No migrant worker or member of his or her family shall be arbitrarily deprived of property, whether owned

individually or in association with others. The property of migrant workers is also protected by a compensation requirement in case of a taking: Where, under the legislation in force in the State of employment, the assets of a migrant worker or a member of his or her family are expropriated in whole or in part, the person concerned shall have the right to fair and adequate compensation (Article 15, sentence 2, ICRAM).

- Under the Convention on the Rights of Persons with Disabilities, 2006 (CRPD), States Parties shall take all appropriate and effective measures to ensure the equal right of persons with disabilities to own or inherit property, to control their own financial affairs, and to have equal access to bank loans, mortgages, and other forms of financial credit, and shall ensure that persons with disabilities are not arbitrarily deprived of their property (Article 12, para. 5, CRPD).

Property as a human right, although not generally accepted as binding law, is considered as invaluable for women and men living in marginal conditions (Howard-Hassmann 2013): persons exposed to racism, rural women, migrant workers, persons with disabilities. From the perspective of legal positivism, it does not matter that some stakeholders in the human rights discourses envisioned a broader, more comprehensive protection of private property. It did not come to pass (Jacobs 2013: S91–S92). What remains, however, is the commitment of UN-sponsored human rights law to protect the right to own property from certain kinds of discrimination against vulnerable human owners.

The fourth element of the golden rule of property as a human right is the *right to work* (Article 23, para. 1, UDHR; Article 6 ICESCR). Adam Smith emphasized: 'The property which every man has in his own labor, as it is the original foundation of all other property, so it is the most sacred and inviolable' (Smith 1776: 120). With good reasons, a leading human rights handbook puts the prohibition of slavery, the right to work, and the protection of property in the same chapter about the 'protection of the human person in the economic sphere' (Kälin and Künzli 2009: 420–439). The right to work correlates with the prohibition of slavery because voluntary work is possible only for women and men who are free to choose their occupation. The right to work correlates with the right to own property because owning the means of production—for example, an artisan's toolbox or a peasant's hoe—is the foundation of work with the lowest degree of exploitation. The right to work also correlates with the right to own property because paid labor is the most important prerequisite of acquiring property. Finally, the right to work is linked to the right to an adequate standard of living. Article 11 ICESCR should be read in the light of the preamble which emphasizes 'that the individual having duties to other individuals and to community to which he belongs, is under a responsibility to strive for the promotion and observance of the rights recognized in the present Covenant.' Before a woman or man asks for support under Article 11 ICESCR, she or he must have tried to gain livelihood through work. A certain duty to work—a significant element of property as a universal human right—is the closest that UN-sponsored human rights law gets to Gandhi's 'duty of citizenship of the world' (UNESCO 1948: 3).

The fifth element of the golden rule of property as a human right is the *right to an adequate standard of living* (Article 25 UDHR; Article 11, para. 1, ICESCR). According to Article 25, para. 1, UDHR, governments have to provide for a basic minimum (Davy 2012: 168–174; Eide and Eide 1999) and fulfill everybody's right to the adequate standard of living. Article 11, para. 1, ICESCR implements the right to an adequate standard of living: 'The States Parties to the present Covenant recognize the right of everyone to an ad-equate standard of living for himself and his family, including adequate food, clothing and housing, and to the continuous improvement of living conditions …' Several non-discrimination conventions reaffirm the right to an adequate standard of living with respect to racial discrimination in housing (Article 5 [e] iii ICERD), women in rural areas (Article 14, para. 2 [h] CEDAW), children (Article 27, para. 1, CRC), or persons with disabilities (Article 28 CRPD).

2.3 Result of Legal Analysis

From the perspective of legal positivism, the analysis of UN-sponsored human rights law has the following result: Property is a universal human right; and property relations are subject to several human rights (Davy 2012: 164–167; OHCHR 2014: para. 72–73). Binding human rights law imposes on States Parties the obligation to respect, protect, and fulfill each human right (Maastricht Guidelines 1997). Property as a human right imposes on States Parties the obligation to respect, protect, and fulfill the golden rule of property as far as the property-related provisions of the UDHR have been transformed into binding human rights through the ICCPR and the ICESCR or one of several UN-sponsored conventions ostracizing the discrimination of vulnerable women and men. In this sense, the golden rule of property as a human right is a bundle of five rights:

- the right not to be owned through slavery, servitude, or compulsory labor;
- the right not to be owned by forced marriage or conjugal slavery;
- the right to own property, if the proprietor is a victim of racial discrimination, a woman, a migrant worker and her or his family, a child, or a person with a disability;
- the right to work, which includes the right of everyone to the opportunity to gain their living by work which they freely choose or accept; and
- the right to an adequate standard of living ('minimal property'), including the right to adequate food and adequate housing.

Universal human rights law must be interpreted with a view to the vast differences between States Parties. Obviously, the culture of land uses and other ownership practices vary worldwide. Universal human rights law has a preference neither for brick houses over mud huts nor for maize over wheat. Therefore, it makes no sense to restrict the States Parties' margin of discretion as to how they respect, protect, and fulfill human rights. Universal human rights also must be interpreted with a view to the economic, social, and political situation of each States Party. Due to widespread poverty, a country may not be able today to fulfill each resident's right to an adequate standard of living. This country still has to undertake steps 'to the maximum of its available resources, with a view to achieving progressively the full realization of the rights' (Article 2, para. 1, ICESCR) and has a duty to the 'continuous improvement of living conditions' (Article 11, para. 1, ICESCR). Informal land uses are of great significance in enjoying some access to the world of things in marginal circumstances (Davy and Pellissery 2013; Huchzermeyer 2011; Meneses-Reyes and Caballero-Juárez 2014).

Property as a human right is different from most constitutional property clauses (van der Walt 1999). On the one hand, property as a human right is broader than most domestic concepts of property. For example, it comprises active duties of the government to provide every person in need with an adequate standard of living. On the other hand, property as a human right is narrower than most domestic concepts of property. Above all, the human right to property protects humans in vulnerable circumstances. Land uses deriving from vanity (Fig. 1, left side) are not the predominant concern of property as a human right. Both differences perhaps explain why human rights are not more popular among property scholars. Only a few authors accept the overlap between property rights and economic or social rights (Simpson 2001: 757). Many reject the idea that the government has a human-rights-based duty to provide some property to everybody lacking an adequate standard of living. Even those, who cherish economic and social rights (Liebenberg 2005), fail to call the right to an adequate living (Article 25 UDHR; Article 11 ICESCR) a property right. Similarly, many property scholars seem to dislike that the universal human right to property is for humans only. Universal human rights are not meant to be rights of corporations (Grear 2006). Although some voices deny private property rights to corporations (Berle and Means 1932), mainstream property theory hardly questions whether the right to own property also protects corporations and legal persons. The reluctance of property scholars to consider property as a human right is both an intellectual and forensic loss.

3 Property and Human Dignity

3.1 Human Rights and Human Dignity

Human rights are not merely a legal concept. In fact, many authors see the significance of human rights mostly in their ideational strength to inspire public discourse (Dean 2007; Sen 2004; Pogge 2002 and 2007; Turner 1993). In this vein, the remainder of this chapter tests the result of the legal analysis from the perspective of political philosophy. The test is based on the self-description of UN-sponsored human rights documents that 'civil, political, economic, social, cultural and other rights and freedoms all … derive from the inherent dignity of the human person and are essential for his free and full development' (Principle VII, para. 3, of the 1975 Helsinki Final Act). How does private property relate to human dignity?

The relationship between human dignity and human rights, although reiterated often in UN documents, is a good example of what David Kennedy (2002: 106) calls the 'ambivalent porosity' of human rights. In other words, the relationship between human dignity and human rights is unclear. What does it mean that human rights 'derive from the inherent dignity of the human person' (Principle VII, para. 3, 1975 Helsinki Final Act)? Perhaps it means that human dignity is the origin of rights which, by the rules of logic or legal doctrine, follow strictly from the interpretation of the legal phrase 'human dignity.' In this vein, we conceive of human dignity as an extralegal authority whose instructions the international community obeys by drafting and ratifying human rights treaties. Human rights would derive from dignity as a strict replication of natural justice demands that leave little sovereignty to the members of the international community. Such an understanding creates a tension between natural justice and democratic sovereignty. Human dignity as the basis of natural rights which determines man-made laws amounts to the 'terrorist language' which Jeremy Bentham (1843: 501) calls 'nonsense upon stilts.' In this vein, the Canadian Supreme Court asserts that 'human dignity is an abstract and subjective notion that … cannot only become confusing and difficult to apply; it has also proven to be an additional burden on equality claimants, rather than the philosophical enhancement it was intended to be' (R. c. Kapp [2008] 2 R.C.S. 483 [504]).

But perhaps Principle VII merely reminds us that human dignity has inspired loosely the creation of rights. From this perspective, dignity can be conceived of as a convenient shell which contains all human rights, for want of a better vessel. Human dignity would serve as an ideational inspiration of rights, but lack any compelling and mandatory content. The framers of international human rights always have emphasized that human rights closely relate to human dignity. The first sentence of the preamble to the Universal Declaration avows 'recognition of the inherent dignity and of the equal and inalienable rights of all members of the human family …' The preambles to the ICCPR and ICESCR both assert that the rights included in the covenants 'derive from the inherent dignity of the human person …' This does not certify, however, that everyone agrees on what the precepts of human dignity are (Morsink 1999: 281–302). International human rights law, as a former president of the American Society of International Law once claimed, finds it difficult 'to mate cannibals and non-cannibals without changing their incompatible attitudes toward cannibalism' (McDougal 1959: 109). Unsurprisingly, the framers of international human rights did not choose God's eternal will, social justice, international solidarity, capitalist ethics, Sharia law, or any other standard popular in only a part of the world. The framers chose human dignity perhaps because human dignity provides a sufficiently vague and ambiguous standard that both 'cannibals and non-cannibals' can accept.

In the following, the results of the legal analysis of property as a human right are tested from the perspective of political philosophy. Does the result, in many ways a huge deviation from constitutional property clauses and from common or private law, conform with the overarching concept of human dignity? By using Margalit's concept of a decent society (Margalit 1996), I would think property as a human right conforms with human dignity if property relations are non-humiliating. I would also think that property as a human right does not conform with human dignity if property relations gave anybody a good reason to feel humiliated. Margalit (1996: 9) defines humiliation as 'any sort of behavior or condition that constitutes a sound reason for a person to consider his or her self-respect injured.' He uses the phrase 'decent society' as orientation for non-humiliating public policies: 'A decent society is one that fights conditions which constitute a justification for its dependents to consider themselves humiliated. A society is decent if its institutions do not act in ways that give the people under their authority sound reasons to consider themselves humiliated' (Margalit 1996: 10–11).

Surely, many other definitions of human dignity exist. George Kateb emphasizes that human dignity is about humanity and the human species: 'The core idea of human dignity is that on earth, humanity is the greatest type of being—or what we call species because we have learned to see humanity as one species in the animal kingdom, which is made up of many other species along with our own—and that every member deserves to be treated in a manner consonant with the high worth of the species' (Kateb 2011: 3–4). Jeremy Waldron combines the moral and legal discourses on dignity. He entertains the idea 'that "dignity" is a term used to indicate a high-ranking legal, political, and social status, and that the idea of *human* dignity is the idea of the assignment of such a high-ranking status to everyone' (Waldron 2012: 47). Anne Phillips understands the relevance of human dignity for the distribution of wealth, but rejects the notion that human dignity provides a standard independent from equality: 'The idea that people need a basic minimum of resources to live a life of human dignity is, in essence, an equality right; it says that all humans need enough to live on, not just the more privileged ones' (Phillips 2015: 101). Margalit, Kateb, Waldron, or Phillips read human dignity in different ways. Non-humiliating policies (Margalit) are not the same as policies that are consonant with the high worth of the species (Kateb), assign a high-ranking status to everyone (Waldron), or observe equality rights (Phillips). Considering the wide range of ideas associated with human dignity, how can philosophy help understand the relationship between human dignity and private property?

To make a test of property as a human right easier from the perspective of political philosophy, the following test adopts Margalit's concept as standard of human dignity. Humiliation, or shame, is a convincing standard of human dignity (Davy 2014a; Lindner 2007; Lindner et al. 2011; Walker et al. 2013). The test could also be run using equality or autonomy or liberty or life as standard of human dignity. In this chapter, however, I apply the standard defined by Margalit (1996).

3.2 Private Property and Human Dignity

Only few human rights documents emphasize explicitly the connection between property rights and human dignity. A notable example is Article XXIII of the American Declaration of the Rights and Duties of Man (1948): 'Every person has a right to own such private property as meets the essential needs of decent living and helps to maintain the dignity of the individual and of the home.' This expression of a human right to property can be called 'minimal property' (Davy 2012: 170; Simpson 2001: 757). Minimal property and human dignity occasionally are observed in the literature: 'As a human right, property should provide the human being with a degree of security to enjoy a life in dignity' (van Banning 2002: 191). Sometimes, the connection between human dignity and use rights is limited to certain natural resources, such as fisheries (Song 2015) or land (FAO 2012: 4; OHCHR 2015). Defining the right to adequate housing in the context of Article 11 ICESCR, the General Comment No. 4 related adequate housing to human dignity: '[T]he right to housing should not be interpreted in a narrow or restrictive sense which equates it with, for example, the shelter provided by merely having a roof over one's head or views shelter exclusively as a commodity. Rather it should be seen as the right to live somewhere in security, peace and dignity' (CESCR 1991, para. 7). This approach has been adopted by several UN-related bodies (e.g., UN Habitat 2007; OHCHR 2014 and 2015). Other voices emphasize the link between property rights, human dignity, and liberty: 'Americans cared about property not because they were materialistic but because they cared about political freedom and personal independence. They cherished property rights as prerequisites for the pursuit of happiness, and property opened up a world of intangible values—human dignity, self-regard, self-expression, and personal fulfillment' (Levy 1988: 175). Presumably, the most comprehensive approach to property and dignity is articulated in the concept of dignity takings: '*Dignity takings* are when a state directly or indirectly destroys or confiscates property rights from owners or occupiers whom it deems to be sub persons without paying just compensation or without a legitimate public purpose' (Atuahene 2014: 3).

Even though some literature on property and dignity can be identified, private property and human dignity are not an ideal marriage. Neither is human dignity a favorite topic of property literature nor private property a favorite topic of dignity studies. Dignity theories often eschew property. The two voluminous handbooks on human dignity recently published by Oxford University Press (McCrudden 2014) and by Cambridge University Press (Düwell et al. 2014) hardly pay attention to the relationship between human dignity and private property. In *The Decent Society*, Margalit (1996: 250–251) mentions property only briefly. He asserts that 'the only way propertyless people can secure their human dignity is by working for pay,' an assertion which implies that there 'is a better way of being independent in the capitalist view—owning property.' Property theories—even Margaret Radin's (1993) treatise on property and personhood—rarely mention human dignity explicitly. Social and economic rights create a bridge between human dignity and private property because the right to work or the right to an adequate standard of living can lead to the building up of an individual's asset base. Yet, Sandra Liebenberg's (2005) path-breaking article on the value of human dignity in interpreting socio-economic rights mentions property not once.

Does this mean that human dignity and private property have little or nothing to say to each other? This chapter asserts a strong, yet uneasy bond between human dignity and a human right to property (Davy 2014a). The bond is particularly relevant in cases of private property in land and other natural resources. Access to land is the most fundamental kind of access to the world of things (Davy 2009 and 2012; De Schutter 2010; OHCHR 2014). The scarcity of land and other natural resources connects land use rights closely to issues of personhood, existence, and human dignity. Consider the four examples of land uses in Fig. 3: The sign put up to discourage trespassers from entering 'The Lagoons' in Vancouver, British Columbia, is an iconic marker of private property and the exclusion of others. But property rights also are relevant for using the commons: Taking a selfie in public is a typical example of exercising use rights in a public park, such as in the park of Schloß Schönbrunn, Wien, Österreich. Marginal land uses depend in particular on location and the spatiality of poverty (Davy 2012; Davy and Pellissery 2013). Informal housing in the proximity of formal housing offers opportunities to deliver menial work to the wealthy neighbors. The photograph from Bengaluru shows an informal shack sitting between two multi-storey apartment buildings: The informal dwellers can expect some business coming their way. *Lindys Hair Salon*, however, is placed in a remote 'temporary' relocation area of Cape Town, colloquially called Blikkiesdorp, where the only customers Lindy can expect are ladies from the surrounding 'blikkies' ('tin cans' in Afrikaans). All of the four photographs illustrate a relationship between access to land and the right to exist.

In *The Devil's Dictionary*, Ambrose Bierce ironized the connection between private property in land and the right to exist: If 'the whole area of *terra firma* is owned by A, B and C, there will be no place for D, E, F and G to be born, or, born as trespassers, to exist' (Bierce 1999: 106). Bierce's satirical comment contains a bitter truth. Refusing to someone the right to exist is the most evil form of violating human dignity. Such refusal does not only occur in genocide, 'ethnic cleansing,' or mass evictions, but may already be embedded in a property system as such. Since the right to exist necessarily involves the right to use land and other natural resources (such as water, air, or sunlight), private property and other ownership practices have an effect on human dignity. Denying somebody minimal use rights in land ('primitive resource rights') equals denying them a 'right to exist' (White 2003: 95). It would be naïve to believe, however, that private property is always antagonistic to human dignity. Some access to the world of things is necessary to lead a dignified life, and secure land rights to all help prevent degrading exclusion (Howard-Hassmann 2013; Jacobs 2013; OHCHR 2014; UN Habitat 2007; UN Habitat & GLTN 2008). This is true for everybody, who can achieve her or his aspirations in life only through the use of land, and this means for everybody.

Fig. 3 Access to land and the right to exist © 2014–2016 Benjamin Davy (Vancouver, Canada; Wien, Österreich; Bengaluru, India; Cape Town, South Africa)

Although human dignity is not limited to owning things, owning nothing at all—having no access to land at all—is a humiliating experience to everybody who has not taken the vows of humility.

3.3 Three Worlds

Bierce toys around with a familiar consequence of private property: the exclusion of others. Exclusion makes property as a human right different from other human rights because human rights draw from the idea that *every* woman and men has them. But if somebody owns property, under certain circumstances, this could exclude others from owning property, at least, from owning the *same* property. A sad example in point is homelessness. A homeless person experiences the exclusionary effect of private property and the enclosure of the commons most dramatically: '[Though] we say there is nothing particularly dignified about sleeping or urinating, there is certainly something deeply and inherently undignified about being prevented from doing so … We should be ashamed that we have allowed our laws of public and private property to reduce a million or more citizens to something approaching this level of degradation' (Waldron 1991: 320).

What is true for the homeless can affect everybody, who suffers from a lack of access and use rights to land. At some point, the exclusion can violate human dignity because if no land is available to be owned, or at least used without interference, the non-owners have a good reason to feel humiliated.

Because of its exclusionary effect, private property is different from other human rights. The freedom of expression, assembly, or religion can be exercised by many without taking away anything from others. For example, one person leads a dignified life and writes more than 1000 Twitter or Facebook messages per day, participates in more political rallies than anybody else, and not worships any deity. Another person, who also leads a dignified life, never expresses an opinion, never participates in a peaceful assembly, and observes religious laws strictly. Although the lives of the two persons are different from each other, we can imagine both lives as dignified. Should we be suspicious about the two persons and human dignity, we probably would not be interested at all in the mere number of messages, assemblies, or religious acts, but in qualitative aspects: Is the first person an atheist because the government prohibits religious practices and punishes worshippers excessively? Is the other person under duress from the government and afraid to speak up her mind in public? As long as coercion is not involved and both persons act on their own free will, we can imagine that they live their lives in dignity. Possibly, they live their lives in the same city or even neighborhood. Only in extraordinary circumstances would the human rights enjoyment of the one person interfere with the human rights of the other person (e.g., by communicating 'fake news' or hate messages). An analysis of the relationship between human dignity and, for example, the freedom of expression, assembly, or religion examines *qualities*, not quantities. In the relationship between human dignity and private property, *quantity* always is crucial. Private property can enable a person to have a dignified life, yet private property can also limit public policies that seek to protect human dignity. Why? Because the current property holders demand that their rights be protected from redistribution.

A model of three worlds—surely we can imagine more worlds, but the three worlds are extremes appealing to political philosophy analysis—illustrates how the (hypothetical) design of private property would entirely contradict human dignity:

- **World One (property monopolization)**: Imagine World One as a world with a property system tailored to the requirements of the Western property paradigm (Epstein 1985; Honoré 1961; Penner 2000). Only one thing is extraordinary about World One: private property in this world is owned by *one* single person, and everybody else in World One owns nothing at all (1 = owns everything; N–1 = own nothing). The non-owners depend in fundamental ways on the one and only owner. They cannot brush their teeth, dress their children, or put food on the table without the owner's permission. Since they own nothing, their access to the world of things—including vital uses of land and other natural resources—is entirely subject to the decisions of the owner, who allows or does not allow everybody else to exist. Even if World One does not accept slavery de jure, by virtue of the over-inclusion of the one and only owner, everybody is de facto held in chattel slavery. Even if the owner is a very generous and equitable master, his all-inclusive property rights deny agency and the right to existence to everybody else. Property monopolization is humiliating to the non-owners. If only one person owns everything, private property encroaches on human dignity.

- **World Two (radical property redistribution)**: The coexistence of private property and human dignity demands a non-monopolistic distribution of access rights to the world of things. The most non-monopolistic distribution is an equal distribution. Imagine World Two, an egalitarian world that demands a strictly equal distribution of private property among its members (the share of 1 = entire wealth/N). Does an equal distribution of such rights guarantee an absence of conflicts between human dignity and private property? World Two allows no citizen to own more or less than anybody else. Let us imagine some mechanism in place that, after dark, redistributes private property according to the strictly egalitarian principle. Persons, who gave away everything today in order to live a more spiritual life, or persons, who have risked and lost everything, will find their property restored next morning. The risk-takers will find this comfortable, but the voluntary poor, ascetics, and mendicant friars are weighed down by uninvited wealth. Moreover, the operators of successful businesses lose all of their profits in excess of the equal share of private property. In other words, the egalitarian property redistribution only favors those, who take risks unsuccessfully, and discourages individual efforts to become a better—and wealthier—person. Since everybody must own an equal amount of property, World Two discourages entrepreneurship and hard work. This is unsatisfying and, presumably, a good reason for many in World Two to feel humiliated. A strictly equal distribution of access rights to the world of things, even if it avoids some hardships of an unequal distribution, contravenes merit-based principles of justice (von Hayek 1976; Nozick 1974) as well as the freedom to abstain from material wealth. A strictly egalitarian society that redistributes wealth in a totalitarian fashion, even if done gently, violates human dignity. Private property allows individuals to trade and barter, enjoy the fruits or their labor, decide whether to consume, save, or invest, or choose between working late and spending family quality time. Surely, not every cent of a person's profit or salary is married to this person's dignity. Human dignity implies that an unequal distribution of private property be determined by the decisions and actions of free individuals. Private property guarantees a person's freedom to tailor his or her life according to his or her needs and preferences.
- **World Three (persistent poverty)**: So, if a society neither allows the monopolization nor requires an equal distribution of private property, has such a society found a viable balance between human dignity and private property? The answer is in the negative. Again, quantity is crucial. Consider a society where many persons own private property, tailored to the requirements of the Western property paradigm (Epstein 1985; Honoré 1961; Penner 2000), in a variety of quantities. Some persons, however, own very little or nothing at all. The members of the ownership segment of society enjoy a differentiated amount

of property, each according to their needs and preferences. As far as their own situation is concerned, the members of the ownership segment of society experience no tension between human dignity and private property. The poor, however, feel differently. It does not matter to them whether the wealth of the nation is owned by one owner or 20 million owners. What matters is that the poor and extremely poor own too little. They cannot brush their teeth, dress their children, or put food on the table without the alms donated by generous compatriots or the cash benefits doled out by the social welfare office. Persistent poverty is degrading and humiliating (Davy 2009 and 2014a; Gubrium et al. 2014; Pogge 2002 and 2007; Waldron 1991; Walker et al. 2013). Persistent poverty is not acceptable because 'respect for human dignity requires that we pay close attention to conditions of material disadvantage and its impact on different groups in our society'(Liebenberg 2005: 9). Clearly, the poor do not need to be enthroned as the one and only owner (as in World One) or participate in a strictly equal distribution of private property (as in World Two) to have their human dignity restored. Yet, the poor need some access rights to the world of things and to receive these rights in a non-humiliating fashion.

The three worlds illustrate the complex relationship between human dignity and private property. In some cases, the existence of private property—as an institution as well as an individual right—is a prerequisite of a dignified life, a life without humiliation. In other cases, private property threatens human dignity because it helps establish and maintain a revoltingly uneven and humiliating power relation. Also, human dignity and private property often co-exist in a state of indifference. Limiting our attention to such indifference, we are led to believe that there is little or nothing to learn from examining human dignity and private property. Yet, even apparently 'neutral' property can violate human dignity, if the given distribution of private property denies the poor and extremely poor vital access rights to the world of things. A homeless person, starving after 2 days of having had neither food nor water, has good reasons to feel humiliated.

3.4 The Core, the Floor, and the Ceiling: Basic Ideas

What do we learn from the model of three worlds? Private property and human dignity defy clear-cut classifications. Yet, human dignity provides a compelling framework for assessing property rights and distinguishing between the essential and the intolerable access to the world of goods. When do we own too little or too much? A comparison of luxury and destitution (see Fig. 1) emphasizes that dignity and property are related to each other. The simplifying model of the three worlds illustrates what this relationship means. Many property theories are monorational (Davy 2012: 66–67) and focus only on one of the three worlds. Property as a human right needs to account for all three. Being acceptable as human means that no one has too much, everyone has enough, and no one has too little. This is a dire message to the inhumanely wealthy: You are rich, but cannot be accepted as human because you have appropriated so much more than your share. This is also a dire message to the poor and extremely poor: You are so poor that you cannot be considered as human (and human rights, with their generous 'dignity' or 'equality' language, have betrayed you). Governments that wish to comply with universal human rights can accept neither. Yet, governments are limited in their ability to restore human dignity through egalitarian redistribution of wealth. Unless they also respect liberty, government schemes interfere with the humanity of all citizens subjected to their mandatory happiness.

World One teaches us that non-humiliating property needs a kind of limit or restraint. Only under certain circumstances can we accept property as 'that sole and despotic dominion which one man claims and exercises over the external things of the world, in total exclusion of the right of any other individual in the universe' (Blackstone 1766: 2 [Book II, Chapter 1]). Would this 'sole and despotic dominion' be exercised only by a single owner, everybody else would be humiliated. Nevertheless, nothing in the way the Western property paradigm defines 'property' avoids property monopolization. Neither constitutional property nor property under common or private law demands that the world of things be owned by many. No failsafe mechanism in property law prevents that everything is owned by only one person. Such a mechanism would be similar to fair trade laws which ban business monopolies or the land ceilings in some Indian land reform laws. Still, the Western property paradigm assumes that private property is owned by many (von Hayek 1944: 136). In the case of land, this assumption relies on the liberty of landowners and the forces of land markets. No Western property scholar endorses World One, a world in which all land is owned by only one proprietor. Quite the opposite, libertarians expect a beneficial diversity in ownership: Landowners, who are using their liberty and property wisely, create affluence through competition and, as if guided by an invisible hand, maximize the wealth of nations (Smith 1776: 292; von Hayek 1976: 107–132). Only under these circumstances can property's lack of temperance be accepted. This is the (implied) ***ceiling*** of private property: In order to be compatible with human dignity, property must be owned not only by one single owner, but by many. Or, in other words, nobody must own too much.

But how many more than one woman or man must be also landowners to prevent the humiliation of the landless and of those, who own no property at all? World Two responds to the question with radical property redistribution. Human dignity is sometimes associated with equality (Phillips 2015: 101). The highest degree of equality, with respect to property in land, is achieved by an equal distribution of land. In World Two, private property is equipped with two mechanisms that prevent an unequal distribution of land and other things: One, a measuring tool that determines each person's share, and two, a mechanism for daily redistribution. Both mechanisms have the same purpose: annihilating difference. Because of its totalitarian effect, many egalitarians recommend more sophisticated versions of equality (White 2003). In reality, property redistribution uses more costly and less elegant methods than World Two, such as land taxes or agrarian reform. The humiliation inflicted by World Two teaches us about the core of private property:

The ***core*** of private property is individual freedom regarding decisions and actions taken with respect to the world of things: 'Without property, real and personal, one could not enjoy life or liberty, and could not be free and independent. Only the property holder could make independent decisions and choices because he was not beholden to anyone; he had no need to be subservient' (Levy 1988: 175). World Two is more desirable than World One because it houses many owners, in fact everybody is an owner. Yet, World Two is unacceptable: It fundamentally denies difference although being different is essential for being human. Non-humiliating property must account for individual liberty. The German Federal Constitutional Court defines the core of private property succinctly: 'Property particularly secures the liberty of rights holders with respect to their assets and enables them to create for themselves an autonomous existence … Property is supposed to be the bedrock of the agency of all private owners, who may use their property for their autonomous private interest' (Bundesverfassungsgericht, 17 December 2013, Garzweiler [author's translation]). Similarly, the personhood theory of property emphasizes that private property relations are closely linked to individual liberty and personhood. Property rights needed by the owner to develop her personality and to function within society require particular protection (Radin 1993: 53). From the perspective of Martha Nussbaum's and Amartya Sen's capabilities approach, the core of private property is related to 'valuable functionings' (Sen 1992: 49). Item No. 10 on Nussbaum's list of central human capabilities, dealing with the 'control of one's environment,' includes the capability to 'being able to hold property (both land and movable goods), and having property rights on an equal basis with others' (Nussbaum 2006: 77). The core of private property, in other words, does not depend on having exactly the same as others, but on having *enough* for leading a life in dignity.

Apart from ascetics and mendicant friars, no one can lead a life in dignity without access to the world of things. World Three teaches us about the indignity of persistent poverty. It also teaches us about the irrelevance of the distribution of wealth—whether property is held only by one, by some, or by many owners—in the face of poverty. In *Citizenship and Social Class*, T.H. Marshall presents a sociological concept of citizenship that starts from an egalitarian position, yet progresses into a theory of differentiated inclusion and exclusion (Marshall 1950). Citizenship guarantees to everybody certain rights, yet it also permits a fair degree of inequality. Citizenship means to belong to a 'society in which class differences are legitimate in terms of social justice, and in which, therefore, the classes cooperate more closely than at present to the common benefit of all' (Marshall 1950: 62). How can class differences be legitimate in terms of social justice and even encourage social co-operation? Marshall's answer is intriguingly simple: Class differences are legitimate as soon as social rights ensure that nobody is left behind. Marshall described a social floor, the only acceptable reaction to World Three, which he called the 'social element' of citizenship: 'By the social element I mean the whole range from the right to a modicum of economic welfare and security to the right to share to the full in the social heritage and to live the life of a civilized being according to the standards prevailing in the society' (Marshall 1950: 11).

The International Labour Organization uses the phrase 'social floors' in a recent initiative, but avoids to address issues of private property or land tenure (Social Protection Floors Recommendation, 2012 [No. 202]). Brian Simpson asserts that everyone's right to 'at least a basic minimum of property' expresses 'a notion of human dignity, or the belief that the institution of private property [is] a prerequisite to human freedom' (Simpson 2001: 757). With respect to the human right to property, the concept of a social floor recognizes that human dignity is violated by persistent poverty, but not by the fact that some own more than others. As long as disparity in the distribution of wealth does not amount to intolerable property monopolization (World One), human dignity is not affected by income or wealth disparity. Human dignity is greatly affected, however, if not everybody owns a 'modicum of economic welfare and security.' Subsequently, the right to an adequate standard of living (Article 11 ICESCR) calls for a modicum of social assistance (Van Genugten and Perez-Bustillo 2001; Kälin et al. 2004: 187–309) or minimal property (Davy 2012 170; Simpson 2001: 757). The right to an adequate standard of living has a spatial dimension, in particular with respect to food and housing (Carter 2003: 46–49; CESCR 1991; Davy 2009 and 2012; Deininger 2003: 51–73; Kolocek 2013 and 2017; OHCHR 2014 and 2015; UN Department 2009: 144; UN Habitat 2007; UN Habitat and GLTN 2008). The right to an adequate standard of living relates to land use because no person can exist without using land (Davy 2009 and 2012; De Schutter 2010; OHCHR 2014; Waldron 1991). Everybody occupies physical space, but the full participation in everyday life also requires that land be available for housing, work, mobility, leisure, and social exchange. The scope and content of the right to minimal access to land may vary and cannot be expressed in square meters or requirements for land rights formalization. Minimal access to land comprises the individual right to all of the land uses which are indispensable for a person to achieve an adequate standard of living (van Banning 2002: 323–336; Sprankling 2014: 130–132).

3.5 *The Core, the Floor, and the Ceiling: Locke's Property Theory*

The concept of human dignity helps understand what property means, to what degree private property is indispensable, and under what circumstances private property harms human dignity. From this understanding rise the core, the floor, and the ceiling as elements of private property that derives from human dignity. Since the three elements are not well accepted in mainstream property theory, it is worth remembering that a very similar idea was already embedded in one of the foundational property narratives. John Locke's account of property, inspired by his social contract theory, contains three layers which conform with the concept of property as a human right that comprises a core, a floor, and a ceiling of private property. Locke's account is, in fact, most helpful for understanding human dignity and private property. By invoking one of the most fundamental texts in the history of property theory, I do not claim that the core, the floor, and the ceiling have been there from the beginning. Many eminent scholars (e.g., Epstein 1985; Levy 1988; Schlatter 1951: 151–161) read Locke very differently from my interpretation. I do not wish to engage in a debate on the 'correct' reading of Locke. I think it is appropriate, however, to acknowledge that the Second Treatise was not merely about curbing the government's power to regulate the use of private property (Epstein 1985: 13). Lockean property is polyrational in the sense that it encompasses several layers.

The first layer is the core. Locke asserts that natural persons have a right in their body and, through their labor, may appropriate land and other natural resources: '[E]very Man has a Property in his own Person [...] The *Labour* of his Body, and the *Work* of his Hands, we may say, are properly his' (Locke 1698: 287 [Book II, § 27]). The core of private property is the ownership in one's body and the right to the fruits of individual manual labor. This combination of property, body, and work surely links private property to human dignity. Even if Locke does not use the word 'dignity,' he and his followers 'regarded property as a basic human right, essential to one's existence, to one's independence, to one's dignity as a person' (Levy 1988: 175). The second layer is the floor. Locke is convinced that substantive property as a natural right is not a matter of convenience and comfort, but of personhood and individual survival. The floor, in his words, is subsistence: 'Men, being once born, have a right to their Preservation, and consequently Meat and Drink, and such other things as Nature affords for their Subsistence' (Locke 1698 II § 25). The third layer is the ceiling: Locke suggests that the right to acquire private property be limited in two ways. First, the 'Lockean proviso' (Nozick 1974: 178–182) assumes that the individual appropriation of private property never must interfere with any other person's ability to acquire property through her body's work: 'Nor was this appropriation of any parcel of Land, by improving it, any prejudice to any other Man, since there was still enough and as good left; and more than the yet unprovided could use' (Locke 1698: 291 [Book II, § 33]). Second, Locke limits the accumulation of private property to what a man needs because it would be 'useless as well as dishonest to carve himself too much, or take more than he needed' (Locke 1698: 302 [Book II, § 51]). Beyond the ceiling, private property is no longer legitimized by Locke's labor theory of property.

A Lockean ceiling is mostly accepted by scholars, who consider the consequences of unbridled appropriation on the natural environment (Judge 2002; Shrader-Frechette 1993; Stevens 1996). The reasons for the fetters Locke put upon appropriation, however, derive not from ecology, but from human dignity. The Lockean proviso acknowledges everybody's right to appropriation, depending on each individual's diligence; the second reservation rules out greed and gluttony as justifications for the acquisition of private property. Depriving anybody from their right to appropriate what they need for 'subsistence' is a violation of human dignity as well as the wasteful and gluttonous appropriation by anybody, who takes excessively more than anybody else. A precise delimitation of what is needed for subsistence or what constitutes gluttony is difficult. Such difficulty, however, does not depreciate the notion of the core, the floor, and the ceiling of private property.

It merely encourages us to look harder for the directions given by the concepts of human dignity and private property. Locke's account of property in the Second Treatise is accepted by many theorists as the eminent concept of private property (Nozick 1974: 174–182; Penner 2000: 187–201), particularly with regard to the United States constitution (Epstein 1985: 16). Yet, some scholars limit their understanding of Locke's theory to a restriction of the government. Appraising Locke's ideas, Richard Epstein (1985: 13) asserts that '[p]rivate property represents the sum of the goods that the individual gets to keep outside of the control of the state.' Obviously, his views contradict, for example, an ecologically sensitive interpretation of John Locke. The 'revisionist analysis of Locke's theory of property rights' (Shrader-Frechette 1993: 65) criticizes a selective reading of the Second Treatise and asserts that 'there is a precedent, in Locke's text, for the community decisions required by land-use planning and for societal limits on the exercise of property rights' (Shrader-Frechette 1993: 78).

4 Why not Follow the Golden Rule of Property as a Human Right?

The result of the legal analysis of the human right to property and the result of the human dignity test are not fully congruent, yet there are many overlaps. Property as a human right can be understood best as comprising a core, a floor, and a ceiling:

- UN-sponsored human rights law defines a core of private property. The core protects the right to own property (by oneself or in association with others) with regard to the victims of racial discrimination (Article 5 [d] v ICERD), women (Articles 15 and 16 CEDAW), migrant workers (Article 15 ICRAM), or persons with disabilities (Article 12 CRPD). With regard to other owners, Article 17 UDHR has been transformed into binding treaty law only on the regional level (e.g., Article 1 ECHR_P1). Also, the core of private property protects the right to work (Article 6 ICESCR), which already Adam Smith (1776: 120) called 'the most sacred and inviolable' type of property.
- UN-sponsored human rights law defines a floor of private property. Article 11 ICESCR grants the right to an adequate standard of living, among others, the right to adequate food and adequate housing. It does not matter that T.H. Marshall did not call social citizenship 'property'. Social rights like the right to an adequate standard of living are human rights to minimal property (Davy 2012: 181 and 186), even if domestic property law distinguishes between property rights and social rights (Liebenberg 2005). States Parties have an active duty to provide an adequate standard of living to everybody. Every woman and every man 'shall be able, without shame and without unreasonable obstacles … to enjoy their basic needs under conditions of dignity' (Eide 2001b: 133).
- UN-sponsored human rights law defines a ceiling to private property with regard to the right not to be owned. Human rights law prohibits slavery, servitude,

forced labor, and forced marriages. Women, men, and children cannot be owned under the golden rule of property as a human right. It remains unclear whether human rights law also provides a ceiling to the ownership of land and other natural resources. For example, the second sentence in Article 1, para. 2, ICESCR demands: 'In no case may a people be deprived of its own means of subsistence.' This sounds like a ban on World One, but not like an individual right.

The golden rule of property as a human right (Davy 2012) derives from human dignity. With respect to UN-sponsored human rights, the implementation of the golden rule through binding international treaties is unfinished business. Surely, many open questions will provide food for thought as to how best organize everybody's access to the world of things, and to land. For example, a recent debate on a right to land is based on Article 11 ICESCR and the right to adequate food and adequate housing (De Schutter 2010; OHCHR 2014; Sprankling 2014: 130–132; van Banning 2002: 323–336). In the spirit of this debate, one could presume that a general human right to property exists that guarantees an adequate standard of living (Howard-Hassmann 2013). The purpose of this chapter is, however, to show that property as a human right is even broader. After all, in the light of human dignity, the golden rule of property as a human right provides for a core, a floor, and a ceiling.

Acknowledgements This chapter is benefitting from FLOOR, a research group on financial assistance, land policy, and global social rights (principal investigators: B. Davy, U. Davy, L. Leisering; 2007–2015, partly funded by the German Research Foundation (*Deutsche Forschungsgemeinschaft*—DFG). In particular, I thank DFG for funding my FLOOR sub-project on socio-ecological land policy (DA 849/2–1). I greatly profited from the 2014, 2015, and 2016 workshops preparing a research group on 'Understanding Southern Welfare' at the Center for Interdisciplinary Research (*Zentrum für interdisziplinäre Forschung* – ZiF) at University of Bielefeld. The text draws from my earlier work (Davy 2009; 2012: 164–176; 2014; Davy and Pellissery 2013). I am very grateful to the participants of AESOP, ACSP, ALPS, and PLPR conferences, whose inspiring comments helped me to improve my thoughts. For their assistance, I also thank Valentin Frevel, Melanie Halfter, Daniela Knoop, Michael Kolocek, Astrid Maurer, and Nadine Preuß (TU Dortmund University). I completed work on this chapter while staying at *Caspar Heinrich Klinik*, Bad Driburg (North Rhine-Westphalia, Germany), after suffering an acute myocardial infarction. I am most grateful to the Bielefeld emergency service as well as the doctors and staff of Gilead hospital (Bielefeld) and CHK for keeping my heart beating and my mind feisty.

References

Alexander GS (2009) The social-obligation norm in American property law. Cornell Law Rev 94(4):745–819

Alfredsson G, Eide A (eds) (1999) The Universal Declaration of Human Rights. A common standard of achievement. Martinus Nijhoff, The Hague, Boston, London

Allen T (2007) Property as fundamental right in India, Europe and South Africa. Asia Pac Law Rev 15(2):193–218

Allen T (2010) Liberalism, social democracy and the value of property under the European convention on human rights. Int Comp Law Q 59(4):1055–1078

Ankersen T, Ruppert T (2006a) Tierra y Libertad: the social function doctrine and land reform in Latin America. Tulane Environ Law J 19:69–120
Ankersen T, Ruppert T (2006b) Defending the polygon: the emerging human right to communal property. Oklahoma Law Rev 59(4):681–757
Atuahene B (2014) We want what's ours. Learning from South Africa's land restitution program. Oxford University Press, Oxford
Bentham J (1843) The works of Jeremy Bentham published under the superintendence of his executor, John Bowring, vol II. William Tait, Edinburgh
Berle AA, Means GGC (1932) The modern corporation and private property. Commerce Clearing House, New York, Chicago, Washington
Bierce A (1911/1999) The devil's dictionary. Oxford University Press, New York, Oxford
Blackstone W (1766/1979) Commentaries on the laws of England. Volume II (Of the Rights of Things). With an introduction by A. W. Brian Simpson. University of Chicago Press, Chicago, London
Carter MR (2003) Designing land and property rights reform for poverty alleviation and food security. Land Reform 2:45–57
CESCR (Committee on Economic, Social and Cultural Rights) (1991) General Comment No. 4: the right to adequate housing = CESCR (1992) Report on Sixth Session. E/C.12/1991/4. Annex III: 114–120
Chigara B (2004) Land reform policy. The challenge of human rights law. Ashgate, Aldershot
CHR (Commission on Human Rights) (1954) Report of the Tenth Session. UN-Doc. E/CN.4/705. New York: United Nations
Clayton R, Tomlinson H (2000) The law of human rights, vol 1. Oxford University Press, Oxford, New York
Davy B (2009) The poor and the land: poverty, property, planning (centenary paper). Town Plann Rev 80(3):228–265
Davy B (2012) Land policy. Planning and the spatial consequences of property. Ashgate, Farnham, Burlington, VT
Davy B (2014a) Non-humiliating plans! A human rights approach. FLOOR Working Paper No. 20 (www.floorgroup.raumplanung.tu-dortmund.de/FLOOR_Working_papers/FLOOR_WP020_B_Davy_Non-humiliating_plans.pdf; accessed Jan 2017)
Davy B, Pellissery S (2013) The citizenship promise (un)fulfilled: the right to housing in informal settings. Int J Soc Welf 22:S68–S84 (In: Davy B, Davy U, Leisering L [guest editors] Exploring global social citizenship: Human rights perspectives)
Davy U (2013) Social citizenship going international: changes in the reading of UN-sponsored economic and social rights. Int J Soc Welf 22:S15–S31
Davy U (2014b) How human rights shape social citizenship: on citizenship and the understanding of economic and social rights. Wash Univ Glob Stud Law Rev 13(2):201–263
Dean H (2007) Social policy and human rights: re-thinking the engagement. Soc Policy Soc 7(1): 1–12
Dehaibi L (2015) The case for an inclusive human right to property: social importance and individual self-realization. W J Legal Stud 6(1):1–22
Deininger K (2003) Land policies for growth and poverty reduction. World Bank, Oxford University Press, Washington, Oxford
De Schutter O (2010) The emerging human right to land. Int Commun Law Rev 12:303–334
Dolidze A (2016) Promise and perils of the international human right to property. Univ Pac Law Rev 47(2):169–182
Düwell M, Braarvig J, Brownsword R, Mieth D (eds) (2014) The Cambridge handbook of human dignity: Interdisciplinary perspectives. Cambridge University Press, Cambridge
Eide A (2001a) Economic, social and cultural rights as human rights. In: Eide et al. (eds), pp. 9–28
Eide A (2001b) The right to an adequate standard of living including the right to food. In: Eide et al. (eds), pp 133–148
Eide A, Wenche BE (1999) Article 25. In: Alfredsson G, Eide A (eds), pp 523–550

Eide A, Krause C, Rosas A (eds) (2001) Economic, social and cultural rights, 2nd edn. Martinus Nijhoff, Dordrecht, Boston, London
Epstein R (1985) Takings. Private property and the power of eminent domain. Harvard University Press, Cambridge, MA, London
FAO (Food and Agriculture Organization of the United Nations) (2012) Voluntary guidelines on the responsible governance of tenure of land, fisheries and forests in the context of national food security. FAO, Rome
Frulli M (2008) Advancing international criminal law: the special court for Sierra Leone recognizes forced marriage as a 'new' crime against humanity. J Int Crim Justice 6:1033–1042
Godden L, Tehan M (eds) (2010) Comparative perspectives on communal land and individual ownership. Routledge, Abingdon, New York
Grear A (2006) Human rights—human bodies? Some reflections on corporate human rights distortion, the legal subject, embodiment and human rights theory. Law Critique 17:171–199
Gubrium E, Pellissery S, Lødemel I (eds) (2014) The shame of it. Global perspectives on anti-poverty policies. Policy Press, Bristol
Hardoon D (2017) An economy for the 99%. Oxfam Briefing Paper. Oxford, Oxfam International
Henkin L (1979) International human rights as 'rights'. Cardozo Law Rev 1(2):425–448
Honoré AM (Tony) (1961) Ownership. In: Guest AG (ed) Oxford essays on jurisprudence. Oxford University Press, Oxford, 106–147
Howard-Hassmann RE (2013) Reconsidering the right to own property. J Human Rights 12:180–197
Huchzermeyer M (2011). Cities with 'slums.' From informal settlement eradication to a right to the city in Africa. UCT Press, Claremont
Jacobs HM (2013) Private property and human rights: A mismatch in the 21st century? Int J Soc Welf 22 (Supplement 1) S85–S101 (In: Davy B, Davy U, Leisering L [guest editors] Exploring global social citizenship: Human rights perspectives)
Joireman SF, Brown J (2013) Property: human right or commodity. J Hum Rights 12:165–179
Judge Rebecca P (2002) Restoring the commons: toward a new interpretation of locke's theory of property. Land Econ 78(3):331–338
Kälin W, Künzli J (2009) The law of international human rights protection. Oxford University Press, Oxford, New York
Kälin W, Müller L, Wyttenbach J (eds) (2004) The face of human rights. Lars Müller, Baden
Kateb G (2011) Human dignity. Cambridge, Belknap Press of Harvard University Press, MA, London
Kelsen H (1960) Reine Rechtslehre. Mit einem Anhang: das Problem der Gerechtigkeit, 2nd edn. Verlag Franz Deuticke, Wien
Kennedy David (2002) The international human rights movement: part of the problem? Harvard Hum Rights J 15:101–126
Kolocek M (2013) The human right to housing in the 27 member states of the European Union. Eur J Homelessness 7(1):135–154
Kolocek M (2017) The human right to housing in the face of land policy and social citizenship. A global discourse analysis. Palgrave, Houndsmill, Basingstoke
Krause C (2001) The right to property. In: Eide et al. (eds), pp. 191–201
Krause C, Alfredsson G (1999) Article 17. In: Alfredsson G, Eide A, pp. 359–378
Levy LW (1988) Property as a human right. Const Commentary 5(1):169–184
Liebenberg S (2005) The value of human dignity in interpreting socio-economic rights. S Afr J Hum Rights 21(1):1–31
Lindner EG, Hartling LM, Spalthoff U (2011) Human dignity and humiliation studies: a global network advancing dignity through dialogue. Policy Futures in Educ 9(1):66–73
Lindner EG (2007) In times of globalization and human rights: does humiliation become the most disruptive force? J Hum Dignity Humiliation Stud 1(1):1–30 (online: www.humilliation studies.upeace.org/; last accessed Jan 2017)
Locke J (1698/1991) Two treatises of government: in the former, the false principles and foundation of Sir Robert Filmer, and his followers, are detected and overthrown. In: Laslett P (ed), The latter

is an essay concerning the true original, extent, and end of civil-government. Cambridge University Press, Cambridge
Maastricht Guidelines (1997) Maastricht guidelines on violations of economic, social and cultural rights. Human Rights Quarterly 20 (1998) 691–705. (Also published in: Committee on Economic, Social and Cultural Rights. Substantive issues arising in the implementation of the International Covenant on Economic, Social and Cultural Rights, 2 Oct 2000, E/C.12/ 2000/13: 16–24)
Margalit A (1996) The decent society (trans: Goldblum N). Cambridge, Harvard University Press, MA, London
Marshall TH (1950) Citizenship and social class and other essays. Cambridge University Press, Cambridge
McCrudden C (ed) (2014) Understanding human dignity. The British Academy/Oxford University Press, Oxford
McDougal MS (1959) Perspectives for an international law of human dignity. Am Soc Int Law Proc 53:107–132
Meneses-Reyes R, Cabellero-Juárez JA (2014) The right to work on the street: Public spaces and constitutional rights. Plann Theor 13(4):370–386
Mirow MC (2010) The social-obligation norm of property: Duguit, Hayem, and others. Fla J Int Law 22(2):191–226
Morsink J (1999) The Universal Declaration of Human Rights. Origins, drafting, and intent. University of Pennsylvania Press, Philadelphia
Nozick R (1974) Anarchy, state, and utopia. Blackwell, Oxford, United Kingdom – Cambridge, Massachusetts
Nussbaum MC (2006) Frontiers of justice. Disability, nationality, species membership. Belknap Press, Cambridge, MA, London
OHCHR (Office of the UN High Commissioner for Human Rights) (2014) Report of the United Nations High Commissioner for Human Rights. E/2014/86
OHCHR (Office of the UN High Commissioner for Human Rights) (2015) Land and human rights: standards and applications. OHCHR, Geneva
Ondetti G (2016) The social function of property, land rights and social welfare in Brazil. Land Use Policy 50:29–37
Ovey C, White R (2006) Jacobs and White, The European Convention on Human Rights, 4th edn. Oxford University Press, Oxford, New York
Penner JE (2000) The idea of property in law. Oxford University Press, Oxford
Perlman J (2010) Favela. Four decades of living on the edge in Rio de Janeiro. Oxford University Press, Oxford
Phillips A (2015) The politics of the human. Cambridge University Press, Cambridge
Ploeger HD, Groetelaers DA (2007) The importance of the fundamental right to property for the practice of planning: an introduction to the case law of the European Court of Human Rights on Article 1, Protocol 1. Eur Plan Stud 15(10):1423–1438
Pogge T (2002) World poverty and human rights. Cosmopolitan responsibilities and reforms. Polity, Cambridge
Pogge T (ed) (2007) Freedom from poverty as a human right. Who owes what to the very poor? Oxford University Press, Oxford, New York
Posner RA (2007) Economic analysis of law, 7th edn. Aspen, New York
Radin MJ (1993) Reinterpreting property. University of Chicago Press, Chicago, London
Roy A (2005) Urban informality. Toward an epistemology of planning. J Am Plann Assoc 71(2) 147–158
Roy A, AlSayad N (2004) Urban informality. Transnational perspectives from the Middle East, Latin America, and South Asia. Lexington, Lanham
Schlatter R (1951) Private property. The history of an idea. Russell & Russell, New York
Sen A (1992) Inequality reexamined. Harvard University Press, Cambridge, MA
Sen A (2004) Elements of a theory of human rights. Philos Public Aff 32(4):315–356
Shahinian G (2009) Report of the Special Rapporteur on contemporary forms of slavery, including its causes and consequences. Human Rights Council, 12th Session. A/HRC/12/21

Shahinian G (2010) Report of the Special Rapporteur on contemporary forms of slavery, including its causes and consequences. Human Rights Council, 15th Session. A/HRC/15/20
Shea TJ (1956) Implementing land reform in India. 25(1):1–8
Shrader-Frechette K (1993) Locke and limits on land ownership. In: Caldwell LK, Shrader-Frechette KS (eds) (1993) Policy for land. Law and ethics. Rowman & Littlefield Publishers, Lanham, Maryland, 65–83
Simpson AWB (2001/2010) Human rights and the end of empire. Britain and the genesis of the European Convention. Oxford University Press, Oxford
Singer JW (2000) Entitlement. The paradoxes of property. Yale University Press, New Haven, London
Singer JW, Beermann JM (1993) The social origins of property. Can J Law Jurisprud 6(2):217–248
Smith A (1776/1993) An inquiry into the nature and causes of the wealth of nations (edited by: Sutherland K). Oxford University Press, Oxford, New York
Song AM (2015) Human dignity: a fundamental guiding value for a human rights approach to fisheries? Marine Policy 61:164–170
Sprankling JG (2014) The international law of property. Oxford University Press, Oxford
Stevens JB (1996) John Locke, environmental property, and instream water rights. Land Economics 72(2):261–268
Tomuschat C (2008) Human rights. Between idealism and realism. 2nd edition. Oxford University Press, Oxford, New York
Turner BS (1993) Outline of a theory of human rights. Sociology 27(3):489–512
UN Department (of Economic and Social Affairs) (2009) Rethinking Poverty. Report on the World Social Situation 2010. New York, United Nations
UN Habitat (2007) Enhancing urban safety and security. Global report on human settlements 2007. UN Habitat & Earthscan, London—Sterling, VA
UN Habitat & GLTN (Global Land Tool Network) (2008) Secure land rights for all. UN Habitat, Nairobi, Kenya
UNESCO (1948) Human rights. Comments and interpretations. With an introduction by Jacques Maritain. UN-Doc. UNESCO/PHS/3(rev.)
van Banning TRG (2002) The human right to property. Intersentia, Antwerpen, Oxford, New York
van der Walt A (1999) Constitutional property clauses. A comparative analysis. Dordrecht, Kluwer Law International
van der Walt A (2005) Constitutional property law. Juta, Cape Town
van der Walt A (2009) Property in the margins. Hart, Oxford, Portland
van der Walt AJ, Viljoen S (2015) The constitutional mandate for social welfare—systemic differences and links between property, land rights and housing rights. Potchefstroom Electron Law J (Potchefstroomse Elektroniese Regsblad) 18(4):1035–1090
van Genugten W, Perez-Bustillo C (eds) (2001) The poverty of rights. Human rights and the eradication of poverty. Zed Books, London, New York
von Hayek FA (1944/2007) The road to serfdom (edited by: Caldwell B). University of Chicago Press, Chicago
von Hayek, FA (1976) The mirage of social justice. In: Hayek FA (1982) Law, legislation and liberty. A new statement of the liberal principles of justice and political economy, vol II. Routledge & Kegan Paul, London
Waldron Jeremy (1991) Homelessness and the issue of freedom. Univ California at Los Angeles Law Rev 39:295–324
Waldron Jeremy (2012) Dignity, rank, & rights. Oxford University Press, Oxford, New York
Walker R, Kyomuhendo GB, Chase E, Choudry S, Gubrium EK, Nicola JY, Lødemel I, M L, Mwiine A, Pellissery S, Ming Y (2013) Poverty in global perspective: Is shame a common denominator? J Soc Policy 42(2):215–233
White S (2003) The civic minimum. Oxford University Press, On the rights and obligations of economic citizenship. Oxford

Evolution of Property Rights in India

Madhumita Datta Mitra

1 Introduction

Right to property is framed as a human right under the Universal Declaration of Human Rights[1] and is recognized as a fundamental right in most democracies. It is one of the most controversial of rights, always in need of an appropriate definition suited to a nation's political, social and economic conditions.[2] While all liberal constitutions allow for certain reasonable restrictions on an absolute right to property for some public good, the challenge facing every country is where to draw the line against state interference into a person's right to own and enjoy property.

In 1950, independent India drafted into its new Constitution a set of fundamental rights for its citizens to free speech, peaceful assembly, association, to move freely throughout the territory, to reside and settle in any part of the country, "to acquire, hold and dispose of property", and to practice any profession, or carry on any

The original paper titled "*Evolution of property rights in India: Lessons from the past, possibilities for the future*" was published by the Liberty Institute, New Delhi, under its Right to Property Project which was supported by the Friedrich Naumann Foundation for Freedom.

Madhumita Datta Mitra is an Independent Legal Consultant and Research Fellow to Liberty Institute's Right to Property Project.

[1]Universal Declaration of Human Rights, Article 17, "*(1) Everyone has the right to own property alone as well as in association with others; (2) No one shall be arbitrarily deprived of his property*".

[2]Definitional issues have ensured that right to property has not been included in the International Covenant on Civil and Political Rights and International Covenant of Economic, Social and Cultural Rights.

M.D. Mitra (✉)
Liberty Institute, New Delhi, India
e-mail: madhumita.mitra@gmail.com

S. Pellissery et al. (eds.), *Land Policies in India*, India Studies in Business and Economics, DOI 10.1007/978-981-10-4208-9_2

occupation, trade or business. The Constitution also gave the nation an independent judiciary.

Of all the fundamental rights enshrined in the Indian Constitution, the right to property has been persistently under attack from the executive. Political philosophies of the day claimed a need to set right historical wrongs. Whittling down property rights through repeated subversion of the Constitution was the chosen path. This pitted the executive against a judiciary, which believed itself to be the final arbiter on the Constitution as framed by the founding fathers.

Undermining of the right to property as a fundamental right precipitated by a weak rule of law regime saw a corresponding rise in the abuse of the eminent domain power. The justification for dilution of the right to property for a more equitable distribution of land by taking from the large landlords, gave way to acquisition of land from small and marginal farmers, for projects and activities that benefit the rich and powerful. This led to a growing sense of injustice and numerous public protests.

This paper will trace the evolution of the right to property in India under the Constitution of India since 1950 and through the substantial and often conflicting jurisprudence. The paper will look at the executive's role in the gradual dilution and eventual elimination of the right to property as a fundamental right through the play of politics of equity and distributive justice. Was the Supreme Court's assertion of its supremacy over the Parliament's powers to determine the extent of property right commensurate with the Court's abdication of its review powers in the face of gross abuse of eminent domain?

The property rights story in India is characterized by the dilution of the right to property in the first 30 years, driven by socialist ideology and a sense of distributive of justice, as much as populism, and the corresponding abuse of the land acquisition laws. The next 30 years illustrate how the wheel has turned as citizenship deepened. The poorest are at the forefront demanding protection of their property rights and reinforcing the criticality of rule of law.

2 Evolution of Property Rights in India: Pre-independence

The concept of private property as understood in today's constitutional sense evolved with the interpretation of classical Hindu law by judges of the British Empire. The English common law practices ironed out conflicting texts and divergent customary rules prevailing across India and codified problematic elements of a Hindu's right to property and its alienation (Gandhi 1985).[3]

[3]The earliest record of the concept of private property in India is in the Manusmriti, *The Code of Manu*, a body of ancient Sanskrit texts detailing religious and legal duties of Hindus.

Muslim rulers[4] had introduced the *Jagirdari* system of creating temporary alienations on military-revenue considerations, which evolved in the sixteenth century. *Jagirs* (land holdings) were granted to nobles, scattered away from each other to prevent consolidation by the assignees (Gandhi 1985). British rulers inherited the existing land settlement systems of the Mughals that covered much of the Indian sub-continent. Waning Mughal rule had made the *jagirdars* de facto owners of the land. It was politically expedient for the colonial rulers to continue dealing with them to generate land revenue. By imposing the English common law to determine property relationships, the British ironically laid the ground for recognition of private property rights in India.

In 1793, the British government granted Permanent Settlements to *zamindars* (landed aristocrats)[5] in the region of Bengal with ownership rights over land. The settlement was extended to Bihar, Madras and Orissa. Modified versions of such settlements, including short-term alienations, were created in other parts of India also (Gandhi 1985; Mearns 1999).[6] The common feature of these diverse land tenure systems was that the *zamindars* did not technically own the land and the tillers of the land were tenants of the *zamindars*.[7]

The concept of eminent domain as an attribute of State sovereignty was first introduced by the British through the Bengal Regulation I of 1824, which authorized compulsory acquisition of private property by the State.[8] The Land Acquisition Act of 1894 empowered the State to acquire private land for a 'public

---

[4]Muslim rule in the Indian sub-continent was spread roughly between tenth to eighteenth centuries.

[5]The term '*zamindar*' is broadly used for 'intermediaries' across varied tenure systems, who administered land on behalf of the rulers, but did not own it.

[6]Broadly, three different types of revenue systems were introduced by the British, which evolved into the land tenure systems that independent India inherited. The *Zamindari* system introduced around 1793, prevailed over most of North India, including present-day Uttar Pradesh (except Avadh and Agra), Bihar, West Bengal, most of Orissa, and Rajasthan (except Jaipur and Jodhpur). The *Ryotwari* system, introduced in Madras in 1792 and in Bombay in 1817–18, held sway over most of South India, including present-day Maharashtra, Karnataka, Tamil Nadu, Kerala, Andhra Pradesh, and most of Madhya Pradesh and Assam and also the princely states of Jaipur and Jodhpur in Rajasthan. The *Mahalwari* system was introduced between 1820 and 1840 to the present-day Punjabs in Pakistan and India, and Haryana, parts of present-day Madhya Pradesh and Orissa, and the princely states of Avadh and Agra in Uttar Pradesh.

[7]Permanent Settlements meant that *zamindars* paid revenue fixed in perpetuity to the government, which was at rates higher than what was paid prior to 1793.

[8]Bengal Regulation I, 1824 applied to the Bengal Presidency. Similar laws were enacted for Bombay (Building Act XXVII of 1839) and Madras (Act XX of 1852 adopting sections of the Bengal Regulation I, 1824). Separate amendments brought the railways under these legislations. First consolidated land acquisition law for British India was Act VI of 1857 repealing all previous legislations. See, Law Commission of India, Tenth Report: *Law of Acquisition and Requisition of Land,* 1958.

purpose' on payment of compensation.[9] Constitutional protection of property figured for the first time under the British rule in the Government of India Act of 1935. Expropriation of private property, including land and commercial and industrial undertakings, without 'public purpose' and full compensation was illegal.[10]

3 Indian Constitution and Property Rights

By the end of the British rule, *zamindars* held vast tracts of land with complete control over the tillers' rights. This land was however, hugely fragmented, because of the historical nature of alienations made first by the Mughals and later by the British. In the run-up to the Indian independence in 1947, socialism was the dominant ideology of the Indian National Congress, the party that led India's freedom struggle against British rule. Insecurity of land tenures among the village communities, poverty and indebtedness and recurring famines preoccupied negotiations on law-making with the British to secure independence and later, within the Constituent Assembly drafting the Constitution for independent India.

The Constituent Assembly was strongly divided between government take over of private property and the continuance of property rights as it stood in the 1935 Act. Even among those who favoured expropriation, and no one really opposed abolition of *zamindari*, differences arose over how much compensation should be paid (Austin 1999).[11] The Constitution of India, which came into effect in 1950, was therefore, a compromise. So while the citizens enjoyed fundamental right "to acquire, hold and dispose property" under Article 19(1)(f), Article 19(5) made this right subject to reasonable restrictions in public interest. This fundamental right could also be taken away under Article 31, the eminent domain article, but taking of

---

[9]Land Acquisition Act 1894, originally applied only to British India. The Native States passed their own land acquisition acts, for example, the Hyderabad Land Acquisition Act 1899, the Mysore Land Acquisition Act 1894, the Travancore Land Acquisition Act 1914. See, Law Commission of India, Tenth Report: *Law of Acquisition and Requisition of Land*, 1958.

[10]Government of India Act 1935, "*Section 299 (1): No person shall be deprived of his property in British India save by authority of law; Section 299(2): Neither the Federal nor a Provincial Legislature shall have power to make any law authorizing the compulsory acquisition for public purposes of any land, or any commercial or industrial undertaking, or any interest in, or any company owning, any commercial or industrial undertaking, unless the law provides for the compensation for the property acquired and either fixes the amount of compensation, or specifies the principles on which, and the manner in which, it is to be determined…; Section 299(5): In this section 'land' includes immovable property of every kind and rights in or over such property, and undertaking includes part of an undertaking.*

[11]The Social Revolution and the First Amendment, Chapter 3. While Rajendra Prasad, Jawaharlal Nehru and Sardar Vallabhbhai Patel were on one page that *Zamindari* must be abolished, Mahatma Gandhi had earlier expressed himself against unjustly dispossessing *zamindars* of their property and instead advocated converting their mind-set to holding property in trust for their tenants.

private property could only be 'by the authority of law', 'for public purposes' and on payment of compensation.

Though compensation was a fundamental requirement, there was to be no 'just compensation', only that the law should provide for compensation for the acquired property and either fix the amount or specify the principles of determination of compensation (Singh 2005). The Constitution also placed 'acquisition and requisitioning of property' as a Concurrent List item which meant that both Parliament and the State legislatures could enact laws on the subject. But authority of the Parliament was established as a fundamental principle and legislations passed by the States required Presidential assent.

The founding fathers' primary goal was to ensure social engineering through agrarian reforms.[12] Land was made a 'state subject' by the Government of India Act 1935, and this position continued under the Indian Constitution. Individual States therefore, enacted a large number of land reform legislations essentially to abolish intermediary tenures, regulate the size of holdings (to enable ceiling-surplus redistribution of land to the landless), and for consolidation (of fragmented land holdings) and settlement of tenures/ownership.

A series of judgments from the Supreme Court and High Courts in the first years of the Constitution belied the expectation of the Constituent Assembly that the government would be allowed a free hand with its social engineering. Courts repeatedly struck down laws enacted by the State Legislatures as *ultra vires* of fundamental rights and rule of law principles of the new Constitution.

4 Individual Right Versus Community Rights: Constitution Amendments 1951–1964

The court rulings hit three property issues—expropriation of *zamindari* land on abolishing of *zamindari*, takings under police power and nationalization of trade and business to effect government control over economy, defeating Prime Minister J. L. Nehru's expectations that the courts would endorse his philosophy that no individual could override the rights of the community (Austin 1999).

The First Amendment to the newly minted Constitution in 1951 was meant to remove hurdles posed by the judiciary on 'dilatory litigation'.[13] Article 31A barred judicial review of any fundamental right violation as a result of an eminent domain

[12]Government's land reforms agenda had five components: Abolition of the Intermediaries; Tenancy Reforms; Ceiling on landholdings; Consolidation of holdings; Compilation and updating of land records.

[13]Two rulings of the Patna High Court invalidated the Bihar Management of Estates and Tenures Act 1949 for violating Articles 19(1)(f) and 31 (*Sir Kameshwar Singh (Darbhanga) vs The Province of Bihar*, AIR 1950 Patna 392) and the Bihar Land Reforms Act 1950 for determining compensation that infringed Article 14 as unequal treatment (*Kameshwar Singh vs State of Bihar*, AIR 1951 Patna 91).

exercise. Article 31B was inserted creating the Ninth Schedule in the Constitution to prohibit courts from questioning agrarian land reform legislations inserted in the Schedule.[14]

In 1953, the Supreme Court held that the compensation provided for acquisition of private land to rehabilitate refugees was inadequate and defined compensation as "a just equivalent of what the owner has been deprived of".[15] In another case relating to placing a company under government-appointed agents, the Supreme Court said it amounted to deprivation of property for which government was liable to compensate the shareholder.[16] The Supreme Court also struck down government takeover of private operators from running buses on hire on public roads.[17]

The Fourth Constitution Amendment in 1955 therefore, amended Article 31A to protect government takeover of management of companies. If ownership of property was not transferred to the government, it would not amount to compulsory acquisition even though the person was deprived of his property.[18]

The Seventh Constitution Amendment in 1956 harmonised multiple entries in the Seventh Schedule on the single subject of acquisition and requisition of property and deleted similar entries in the Union and State Lists to remove technical difficulties in legislation. Entry 42 was broadly framed in the Concurrent List as '42. Acquisition and requisition of property'. Parliament's authority over legislations passed by the States was maintained.

The Seventeenth Constitution Amendment in 1964 was a sign of an all-out turf war between the executive and the judiciary that had less to do with property rights. The Supreme Court had declared Kerala Agrarian Relations Act 1961 unconstitutional and not protected from judicial scrutiny by the amended Article 31A. Granville Austin writes that the Court may have been 'splitting hairs' by picking on what was more of a nomenclature issue and not unusual, given the variety of land tenure systems in the country.[19] This Amendment broadened the definition of 'estate' to include tenure systems like *inam*, *jagir*, land held under *ryotwari* settlement and any equivalent 'estate' in local law. Small holders of land within the

---

[14]A first list of 13 agrarian laws from the States of Bihar, Bombay, Madhya Pradesh, Madras, Uttar Pradesh, etc. were placed in the newly created Ninth Schedule.

[15]*State of West Bengal vs Bela Banerjee & Ors.*, AIR 1954 SC 170-2.

[16]*Dwarkadas Srinivas vs Sholapur Spinning and Weaving Co.*, AIR 1954 SC 199; *State of West Bengal vs Subodh Gopal Bose,* 1954 SCR 587.

[17]*Saghir Ahmad vs The State of Uttar Pradesh*, 1955 SCR 707.

[18]The Constitution (Fourth) Amendment Act 1955. Seven more laws were added to the Ninth Schedule, four of which dealt with non-agricultural property (including the law questioned in the *Bela Banerjee* case, the West Bengal Land Development and Planning Act 1948) and three concerned business regulations "in order to put an end to the dilatory and wasteful litigation and place these laws above challenge in the courts".

[19]*Karimbil Kunhikoman vs The State of Kerala*, 1962 Supp (1) SCR 829. The Court said that lands held by *ryotwari pattadars* (holders) are not 'estates' under Article 31A(2)(a) and that under Article 14, compensation principles between affected categories were discriminatory. In *Krishnaswami vs State of Madras*, AIR 1964 SC 1515, the Supreme Court also invalidated the Madras Land Reforms Act 1961.

ceiling limits were protected from land acquisition or at least were entitled for full compensation (Austin 1999).[20]

5 Golak Nath, Bank Nationalizations and Princely Privileges: Constitution Amendments 1971–72

In 1965, the Supreme Court again interfered with the expanded definition of the term 'estate' in Article 31A and declared that Article 31(2) required payment of a just equivalent compensation for expropriated property.[21] But the turning point in executive-judiciary conflict came with the Court's decision in the *Golak Nath* case.[22] The Court ruled through a wafer thin majority, six to five, that fundamental rights, including the right to property, were 'primordial rights necessary for the development of the human personality' and were given a 'transcendental position' in the Constitution. Parliament's power to amend the Constitution could not therefore be used to abridge the fundamental rights. The Court then declared the First, Fourth and Seventeenth Constitution Amendments unconstitutional and reaffirmed the supremacy of fundamental rights in general and right to property in particular. But taking a step backward, the Court allowed these Constitutional amendments to remain valid till the date of its decision through the doctrine of 'prospective overruling'.[23]

The *Golak Nath* case set off 'the great war' compared to the 'earlier skirmishes' between the Parliament and the judiciary over supremacy. The Indira Gandhi led Congress government believed that its socialistic goals could not be realized unless the right to property was modified. The Objects and Reasons of the Twenty-fourth Constitution Amendment Act 1971 directly referred to the *Golak Nath* judgment. "[t]he result of the judgment is that Parliament is considered to have no power to take away or curtail any of the fundamental rights guaranteed by Part III of the Constitution even if it becomes necessary to do so for giving effect to the Directive Principles of State Policy and for the attainment of the objectives set out in the Preamble to the Constitution." The amendment therefore, aimed at making all

---

20The Constitution (Seventeenth) Amendment Act 1964, also inserted 44 new laws in the Ninth Schedule.

21*Vajravelu vs Special Deputy Collector, West Madras*, AIR 1965 SC 1017.

22*Golak Nath vs State of Punjab*, 1967 2 SCR 763. The appellants had challenged the order of the Collector declaring their land holdings surplus under Punjab Security of Land Tenures Act 1953, the violation of their fundamental rights under Article 19(1)(f) and (g) and Article 14 and sought to declare the 1st, 4th and 17th Constitution Amendments as *ultra vires*. 17th Amendment had placed the Punjab Security of Land Tenures Act 1953 in the Ninth Schedule.

23*Golak Nath vs State of Punjab,* 1967 2 SCR 763. Two earlier judgments of the Supreme Court had held that Parliament had the power to amend the fundamental rights as it did by the 1st, 4th, 17th Constitutional Amendment. See, *Shankari Prasad vs Union of India* 1952 SCR 89 and *Sajjan Singh vs Union of India* 1965 1 SCR 933.

fundamental rights amendable to give effect to the Directive Principles of State Policy (Directive Principles).[24] It excluded amendments from the reach of Article 13, which does not permit making of any law infringing fundamental rights.

To counter "a property oriented and capricious judiciary" (Austin 1999) the Twenty-fifth Amendment Act in 1972 was aimed at reasserting the supremacy of eminent domain expropriations with or without compensation, against some Supreme Court decisions on the nationalization of certain private enterprises.[25] The amendment replaced the term 'compensation' by the word 'amount' in Article 31(2) payable for compulsorily acquired property. Courts were barred from questioning the 'amount' on grounds that it was not adequate or paid other than in cash putting to rest the tendency of courts to invalidate legislations on grounds of inadequate compensation. A new Article, 31C, was inserted giving the Directive Principles precedence over the fundamental rights, and included an 'escape clause' (Austin 1999, pp. 244–245) stating that no law declaring its purpose to be fulfilling the Directive Principles in Article 39(b) and (c) could be challenged in court on the ground that it did not do so. Article 14 (equality before the law), Article 19 (the freedoms article) and the property terms of Article 31 were made subordinate to the most classically socialist of the Directive Principles and an entire category of legislation placed beyond judicial review.

The Twenty-fifth Amendment in effect put a closure on the confusion over what the law was in case of government acquisition of private property. Court rulings were inconsistent on the First and Fourth Amendments as to the extent of judicial review on the Ninth Schedule laws and adequacy of compensation. The government too contributed to the adverse rulings by calculating questionably low compensation in several cases "either from zealousness or carelessness".[26] Further, none of the constitution amendments had removed the word 'compensation' from Article 31,

---

[24]The Constitution of India 1950, Directive Principles of State Policy is contained in Part IV of the Constitution, these are a set of non-justiciable principles or standards covering social, economic and political justice, administrative, environment and culture, peace and security, necessary for governing the country.

[25]*Rustom Cavasjee Cooper vs Union of India* (1970 3 SCR 530) (popularly known as the *Bank Nationalization* case). In this case, the Supreme Court declared the Banking Companies Act 1969 invalid by which 14 banks were nationalized, for violating fundamental rights. The Statement Of Objects And Reasons of the 25th Amendment mentioning the *Bank Nationalization* case, stated "[T]hus in effect the adequacy of compensation and the relevancy of the principles laid down by the Legislature for determining the amount of compensation have virtually become justiciable inasmuch as the Court can go into the question whether the amount paid to the owner of the property is what may be regarded reasonably as compensation for loss of property."

[26]In *State of Gujarat vs Shantilal Mangaldas*, 1969 (3) SCR 341, for example, the Court said, "If compensation was not illusory, it would not be justiciable". In *Vajravelu vs Special Deputy Collector, West Madras*, AIR 1965 SC 1017, the Court held that "Legislature in making a law of acquisition or requisition shall provide for a just equivalent of what the owner has been deprived of or specify the principles for the purpose of ascertaining the 'just equivalent' of what the owner has been deprived of." In *Union of India vs Metal Corporation of India Ltd.*, (1967) 1 S.C.R. 255, the Court held that principles for determination of compensation was irrelevant and compensation illusory.

"inviting judicial supposition that the government intended payment of equivalent value of property taken." (Austin 1999). The Twenty-fifth Amendment thus cleared the way for over hundred nationalization laws in coal, coking coal, copper mines, steel plants, textile mills and shipping lines.

The Twenty-sixth Constitution Amendment Act in 1971, also concerning property rights, derecognized former Princes of Indian princely States, ended their privileges and abolished their privy purses. This amendment followed the Supreme Court nullifying a Presidential order of 1970, which had derecognized erstwhile Princes.[27]

6 Fundamental Rights Case and the Forty-Second Amendment 1977

It came to be known as the Fundamental Rights case not because of what the judges of the Supreme Court wrote in the judgment, but what the judges interpreted of the judgment in subsequent cases. The *Kesavanada* judgment[28] delivered on 24 April 1973 became a significant moment in India's constitutional history when the Supreme Court held that there was a 'basic structure' of the Constitution and that it could not be altered. All Constitution amendments after the date of this judgment, which alter the 'basic structure', can be challenged as *ultra vires*.

The judgment was highly controversial and the judges divided on political lines. The 'View by the Majority' statement by seven of the 13 judges and signed by nine, holding that "Article 368 does not enable Parliament to alter the basic structure or

[27]The Constitution (Twenty Sixth) Amendment Act 1971 amended Article 363 of the Constitution which gave special privileges to erstwhile princely states of India which merged with the Indian State after independence in 1947. Privy purses were payments made to royal families of these princely states to compensate for loss of ruling rights. See, *H.H. Maharajadhiraja Madhav Rao Jiwaji Raoscindia Bahadur vs Union of India*, 1971 SCC (1) 85. Supreme Court struck down Presidential Orders of 6 September 1970 as illegal and inoperative and "the petitioners will be entitled to all their pre-existing rights and privileges including right to privy purses, as if the orders have not been made." See also Datar (2013).

[28]*Kesavananda Bharati vs The State of Kerala*, 1973 4 SCC 225. The main petitioner, Swami Kesavananda Bharati, head of a religious sect (mutth) in Kerala challenged the Kerala government's attempt under two State land reforms legislations to impose restrictions on the management of its mutth properties. Other petitioners included land owners affected through compulsory acquisition or operation of ceiling laws, owners of companies nationalized and erstwhile rulers of princely states. The State government invoked its authority under Article 31 (eminent domain) but the lawyers to the main petitioner, led by Nani Palkhivala, fought the petition under Article 29 (right to manage religiously owned property without government interference) and also challenged the constitutionality of three amendments, the 24th, 25th and 29th (the last one placed the Kerala Land Reforms Act 1969 in the Ninth Schedule).

framework of the Constitution" was as dubious as it was confusing (Austin 1999).[29] The majority decision of the court upheld the constitutionality of the Twenty-fourth and Twenty-fifth Amendments, but struck down Article 31C's 'escape clause'.[30]

On a reading of the judgment it is not clear whether fundamental rights were meant to be part of the so-called 'basic structure'. The doctrine finds mention in the separate opinion of Justice H.R. Khanna without any reference to the fundamental rights. Justice Khanna resolved this contradiction by 'a strange exercise' of clarifying his own judgment 2 years later in the *Indira Gandhi* case![31]

The *Kesavananda* verdict caused the government to wreck vengeance on the judiciary through the Forty-second Amendment in 1977, at a time when national Emergency was in force across India. The judgment was invalidated and the Parliament granted itself unrestrained powers to amend any part of the Constitution without judicial review.[32] The amendment also restricted and stripped courts including the Supreme Court, of many of their powers, and gave primacy to the Directive Principles over the fundamental rights.[33]

7 Abolition of Right to Property: The Forty-Fourth Constitution Amendment 1978

Suppression of civil liberties in the 2 years of Emergency (1975–1977) intensified the efforts by the Janata government to undo the harm wrought by the Forty-second Amendment. But the Objects and Reasons of the Forty-fourth Constitution Amendment Bill made it clear that the right to property was not to be accorded the

---

[29]13 judges delivered 11 opinions and the "View by the Majority" statement followed the opinions at the end of the judgment. The opinions were lengthy and lacked precision about what was actually decided. This was slightly mitigated by the 'conclusions' which summarized opinions, but they conflicted with the statement signed by nine judges and had discrepancies when compared to their individual opinions. Without the statement there would not have been a court 'decision' in any comprehensible sense.

[30]The Constitution of India, Article 31C, "*... and no law containing a declaration that it is for giving effect to such policy shall be called into question in any court on the ground that it did not give effect to such policy*".

[31]*The Kesavananda Bharati Case: The untold story of struggle for supremacy by Supreme Court and Parliament*, Andhyarujina (2011), Chapter VI. See, *Indira Gandhi vs Raj Narain*, 1976 2 SCR 347. In fact, Justice Khanna upheld Article 31C which had immunized any law from the challenge of Articles 14, 19 and 31 if it were made in pursuance of Articles 39(b) and (c) of the Directive Principles and also held valid the 29th Constitution Amendment Act 1972 which gave protection to the Kerala Land Reforms laws in the Ninth Schedule, subject of challenge in the *Kesavananda* case.

[32]The Forty Second Constitutional Amendment Act 1977, the amendment to Article 368 prevented any constitutional amendment from being "*called in question in any Court on any ground*".

[33]The Forty Second Constitutional Amendment Act 1977, "*No law implementing any of the Directive Principles could be declared unconstitutional on the grounds that it violated any of the Fundamental Rights.*"

honour of a fundamental right. "In view of the special position sought to be given to fundamental rights, the right to property, which has been the occasion for more than one amendment of the Constitution, would cease to be a fundamental right and become only a legal right. Necessary amendments for this purpose are being made to Article 19 and Article 31 is being deleted…Property, while ceasing to be a fundamental right, would, however, be given express recognition as a legal right, provision being made that no person shall be deprived of his property save in accordance with law" (Austin 1999, pp. 421–422).[34]

The Forty-fourth amendment thus, completely took away what remained of the fundamental right to property, to buy, keep and sell properties, within reasonable restrictions, by deleting Articles 19(1)(f) and 31. There was no longer any fundamental right to compensation or amount payable in lieu of expropriation. Article 300A was introduced as an enabling constitutional right, that "[n]o person shall be deprived of property save by authority of law". Only two exceptions to the right to property remained—first, minorities could establish educational institutions and second, the right to compensation at market value for persons who held land for personal cultivation within the ceiling limit.

8 Legacy of *Kesavananda*, Article 300A and the Right to Property

In 1980, the Supreme Court re-established its power as the protector of the Constitution in the *Minerva Mills* case, by declaring unconstitutional the part of the Forty-second Amendment, which prevented any constitutional amendment from being "called in question in any Court on any ground". The Court also struck down the amendment that gave precedence to the Directive Principles over the fundamental rights[35] and reiterated that, "[A]ll constitutional amendments made after the decision in *Kesavananda Bharati* case would have to be decided by reference to the 'basic structure' doctrine…".[36]

[34]Ironically, it was not the Congress government, the judiciary's bête noir on all the property battles since 1950, which deleted the right to property, but the successor Janata government. Janata Party's election manifesto promised to remove the fundamental right to property and retain it as a statutory right. The principal rationale for the move was to protect other fundamental rights as right to property was the cause of many amendments and conflicts with the judiciary. The Party may have used removal of right to property as a fundamental right as an inducement for the support of the communist parties and others.

[35]Though Article 31C was later interpreted in other Supreme Court cases, the extent to which fundamental rights in Article 14 and 19 may be overridden in pursuit of the DP remains unclear even today.

[36]*Minerva Mills vs Union of India*, 1980 3 SCC 625. Government assumed management and then nationalized privately owned mills under the Sick Textiles Undertaking (Nationalization) Act 1974, which was challenged in the Minerva Mills case by the mills' previous owners.

With the *Minerva Mills* case and the sobering experience of the Emergency, the right to property ceased to be a matter of contest between the government and the judiciary. *Kesavananda* had held, unanimously, that fundamental right to property was not a basic feature of the Constitution. The judiciary had thus conceded that determination of the extent of the right to property was the domain of the executive, but held its ground that it had the power of judicial review through the 'basic structure' doctrine. The Parliament had wrested the powers to amend the Constitution so long as it did not violate the 'basic structure', and to exercise eminent domain under the authority of any law. "The great contests over property rights in cases like *State of West Bengal vs Subodh Gopal Bose*, *State of West Bengal vs Bela Banerjee*, *K.K. Kochuni vs State of Kerala*, *P. Vajravelu Mudaliar vs Special Deputy Collector*, *R.C. Cooper vs Union of India*, became a matter of the past and irrelevant to the future. In retrospect it seems strange how much the Supreme Court was preoccupied with the sanctity of property rights and the challenge to economic laws and policies of Government and how little it was concerned with the personal rights of individual during the period from 1954 to 1976" (Andhyarujina 2011).

The constitutional history of right to property is really one of interpreting the power of the Parliament to amend the Constitution under Article 368. This was accomplished by determining whether Directive Principles could be given effect vis a vis the right to property under Articles 19(1)(f) and 31 and by the interpretation of the term 'compensation'. The political and social consensus on the limited value of the right to property was accepted by different political views that its extinguishment was necessary for social and economic objectives.

After 1978, all types of deprivation of property are made under Article 300A. The only exceptions require the State to ensure that "the amount fixed or determined" for acquisition of property of a minority educational institution, shall not "restrict or abrogate the right guaranteed" by Article 30(1)[37] and, second that, "[P]ayment of compensation at a rate which shall not be less then the market value thereof" is guaranteed to the land loser who held land "within the ceiling limit" and "in his personal cultivation".[38] These exceptions imply that the State is not obligated to pay compensation for any property acquired under Article 300A.

The law of the land was crystallized in a 1995 case[39] where the Supreme Court unequivocally held that the right to property is not a 'basic feature' and is therefore, not a fundamental right under the Constitution. The Court held that judicial interpretation should not be a tool to reinduct the doctrine of compensation as concomitance to acquisition or deprivation of property under Article 300A. The Court even

[37]See, The Constitution of India 1950, Article 30(1A) read with Article 30(1).

[38]See, The Constitution of India 1950, Article 31A(1).

[39]*Jilubhai Nanbhai Khachar vs State of Gujarat*, 1995 Supp (1) SCC 596.

refused to entertain the contention that different principles of compensation provided by different laws were discriminatory and therefore, a violation of Article 14.

In 2010, the Supreme Court again missed an opportunity to read the right to property as a fundamental right on the basis of the *IR Coelho* decision (discussed later). The Court declined to invalidate the Forty-fourth Amendment and restore the fundamental right to property without considering the merits of a Writ Petition, in which, the petitioner, Sanjiv Agarwal, had cited indiscriminate violation of eminent domain and argued that large-scale displacements caused by projects like the Narmada dam, Special Economic Zones and land acquisition instances in West Bengal had dispossessed the poor.[40]

9 The Ninth Schedule: A Bottomless Pit

The constitutional history of right to property is incomplete without a discussion on the Ninth Schedule. With the fundamental right to property gone, the Ninth Schedule containing laws, which cannot be declared void on the ground that they violated any fundamental right, has become a bottomless pit to protect laws "regardless of their quality or legality… and for laws to serve personal interests of the powerful."[41] The Ninth Schedule laws fall in the categories of land redistribution, nationalization of private industries, tenancy, and rent and price controls enacted by Central and State governments. The Schedule has also been used to protect laws on elections and reservation policies. The current tally of the Ninth Schedule laws is 284 which include about 150 amendment acts.

Article 31B, the source of the Ninth Schedule was not discussed in *Kesavananda*. It came up for consideration in *Waman Rao vs Union of India*,[42] where the Supreme Court upheld validity of the First Amendment that introduced this Article and the Ninth Schedule in the Constitution and decided not to allow questioning of any law inserted after 24 April 1973 (date of the *Kesavananda* decision).

---

[40]*Sanjiv Agarwal vs Union of India* (2010) in Writ Petition (C) No. 464 of 2007. See also Agrawal (2014) where the author quotes the Chief Justice of India saying in Court that, "It has to be read along with the 42nd Amendment by which the word 'socialist' was inserted in the Preamble to the Constitution. If your contention is to be accepted, then we will have to reverse earlier judgments on property rights. Recently, we dismissed the Gudalur Janmam petition seeking similar relief. We can't reopen the issue."

[41]*Working a Democratic Constitution, A History of the Indian Experience*, Austin (1999). The Social Revolution and the First Amendment, Chapter 3.

[42]1981 2 SCC 362.

In *IR Coelho* (2007), the Supreme Court held that "*Kesavananda Bharati's* case cannot be said to have held that fundamental rights chapter is not part of basic structure." The validity of each new constitutional amendment is to be judged on its own merits and the actual impact of the law on the fundamental rights has to be considered to determine whether or not it destroys the 'basic structure'. So all post-24 April 1973 laws, including those protected by the Ninth Schedule, have to be tested on the touchstone of the basic or essential features of the Constitution as reflected in Article 21 read with Article 14, Article 19, and the principles underlying them.[43]

Yet, a subsequent bench in 2010 equivocated on the issue when applying *IR Coelho's* principles on the validity of another law which was placed in the Ninth Schedule after 24 April 1973.[44] The Court held that the validity of a law put in the Ninth Schedule would be invalidated only if it breached some 'overarching principles' like secularism, democracy, separation of powers, power of judicial review, rule of law and 'egalitarian equality'. The concept of 'overarching principles' was evolved in an earlier case presumably to dispel the uncertainty caused by the Court's own subjective and confusing articulation of the 'basic structure' doctrine.[45]

These rulings on the Ninth Schedule *vis a vis* the fundamental rights are irrelevant to the right to property as it is no longer a fundamental right. The need to keep 'progressive legislations' on land reforms out of the purview of judicial scrutiny was felt necessary at a time when the right to property could be asserted as a fundamental right. Other Ninth Schedule legislations added, when India was riding high on a socialist style planned economy and needed to control a concomitant rise in black markets, and were open to challenges for infringement of other fundamental rights, are no longer valid in the current economic scenario. Even post *Kesavananda*, by which time it was clear that right to property was not even a basic feature of the Constitution, laws continued to be inserted in the Schedule.[46]

---

[43]*I.R. Coelho (Dead) By LRs vs State of Tamil Nadu & Ors.*, 2007 2 SCC 1. To clear the inconsistencies of the *Waman Rao* case, the case was referred to a Constitution Bench of nine judges in 1999. The issue related to a law passed by the Tamil Nadu assembly that was invalidated prior to the *Kesavananda* verdict for violation of fundamental rights, but was placed in the Ninth Schedule later.

[44]*Glanrock Estate (P) Ltd. vs The State of Tamil Nadu*, 2010 10 SCC 96. Gudalur Janmam Estates (Abolition and Conversion into Ryotwari) Act 1969 failed to meet the benchmark of the 'overarching principles'.

[45]*M. Nagaraj vs Union of India*, 2006 8 SCC 212. See also, *The Keshavananda Bharati Case: The untold story of struggle for supremacy by Supreme Court and Parliament*, Andhyarujina (2011), Chapter X. The Court held that Article 14 by itself was not a basic feature of the Constitution, but was only a principle of formal equality. The principle of "egalitarian equality" was an "overarching principle" of the Constitution, like democracy, secularism, rule of law, etc.

[46]The 47th Constitution Amendment 1984, the 66th Constitution Amendment 1990, 76th Constitution Amendment 1994, 78th Constitution Amendment 1995, have inserted laws in the Ninth Schedule.

Yet the Supreme Court did not throw the Ninth Schedule out of the Constitution in these cases. But it is interesting to note the decline in the use of the Ninth Schedule in the last two decades, clearly the outcome of increased judicial scrutiny.[47]

10 Conclusion

Ownership of property has been critical in determining the power and political evolution of society from ancient times. With increasing number of people owning property, land and other assets, the demand for political participation in decision-making has increased. From the initial days of democracy in ancient city states in Greece, to Magna Carta in England in 1215 AD, the American revolution in 1776, and expansion of voting rights in the nineteenth-century Europe, all reflected the growing aspiration of people to participate as equals in the political process, based on property ownership.

In 1950, the Indian Constitution recognized right to property as a fundamental right. It also adopted universal adult franchise. Constituent Assembly debates inform that right to property was incorporated as a compromise to ensure that the rich and powerful political elites are not alienated. On the other hand, universal adult franchise was adopted to ensure widest political participation, and thus providing legitimacy to the new order emerging from the end of colonial rule.

The progressive dilution and then finally deletion of the right to property created perpetual scarcity of land, as land and property market got strangulated. The scarcity fuelled corruption and gave rise to an unholy nexus between the economically powerful and politically connected through the rampant misuse of the land acquisition laws.

A fundamental shift in the political consciousness is taking place in India today regarding property rights. While restoration of right to property as a fundamental right in the Constitution is still not on the table, the demand for protection property rights, particularly of the poor, can no longer be brushed aside. Political devolution to the States, where land could become a key feature of the local governments, with State and Central government exercising residual authority is a future to look forward to in a deepening democracy. This paper is a small effort towards the process of improving our understanding of the legal evolution of property rights in India and how it can shape a just and productive future for the country.

[47]The last time a law was added to the Ninth Schedule was in 1995.

References

Agrawal S (2014) The Indian federalists—the original will of India's founding fathers. Notion Press, Delhi

Andhyarujina TR (2011) The Kesavananda Bharati case: the untold story of struggle for supremacy by Supreme Court and Parliament. Universal Law Publishing, Delhi

Austin G (1999) Working a democratic constitution, a history of the Indian experience. Oxford University Press, New Delhi

Datar A (2013) Who betrayed Sardar Patel. The Hindu, 19 Nov 2013

Gandhi AL (1985) Right to property: its changing dimensions. Scientific Publishers, Jodhpur

Mearns R (1999) Access to land in rural india: policy issues and options. World Bank Policy Research Working Paper 2123

Singh J (2005) (Un)constituting property: the deconstruction of the 'right to property' in India. CSLG Working Paper Series, CSLG/WP/04-05

Postcolonial Evolution of Water Rights in India and the United States

Jesse J. Richardson

1 Introduction

Both India and the United States adopted the English common law for water rights upon gaining independence from England, although these events occurred 171 years apart (1776 in the United States, and 1947 in India). By the time India gained independence in 1947, many states in the United States had already evolved away from the English common law for water rights, particularly with respect to groundwater. However, to this day, most states in India have not altered the English common law, despite several prominent problems. This chapter explores the evolution (or lack thereof) of water rights in both countries and attempts to explain the stark differences.

First, the chapter reviews general demographic and water use data from each country to compare the two. Second, a Virginia case is used to illustrate the issues when deciding whether to adopt the English common law. Although the case focuses on groundwater rights, its analysis applies to a broad spectrum of cases. Indian cases do not engage in such analysis, perhaps due to the India Easements Act of 1882.

Next, the chapter addresses surface water. States in India and the eastern United States use riparian rights adopted from the English common law. States in the western United States have, for the most part, rejected riparian water rights for prior appropriation, explaining that the conditions in those states differ so much from the

J.J. Richardson (✉)
West Virginia University College of Law, Morgantown, USA
e-mail: jesse.richardson@mail.wvu.edu

S. Pellissery et al. (eds.), *Land Policies in India*, India Studies in Business and Economics, DOI 10.1007/978-981-10-4208-9_3

conditions in England that a riparian right approach is not appropriate. However, some western states still recognize riparian rights that were established prior to the switch to the prior appropriation doctrine.

Although states in India may recognize that riparian rights fail to adequately address the Indian reality, the country appears to still prefer the "natural flow" theory (*Karathigundi Keshava v. Sunnanguli Krishna Bhatta* 1945). The natural flow theory gives the landowner the right to the full flow of the watercourse. Most states in the United States have switched to the "reasonable use" rule, allowing some reasonable reduction in flow for use of the water by upstream owners.

Next, the chapter discusses percolating groundwater (groundwater not in identified streams or channels). In contrast to surface water, percolating groundwater is considered part of the soil under the absolute dominion rule. This rule, as first stated in *Acton v. Blundell* (1843), is referred to by American courts as the "English Rule." In the United States, however, courts generally have adopted a less severe form of the rule, finding liability for the misappropriation of percolating groundwater only if the act was malicious (Kelly 2016).

In the early 1900s, American courts began to evolve away from the English Rule, with many courts adopting the reasonable use rule, also referred to as the "American Rule." The American Rule limits how water withdrawn from a property may be used (Ibid). In contrast, states in India have remained committed to the absolute dominion rule as stated in the English common law.

The chapter then moves to a discussion of statutory and policy changes to the common law in each country. Both countries have utilized a form of "regulated riparianism" by adopting policy, statutory and regulatory programs to supplement the common law. In India, this movement takes the form of state water policies, guided by a National Water Policy. Most Indian state water policies parallel the 2002 National Water Policy (Government of India, Ministry of Water Resources 2002), which is remarkably similar to the statutes passed in eastern states in the United States. Both provide priorities for water use and allocation (Richardson 2015).

Finally, the chapter concludes by presenting lessons learned from the different paths of the two nations. These lessons can help both nations develop more sustainable water rights systems.

2 Overview of India and the United States

2.1 United States

The United States spans 9,833,517 km^2, including 9,147,593 km^2 of land mass and 685,924 km^2 (6.97%) of water, ranking as the third largest country in the world. The 2010 census estimated the country's population as 309,349,689, also third most in the world. However, with only 35 people per square kilometer, the United States ranks 180th in terms of density. Estimated (2016) GDP (Gross Domestic Product) per capita amounts to $57,220 (10th). Ranked by nominal GDP, the economy is the largest in the world. New York City is the country's largest city, with a population of 8,550,405 (estimated, 2015). The economy experienced rapid growth in the nineteenth century, and is now an established industrialized country with stable overall GDP growth.

The United States includes 50 states, a federal district, five major self-governing territories and a variety of possessions. Water quality law mainly involves national law, whereas water allocation rules mainly occur at the state level. The eastern United States and western United States (roughly divided by the Mississippi River), have different water allocation regimes, with the east primarily governed by riparian or reasonable use rules and the west primarily using prior appropriation. Thirty-one states use riparian rules for surface water and/or groundwater. The remaining 19 states, mainly in the western United States, use prior appropriation, where one acquires a right to use a certain amount of water by using the water. In times of shortage, the water is allocated based on the time that the use was established. Priority is given to the earliest use and then each subsequent use until all of the water is allocated, potentially leaving some later users with no water.

Freshwater withdrawals in the United States totaled 306,000 million gallons (about 1.6 km^3) per day in 2010. Thermoelectric power generators withdrew 38.2% of this total. Irrigation accounted for 37.2% of withdrawals, and 2000 million gallons a day were withdrawn for livestock watering. Therefore, thermoelectric power and agriculture accounted for almost equivalent withdrawals. Of the withdrawals, 75% came from surface water (with 29% of this amount going to agriculture) and 25% came from groundwater (with 64% of this amount going to agriculture).

The climate of the United States varies greatly, ranging from semiarid to arid in much of the West, to Mediterranean on the coast of California, to subarctic Alaska and tropical Hawaii, to humid continental, humid temperate, and humid subtropical in the East. Vast differences in terrain also exist, ranging from mountains to seashores.

2.2 *India*

India is a federal republic governed by a parliamentary system. India ranks as the seventh largest country in the world and spans 3,287,263 km^2. This figure includes 2,864,021 km^2 of land mass and 302,393 km^2 (9.55%) of water. The 2011 Census estimated the country's population at 1,210,854,977, ranking second in the world (first among democracies) and amounting to a density of 389 people per square kilometer, or 31st most dense. The per capita GDP of $1820 ranks 122nd. In 2015, India was the world's seventh largest economy measured by per capita GDP, and third largest measured by Purchasing Power Parity. The largest city, Mumbai, has a population of 18.4 million (estimated, 2013).

India includes 29 states and 7 Union Territories, with state law primarily governing water allocation. Each state has different water rules. In 2010, freshwater withdrawals totaled 2.09 cubic kilometers per day, of which agriculture accounted for 91%, industry 2% and municipalities 7%.[1]

The Indian economy is classified as a newly industrialized country and a developing economy. According to the International Monetary Fund's World Economic Outlook (April 2016), India's economy is the fourth fastest growing in the world. This growth contrasts greatly with the growth of the country's economy during British Rule and in the decades that followed independence.

> There is no doubt that our grievances against the British Empire had a sound basis. As the painstaking statistical work of the Cambridge historian Angus Maddison has shown, India's share of world income collapsed from 22.6% in 1700, almost equal to Europe's share of 23.3% at that time, to as low as 3.8% in 1952. Indeed, at the beginning of the 20th century, "the brightest jewel in the British Crown" was the poorest country in the world in terms of per capita income.
>
> (Singh 2005)

The 30 years following independence have been characterized as showing a "Hindu rate of growth," referring to the extremely low rate of growth compared to other Asian countries (Panigariya 2008)

Like the United States, India hosts a wide variety of climates, "from arid desert in the west, alpine tundra and glaciers in the north and humid rainforests in the southwest and the island territories" (Wikipedia, https://en.wikipedia.org/wiki/Climate_of_India). The landscape also varies from deserts to the Himalaya Mountains.

3 Deviation from the English Common Law in the United States

The decision-making process involved when a United States court deviates from English common law is well illustrated in a Virginia case and laid out below. Indian courts appear to be beginning to approach the English common law in a similar way.

The court first recognized that although Virginia had adopted English common law by statute, its adoption took place in a situation not applicable to the present time or particular state (*Costello v. Frederick County Sanitation Authority* 1999). Although the Rule had been rejected by many states and authorities, the court pointed out that Virginia had adopted the English common law by statute, which might be dispositive (Code of Virginia 1950). However, the court then proceeded to examine the history, intent, and purpose of the statutes (Ibid).

Reviewing case law on interpreting the adoption of English common law, the court stated that the "true holding" of these cases appears to be "that for a common

[1]The data fail to specify whether these figures refer to withdrawals or consumption.

law rule to be binding upon the courts in the Commonwealth of Virginia, it must be one that is well established, that goes back 'to the time that the memory of man runneth not to the contrary' and have a lasting and enduring value which is recognized by the English courts and presumably by many American courts" (*Costello v. Frederick County Sanitation Authority* 1999). In other words, the court suggests that in order to uphold English common law, it must be well established, long-standing and must have present value. Further details from the case state:

> Before English common law can be applied in Virginia it must be analyzed in light of Code § 1-20 and the cases interpreting that code section. According to the code, English common law cannot be applied if it is "repugnant to the principles of the Bill of Rights and the Constitution." Nor can it be applied if it is "altered by the General Assembly." In addition to the statutory provision, *Foster v. Commonwealth,* 96 Va. 306, 31 S.E. 503 (1898), sets forth yet another limitation on the use of English common law. In *Foster,* we considered the predecessor to Code § 1-10. We stated that though the statute, aside from its express limitations, appears to adopt English common law "generally, and without a qualification," this is not in fact the case.
>
> (*Weishaupt v. Commonwealth of Virginia* 1984)

Therefore, that Virginia courts may "adopt from English common law those principles that fit our way of life and … reject those which do not" (*Costello v. Frederick County Sanitation Authority* 1999).

The analysis in *Costello* mirrors that of other courts considering water allocation doctrine. Most courts in the United States do not feel bound to adopt the English common law if such law fails to address the present conditions in that state, even in the face of statutory provisions much stronger than the ones at issue in Virginia.

4 Surface Water

4.1 Introduction

Although some controversy exists as to whether English common law forms the source of riparian water rights (Getzler 2004; Dellapenna 2011), this chapter assumes that riparian water rights originated in English common law. English common law recognized a natural right to water in a watercourse in the 1600s (*Suxy v. Pigot* 1625; Getzler 2004). The right later became to be known as riparian rights, allowing the owner of land abutting a waterway to an uninterrupted flow of the watercourse, regardless of the rights of others (Ibid). Many states in both the United States and India adopted this common law upon independence.

However, after this initial adoption, the states in the two nations parted ways. This section examines how Indian states have remained true to the adopted common law riparian rights, while many states in eastern United States have altered those rights. Further, most states in the western United States have rejected common law riparian rights outright.

4.2 United States

4.2.1 Eastern United States

In the United States, most states in the east use the riparian water rights doctrine, although some states have gone from the "natural flow" rule to the "reasonable use" rule.[2] The natural flow doctrine, also called the "English Rule" in the United States, provides that a landowner has the right to have the water flow through the property undiminished in quality or quantity (Kelly 2016). The reasonable use theory gives each riparian the right to reasonable use of the water, sharing equally with other riparian owners, even if the reasonable use diminishes the natural flow (Ibid).

A total of 30 states use the riparian rights rule for surface water.[3] As originally set out, riparian rights adhered to the natural flow doctrine. However, almost immediately after the English common law was adopted in the United States, courts began to create exceptions to the "natural flow" rule, notably including an exception for domestic use (Ibid). Courts that failed to modify the natural flow doctrine instead generally rejected it. Within just 5 years of the formation of the natural flow theory in the United States, courts had already begun abandoning it for the reasonable use doctrine (*Cooper v. Hall* 1832). Horowitz opined that the evolution from natural flow to reasonable use originated in American courts as a way to advance development given the circumstances of the nation at that point (Horowitz 1977).

Similar to natural flow, many courts have created exceptions for the "reasonable use" rule. "Natural flow" and "reasonable use" have therefore become nearly indistinguishable (Ibid). The natural flow theory is still promoted by some scholars, and the term is still used by some courts, mostly to support aesthetic or ecological concerns (Ibid).

4.2.2 Western United States

When the western United States began to experience conflicts over water allocation, some states initially adopted riparian rights. However, most of these states quickly switched to the prior appropriation doctrine, where water rights are not tied to land ownership, but are instead based on the "first in right, first in time" principle. Other western states adopted prior appropriation from the outset. Although in many of

[2]No source documents which states have made the switch, but the literature appears to assume that most or all states in the United States now use the reasonable use riparian rights doctrine, or have modified the natural flow rule to the degree that it now appears identical to the reasonable use rule.

[3]Alabama, Arkansas, Connecticut, Delaware, Georgia, Hawaii, Illinois, Indiana, Iowa, Kentucky, Louisiana, Maine, Maryland, Massachusetts, Pennsylvania, Rhode Island, South Carolina, Tennessee, Vermont, Virginia, West Virginia and Wisconsin.

these cases, the state had arguably adopted the English common law rule of riparian rights, leaving courts to use various methods to avoid that imposition.

The doctrine of prior appropriation is defined as follows:

> A property right in the use of water is created by diversion of the water from a stream (or lake) and its application to a beneficial use. Water can be used at any location, without regard to the position of place of use in relation to the stream. In the event of a shortage of supply, water will be supplied up to a limit of the right in order of temporal priority: the last man to divert and make use of the stream is the first to have his supply cut off.
>
> (Meyers 1971)

Nine states have completely supplanted common law riparian rights with the prior appropriation doctrine (Thompson et al. 2013).[4] Mississippi and Texas also use prior appropriation for surface water (Richardson 2014). Eight western states displaced common law riparian rights, but still honor riparian rights established before the adoption of prior appropriation, or where title was acquired from the federal government (Thompson et al. 2013).[5]

Colorado was the first state to completely supplant common law riparian rights with the prior appropriation doctrine. The Supreme Court of Colorado, despite 1861 and 1862 Territorial Acts that appeared to adopt the riparian rule, concluded that the English common law simply did not fit the very different conditions in that state.

> the common law doctrine giving the riparian owner a right to the flow of water in its natural channel upon and over his lands, even though he makes no beneficial use thereof, is inapplicable to Colorado. Imperative necessity, unknown to the countries which gave it birth, compels the recognition of another doctrine in conflict therewith. And we hold that, in the absence of express statutes to the contrary, the first appropriator of water from a natural stream for a beneficial purpose has, with the qualifications contained in the constitution, a prior right thereto, to the extent of such appropriation.
>
> (*Coffin v. Left Hand Ditch Co.* 1882)

In an even clearer example of dismissing an earlier adoption of the English common law, the Nevada Supreme Court, overruling a prior decision, declared that prior appropriation had always been the "universal custom" in the West, and in Nevada (*Jones v. Adams* 1885). Just 13 years earlier, the court had ruled that the English common law of riparian rights applied in that state (*Vansickle v. Haines* 1872).

Justice Holmes perhaps best stated the American approach to the adoption of English common law of water allocation. In a United States Supreme Court case addressing a claim that Arizona territorial law that adopted the common law of England, with some limitations, Justice Holmes stated that adopting English common law does not mean "that patentees of a ranch on the San Pedro are to have

---

[4]Alaska, Arizona, Colorado, Idaho, Montana, Nevada, New Mexico, Utah and Wyoming are known as "Colorado doctrine states", as Colorado was the first state to eliminate riparian rights and replace that system totally with prior appropriation.

[5]California, Kansas, Nebraska, North Dakota, Oklahoma, Oregon, South Dakota and Washington are known as "hybrid doctrine" states.–.

the same rights as owners of an estate on the Thames" (*Boquillas Land & Cattle Co. v. Curtis* 1909). Instead, the law merely adopted a "general system," as opposed to another general system (in this case, Spanish-Mexican) (Ibid).[6]

4.3 India

Common law has governed water allocation in India since at least the late nineteenth century (Cullet and Koonan 2011). Surface water rights in India are connected to ownership of land and are usufructuary rights, meaning that the landowner can use the water, but do not own the water (Ibid). As is typical in riparian rights, the owner of Indian land abutting a surface waterway holds riparian rights, or the right to take water from a stream, with limitations (Iyler 2009, citing *Secy Of State v. Kannepalli Jankiramayya*). Although riparian rights are codified in Section 7 of the Indian Easements Act, 1892, numerous court cases have interpreted and outlined the rights (Cullet and Koonan 2011). Riparian rights constitute property rights, not "mere shadowy privileges" (Iyler 2009).

Illustrations (h) and (i) to Section 7 of the Indian Easements Act, 1892, appear to codify the natural flow form of riparian rights. However, illustration (j) acts to limit the doctrine by requiring "material injury" to the downstream owner for a cause of action, at least in certain situations.

Section 7(b) of the Indian Easements Act, 1892, provides that

> Easements are restrictions of one or other of the following rights (namely):
>
> (a) Exclusive right to enjoy. - The exclusive right of every owner of immovable property (subject to any law for the time being in force) to enjoy and dispose of the same and all products thereof and accessions thereto.
>
> (b) Rights to advantages arising from situation. - The right of every owner of immovable property (subject to any law for the time being in force) to enjoy without disturbance by another the natural advantages arising from its situation.

The pertinent illustrations provide that

> (h) The right of every owner of land that the water of every natural stream which passes by, through or over his land in a defined natural channel shall be allowed by other persons to flow within such owner's limits without interruption and without material alteration in quantity, direction, force or temperature; the right of every owner of land abutting on a natural lake or pond into or out of which a natural stream flows, that the water of such lake or pond shall be allowed by other persons to remain within such owner's limits without material alteration in quantity or temperature.
>
> (i) The right of every owner of upper land that water naturally rising in, or falling on such land, and not passing in defined channels, shall be allowed by the owner of adjacent lower land to run naturally thereto.

---

[6]Courts are split on whether statutes adopting "the common law of England" create riparian rights (Thompson et al. 2013, 207).

(j) The right of every owner of land abutting on a natural stream, lake or pond to use and consume its water for drinking, household purposes and watering his cattle and sheep; and the right of every such owner to use and consume the water for irrigating such land, and for the purposes of any manufactory situate thereon, provided that he does not thereby cause material injury to other like owners.

Explanation. -A natural stream is a stream, whether permanent or intermittent, tide or tideless, on the surface of land or underground, which flows by the operation of nature only and in a natural and known course.

Illustration (h) makes clear that the riparian rule in India uses the natural flow approach (Iyler 2009). Therefore, the riparian owner has the right to have the surface water flow through the property, undiminished in quantity and unpolluted (Ibid). Illustration (j) seems to prioritize natural flow rights by arguably allowing riparian owners, in the first clause, to withdraw as much water as needed for drinking, household purpose, and stock watering. The second clause allows the riparian to use water from the stream for irrigation and manufacturing purposes, but limits that use to those that do not cause "material injury" to other riparians.

Puthucherril argues that illustration (h) limits the right of a riparian to use water for drinking, household, and stock watering purposes to those uses that will not impact natural flow (Ibid). However, at least one court holds otherwise, providing that the use of water for domestic purposes may impact natural flow without liability (*State of Bombay v. Laxman Sakharam Pimparkar* 1960).

Note, however, that Section 2(a) of the Indian Easements Act, 1892, arguably prevents states from regulating surface water.[7] Section 2 (a) provides that

[n]othing herein contained shall be deemed to affect any law not hereby expressly repealed; or to derogate from - (a) Any right of the Government to regulate the collection, retention and distribution of the water of rivers and streams flowing in natural channels, and of natural lakes and ponds, or of water flowing, collected, retained or distributed in or by any channel or other work constructed at the public expense for irrigation.

4.4 Conclusion

While courts in the eastern United States acted fairly quickly to move away from the natural flow rule in the English common law rule of riparian rights, by either swallowing the rule with exceptions or by outright rejecting the rule in favor of prior appropriation, Indian courts, as well as the legislature, have conformed to the natural flow rule. Courts in the United States appear to feel free to adapt the common law rule to the unique circumstances of the time and the location. United States courts also freely adapt water rights to the desires of the community (such as advancing the rights of industry to use the water).

[7]See, e.g., Gronwall (2008), at 339.

The Indian Easements Act, 1892, may explain the hesitance of Indian courts to likewise mold water rights to the conditions of the place and time. The national legislature may need to originate change in water rights in India.

5 Groundwater

5.1 Introduction

"[T]he rules governing subterranean water may vary depending on whether the water is "percolating" water (*i.e.,* water that seeps through the land without following a well defined course or channel) or underground water that is flowing through a reasonably well defined channel or course" (*Costello v. Frederick County Sanitation Authority* 1999, citing *Miller v. Black Rock Springs Improvement Co.* 1901).

The English common law considers percolating groundwater part of the soil and owned by the owner of the surface (*Acton v. Blundell* 1843). Disputes over groundwater withdrawals were rare, and usually occurred in the context of a landowner pumping large amounts of groundwater to rid the land of the water in order to mine minerals or use the land in some other way that required eliminating the water (Kelly 2016). English courts reasoned that since groundwater could not be seen, the properties of groundwater were not known well enough to attempt to regulate groundwater separately from the soil (Ibid). This rule has been called the English Rule and the absolute dominion rule.

Even though the understanding of groundwater has advanced significantly over the years, English courts still utilize this rule (Ibid). The rule was utilized as recently as 1987 in a case involving subsidence of neighboring property due to groundwater pumping:

> As the law stands, the right of the landowner to abstract subterranean water flowing in undefined channels beneath his land … appears to us, in the light of [common law] authorities, to be exercisable regardless of the consequences, whether physical or pecuniary, to his neighbors. Whether or not this state of the law is satisfactory is not for us to say.
>
> (*Stephens v. Anglian Water Authority* 1987)

However, the rule in England has been limited in certain ways, by changing the rule for water pollution and giving local governments certain powers (Kelly 2016). English courts apply a strict liability rule to groundwater pollution (Ibid). In addition, royal and local governments also hold "extensive administrative powers" (Ibid). However, as this section sets out, India appears to still apply the English common law rule for groundwater allocation without limitations.

5.2 United States

Courts in the United States still refer to the rule as the "English Rule," even though one case in the United States appears to have adopted the rule prior to *Action v. Blundell* (Ibid).[8] "In a nutshell, the English Rule permits a landowner unlimited exploitation of the water found beneath his land. He may utilize as much of the subterranean water as he cares to for any purpose irrespective of the effect upon adjoining landowners" (*Costello v. Frederick County Sanitation Authority* 1999). One court, in adopting the rule, explained that properties applying to groundwater "are so secret, occult and concealed, that an attempt to administer any set of legal rules in respect to them would be involved in hopeless uncertainty" (*Frazier v. Brown* 1861).

Twenty-eight states in the United States originally adopted the "English Rule," or the rule of absolute dominion. However, in late 1800s and early 1900s, the courts began to reject the English Rule (Levine 1984). Although the cases often fail to clearly express a rule, and disagreement exists with respect to which states retain the English Rule, the author's research ascertains that 11 states still use the rule.[9]

Seventeen states, mostly in the east, and mostly replacing the English Rule, have adopted the "American Rule," or the "reasonable use" rule.[10] This rule limits use to beneficial uses having a reasonable relationship to the use of the overlying land (Levine 1984). Unreasonable withdrawals for use on a parcel other than that from which the water was withdrawn are prohibited (*Costello v. Frederick County Sanitation Authority* 1999).

Courts have found the English Rule to be "archaic" and not suited to the particular conditions in the United States (Ibid):

> The English Rule is clearly the "English common law" rule, but it was developed in the 19th century in a land which, if anything, has too much water as opposed to too little. The fact that the English Rule has been rejected by most American states and by the drafters of the Restatement of Torts, Second is circumstantial evidence that the absolutist English rule in all of its Draconian splendor may not be a suitable rule for application in Virginia.
>
> (Ibid)

Brentwood and Robar (2004) note that "the form and volume of groundwater found in a particular region and the period in which the region was settled" provide

---

[8]See *Greenleaf v. Francis*, 35 Mass. (18 Pick.) 117 (1836).

[9]Connecticut, Georgia, Indiana, Louisiana, Maine, Massachusetts, Minnesota, Mississippi, Rhode Island, Texas and Vermont have either adopted the rule or expressed a preference for the rule. Note that Vermont purpors to replace the English rule, by statute, with the correlative rights rule, but the statute has not yet been applied. Note also that South Carolina has no meaningful common law for groundwater.

[10]Alabama, Arizona, Arkansas, Delaware, Illinois, Kentucky, Maryland, Michigan, Missouri, New Jersey, New Hampshire, New York, North Carolina, Oklahoma, Pennsylvania, Virginia, and West Virginia.

a significant indicator of the groundwater rule adopted by a particular state (Gronwall 2008).

New Hampshire was the first state to adopt the American rule, in 1862. Iowa (1894), West Virginia (1905), Kentucky (1908), and Michigan (1915) followed. By the 1930s, the American rule had been adopted by more states than had retained the English Rule (Thompson et al. 2013).

Five states use the correlative rights rule.[11] The correlative rights rule is similar to the reasonable use rule, but does not limit uses to the overlying property and dictates proportional sharing. The reasonable use rule, for example, allows a landowner to consume all of the water, so long as the use is beneficial, while the correlative rights rule prohibits one landowner from consuming more than a fair share.[12]

Ohio and Wisconsin use the Restatement (Second) of Torts rule. The Restatement (Second) of Torts Section 858 provides

> (1) A proprietor of land or his grantee who withdraws ground water from the land and uses it for a beneficial purpose is not subject to liability for interference with the use of water by another, unless
>
> (a) the withdrawal of ground water unreasonably causes harm to a proprietor of neighboring land through lowering the water table or reducing artesian pressure,
>
> (b) the withdrawal of ground water exceeds the proprietor's reasonable share of the annual supply or total store of ground water, or
>
> (c) the withdrawal of the ground water has a direct and substantial effect upon a watercourse or lake and unreasonably causes harm to a person entitled to the use of its water.
>
> (2) The determination of liability under clauses (a), (b) and (c) of Subsection (1) is governed by the principles stated in §§ 850 to 857.

Prior appropriation controls groundwater allocation in 13 states.[13] Finally, Florida law recognizes no common law groundwater rights, relying totally on a regulated riparian regime, while South Carolina has no meaningful common law for groundwater rights.

As states changed from the English Rule to other rules to govern groundwater rights, surprisingly few legal challenges to the change were presented. For the few legal challenges that exist, courts generally found in favor of the government (Kelly 2016).[14]

---

[11]California, Hawaii, Iowa, Oklahoma and Tennessee. Vermont appears to have adopted the rule by statute, but the statute has not yet been applied. Nebraska uses a combination of the reasonable use rule and the correlative rights rule.

[12]See, e.g., the leadings case on correlative rights, *Katx v. Walkinshaw*, 74 P. 766 (Cal. 1903); Lukas (1982).

[13]Alaska, Colorado, Idaho, Kansas, Montana, Nevada, New Mexico, North Dakota, Oregon, South Dakota, Utah, Washington, and Wyoming.

[14]See, e.g., *Crookston Cattle Company v. Minnesota Dept. of Natural Resources,* 300 N.W. 2d 769, 774–775 (replacing the English Rule with a regulated riparian statute does not constitute a regulatory taking or violate equal protection); C.f., *Franco-American Charolaise, Ltd. v.*

The federal government holds little or no role in groundwater management in the United States (Gronwall 2008, citing Brentwood and Robar 2004). "[T]his limitation is not due to any constitutional or legal barriers but rather is self imposed and due to historical and cultural factors" (Ibid).

5.3 India

As in the United States, Indian law distinguishes between groundwater flowing in defined channels and percolating ground water, which does not flow in defined channels. Riparian rights govern the former, while percolating groundwater is considered part of the soil and belongs to the owner of the land (*Mahomedans of Lonar v. Hindus of Lonar* 1945). Paragraph 335 of *Karathigundi Keshava Bhatta v. Sunnanguli Krishna Bhatta* (1945) sets out the English Rule for groundwater in India, making percolating groundwater a "natural right" of the landowner. However, groundwater moves through the land, and Indian law recognizes what is called the rule of capture in the United States. Namely, a right of use of the water exists as the water passes through, but the landowner does not own the water in the ground (*Malayam Patel Basavana Gowd v. Lakka Narayana Reddi* 1921). "There is no limitation on how much groundwater a particular land owner may draw" (*Sukry Kurdepa v. Goondakull* 1872).

Section 7 of the Indian Easements Act, 1892, codifies the English Rule for percolating groundwater. Illustration (g) provides: "The right of every owner of land to collect and dispose within his own limits of all water under the land which does not pass in a defined channel and all water on its surface which does not pass in a defined channel."

"[A]n adjacent landowner has no property in or right to subterranean percolating water until it arrives underneath his soil … therefore no property or right of his is injured by the abstraction of the percolating water before it arrives under his land" (*Bradford v. Pickles* 1895).

Most commentators agree that "Indian law on property in groundwater has not undergone any reforms since colonial times." (Gronwall 2008). Brentwood and Robar (2004) assert that the same cultural and historical factors that limit the role of the national government in groundwater allocation in the United States also applies in India (Gronwall 2008), however, constitutional and legal factors do not prevent a national government role in India (Ibid, citing Brentwood and Robar 2004).

Cases in India, however, are beginning to raise some interesting questions. First, the discussion of how conditions in India so differ from those in England, where there is no Monsoon season and dry season, in *Basavana Gowd v. Narayan Reddi* (1931)

(Footnote 14 continued)

Oklahoma Water Resources Board, 855 P. 2d 568 (finding a regulatory taking where a state statute replaced riparian rights with prior appropriation).

resembles the discussion in many American cases rejecting the English common law. The case involved water percolating in a sandy riverbed during the dry season:

> the underground water to which the English cases apply is usually water between layers of subterranean rock or clay so hidden that no one can guess what their course is. In this country, it is fairly safe to say that the under-current of a river is probably flowing down the river bed and that its course is defined in the sense that one will probably be able to tap it somewhere in the river bed, and the water thus is found in, and has not left, the recognized irrigation source, namely, the river
>
> (Ibid)

The infamous "Coca Cola case" also illustrates the tension in groundwater law in India. This case involved the rights of the landowner to withdraw large amounts of water to use in making beverages. The Perumatty Grama Panchayat had granted the company a permit for electricity to pump groundwater for the plant. When the permit came up for renewal, the Panchayat, citing groundwater depletion, drinking water shortages and environmental issues, denied the permit (Gronwall 2008). The Kerala government ordered the Panchayat to issue the permit, and the Panchayat petitioned the High Court of Kerala (Ibid).

The court decided the question of whether the Panchayat held the authority to cancel the permit based on excessive extraction of groundwater (*Perumatty Grama Panchayat v. State of Kerala* 2004). A Single Bench ruled that the groundwater withdrawal was "breaking the natural water cycle" and that the Panchayat could cancel the permit (Ibid; Gronwall 2008). This decision, however, was overruled by the Division Bench, which found that Panchayat could only prohibit the permit holder from bringing about a drought or causing an imbalance in the water table (*Hindustan Coca-Cola Beverages (P) Ltd. v. Perumatty Grama Panchayat* 2005; Gronwall 2008). The Division Bench rejected the lower court holding and directed the Panchayat to reinstate the license.[15]

The first decision referred to the English Rule, and the inappropriateness of the rule in modern day India:

> The principles applied in those decisions cannot be applied now, in view of the sophisticated methods used for extraction like bore-wells, heavy duty pumps etc. Further, those decisions and the above contentions are incompatible with the emerging environmental jurisprudence developed around Art.21 of the Constitution of India.
>
> (*Perumatty Grama Panchayat v. State of Kerala* 2004)

The Division Bench failed to even refer to the English Rule, referring only to an "assumption" that a landowner can pump groundwater from beneath their property, and a limitation of "reasonableness" (*Hindustan Coca-Cola Beverages (P) Ltd. v. Perumatty Grama Panchayat* 2005). The court then derived the standard of bringing about a drought or an imbalance in the water table (Ibid).

[15]The case was appealed to the India Supreme Court and is still pending.

5.4 Conclusion

Groundwater rights prove to be much more difficult than surface water rights. Courts in the United States have deviated from the English Rule often, and express little or no hesitation in doing so. Including the English Rule (which some commentators opine barely exists anymore as a practical matter), five different doctrines apply to groundwater in the United States. Even though a small number of states retain the doctrine, courts have uniformly criticized the English Rule.

Although the English Rule remains the law of the land in India, some courts, most notably in Kerala, have, at least impliedly, criticized the doctrine and suggested alternative rules. The Indian Easements Act, 1892 also impacts groundwater allocation in India by making courts hesitant to change the doctrine to fit the conditions in India today.

6 Regulated Riparianism

6.1 Introduction

Dellapenna coined the term "regulated riparianism" to refer to state statutory regimes in the United States that supplement or purport to replace common law water rights in the eastern United States (Dellapenna 1985). The term curiously includes groundwater (which is not subject to riparian rights) as well as surface water. The federal (national) government in the United States has failed to directly address water allocation issue, so has not played a role in regulated riparianism in that country.

Regulated riparianism in India appears as water policies issued by the state and national governments. The National Water Policy serves as a model for state policies, in contrast to the lack of involvement by the national government in the United States. This section describes "regulated riparianism" in the United States and India, and concludes that the two regimes are remarkably similar.

6.2 United States

States in the United States have altered the common law water rights rules since colonial times (giving preference to industrial uses) (Kelly 2016). Beginning in 1800s, states began passing statutes that gave preference to agricultural uses of water (Ibid). Statutory preferences have been utilized in eastern (riparian) states but have been unnecessary in the west because prior appropriation bases priority primarily on time only.

Nineteen states have passed water allocation rules in the eastern United States (Richardson 2015). The scope of these statutes varies: many involve permitting systems, and most include exemptions for de minimis uses. Particularly with respect to groundwater, state statutes often establish a procedure for identifying particular geographic areas where the regulations will apply.[16]

The Regulated Riparian Model Water Code exemplifies the state regulations on water allocation. The Model Code provides for the following preferences: (1) water for direct human consumption and sanitation; (2) water for the survival of livestock and crops (including protecting businesses from damage to physical plants and equipment due to lack of water); (3) water to "maximize employment and economic benefits in the context of sustainable development" (Dellapenna 1997). The priorities are subject to ranking by the degree of reasonableness, and temporal priority applies so long as the public interest is served equally by competing uses.

States vary slightly with respect to allocation priorities, but a consensus seems to exist on the priority laid out in the Model Act, with human needs first, followed by livestock, then crops, then other needs (Richardson 2015). The state provisions fail, however, to place limits on the water allocated to these uses, although a "reasonableness" provision may be implied (Ibid).

6.3 India

India first adopted a National Water Policy in 1987. The policy was updated in 2002, and again in 2012. The 2002 plan prioritized water for planning of projects as follows: (1) drinking water; (2) irrigation; (3) hydropower; (4) ecology; (5) agro-industries and nonagricultural industries; and (6) navigation and other uses. These priorities are flexible, however. The 2002 plan also referred to "water zoning," closely linking land use and water use.

The 2012 National Water Policy establishes safe water for drinking and sanitation as a "preemptive" need. Next, three uses constitute high priority allocations: other basic domestic needs (including the needs of animals), achieving food security and supporting sustenance agriculture and minimum ecosystem needs. After these preemptive and high priority needs are met, other water should be allocated to promote its conservation and efficient use. The policy proposed differential pricing for high priority needs and economic pricing for other uses. The policy also emphasized social justice and equity concerns in determining water allocation.

[16]See, e.g., the Virginia Ground Water Management Act of 1992, Virginia Code Ann. §§ 62.1–254, et seq. (authorizing the establishment of ground water management areas).

Eleven states have adopted state water policies.[17] Eight of these policies closely mirror the 2002 National Water Policy.[18]

In addition to state water policies, a "number" of states have adopted state groundwater laws modeled after the Model Bill to Regulate and Control the Development and Management of Groundwater, 2005 (Cullet and Koonan 2011). These laws apply only in designated geographic areas within the state (Ibid). Users within these areas must obtain a permit, and the permit may contain conditions regulating the use of the groundwater (Ibid).

Two state groundwater laws take different approaches than the Model Bill (Ibid). West Bengal's law uses authorities at the state, district, and corporation level, in contrast to the Model Bill's centralized approach (Ibid). The Andhra Pradesh law regulates land, water, and trees in an integrated law, as opposed to the limited scope contemplated in the Model Bill (Ibid).

Puthucherril argues that the riparian doctrine no longer works in India, and that regulated riparianism represents the better way forward (Iyler 2009). He cites the Maharashtra Water Resources Act, 2005, as "one of the first attempts in [India] to introduce regulated riparianism in a comprehensive manner" (Ibid). The Act seeks to equitably and sustainably allocate and manage water through a permitting system (Ibid).

6.4 Conclusion

The regulated riparian provisions in India and the United States are remarkably similar. Groundwater regulation at the state level often involves the designation of specific geographic regions for regulation. Both nations also seem to prioritize human life, animal life, and plant life, in that order within water allocation provisions. However, Indian policies often put humans and animals on equal footing. In addition, policies in India appear to be moving toward limiting agricultural uses (at least for irrigation), while policies in the United States still often give preference to agricultural uses.[19]

The provisions in the United States are statutory and regulatory, while the Indian provisions are policy. Despite this difference, the provisions in neither country have been enforced or even stringently applied. The difficulty of monitoring and enforcing water allocation provisions make the future of these provisions uncertain.

[17]Assam (2007), Himacheal Pradesh (2005), Karnataka (2002), Kerala (2008), Meghalaya (2011), Maharashtra (2003), Madhya Pradesh (2003), Orissa (2007), Punjab (2008), Rajasthan (2010) and Uttar Pradesh (1999). (the numbers in parenthesis refers the year the policy was adopted).

[18]Himacheal Pradesh (2005), Karnataka (2002), Kerala (2008), Meghalaya (2011), Orissa (2007), Punjab (2008), Rajasthan (2010) and Uttar Pradesh (1999). Meghalaya's policy is identical to the 2002 National Water Policy.

[19]However, New Jersey and Georgia have limited agricultural uses.

7 Conclusions and Recommendations

The United States and India both adopted English common law upon declaring their independence from England. However, the two nations have taken very different approaches to the English common law of water allocation in the decades (or centuries) since independence. The national governments in each country have remained in the background. However, the Indian Easements Act, 1892, seems to have had a profound impact on the evolution of water law to the extent it codifies English common law and prevents Indian courts from deviating from the common law. United States courts have freely changed the common law to meet the different conditions and the present time.

With respect to surface water, courts in the United States quickly either amended or abandoned the natural flow rule to allow riparian owners reasonable use of surface water. In the West, courts went further and rejected the riparian doctrine as inapplicable in dry, arid regions. Indian courts have remained loyal to the natural flow doctrine, at least in part due its apparent codification in the Indian Easement Act, 1882.

Groundwater rules prove more difficult, as is the case around the globe. Courts in the United States quickly modified the English Rule, and then moved away from the rule to one of four other doctrines. Although a few states still purport to use the rule, the right to indiscriminately use groundwater has been universally criticized. Even while acknowledging the Indian Easement Act, 1882, Indian courts show more inclination to modify the English common law with respect to groundwater than with surface water, with a handful of cases appearing to attempt modification.

Both countries utilize socalled regulated riparianism, which implements laws and policies that augment, or even purport to supplant, common law rules. The countries are also similar in their provisions on water allocation and state laws that designate particular geographic areas for permitting systems. However, the rules originate with the states in America, while the national government in India provides model policies for the states.

The differences between the United States and India may result from the temporal differences in the ways the two countries have developed. Both countries share similar governance structures (particularly with respect to water allocation) and both countries have diverse climates that vary by region. However, the United States experienced rapid industrialization in the 1800s and early 1900s. This growth clearly influenced water allocation policies. In contrast, India's economy was essentially dormant under British rule and for decades afterwards. Since 1991, however, the Indian economy has grown rapidly, paralleling the growth in the United States a hundred years earlier. The time may be ripe for courts to change common law water rights in India.

Moving forward, the two countries have much to learn from each other. The United States should follow the lead of India and develop model policies and regulations for states to use in regulating water. At present, United States water policy lacks cohesion and unity. Although a parallel to the Indian Easements Act,

1892, appears unlikely (and perhaps undesirable), the federal government could provide technical support and funding as incentives to adopt national priorities and a clearinghouse for information and policies.

In India, amending the Indian Easements Act, 1892, would provide states more flexibility in dealing with water issues. However, amendment of the Act appears unlikely, as the Planning Commission rejected that suggestion when convened to review groundwater rights (Gronwall 2008). In the absence of such amendments, legislatures, and courts should explore conflicts between the English common law of water allocation and other laws and regulations in the states and the nation. Interpretations of the Indian Easements Act, 1892, vary, and the evolution of those interpretations could lead to the evolution of groundwater allocation rules. Looking to the United States courts in the late 1800s and early 1900s, during a time of rapid industrialization, Indian courts should not hesitate to change English common law to fit the needs of present day India (Horowitz 1977).

Finally, the countries can share their experiences with regulated riparianism to develop different approaches to deal with their respective rapidly changing contexts for water allocation. With increasing demands and shortages, and climate change, water law must also evolve to meet the new challenges.

References

Brentwood M, Robar S (eds) (2004) Managing common pool groundwater resources: an international perspective. Praeger, Westport

Code of Virginia (1950) §§ 1–10 and 1–11

Cullet P, Koonan S (eds) (2011) Water law in India: an introduction to legal instruments. Oxford University Press, Delhi

Dellapenna J (1985) Owning surface water in the eastern united states. E Mineral L Found 6: PG

Dellapenna J (ed) (1997) The regulated riparian model water code. American Society of Civil Engineers, New York

Dellapenna J (2011) The evolution of riparianism in the United States Marq L Rev 95:53

Getzler J (2004) A history of water rights at common law. Oxford University Press, Oxford

Government of India, Ministry of Water Resources (2002) National water policy. http://www.indiawaterportal.org/articles/national-water-policy-ministry-water-resources-2002. Accessed 14 Oct 2016

Gronwall J (2008) Access to water: rights, obligations and the Bangalore situation. Linkopeing, LiU-Tryck. http://liu.diva-portal.org/smash/get/diva2:18111/FULLTEXT01.pdf. Accessed 14 Oct 2016

Horowitz M (1977) The transformation of american law, 1780–1860. Harvard University Press, Cambridge

International Monetary Fund (2016) World economic outlook. http://www.imf.org/external/pubs/ft/weo/2016/01/index.htm. Accessed 15 Oct 2016

Iyler R (2009) Water and the laws in India. Sage Publications, New Delhi

Kelly A (ed) (2016) Waters and water rights. Lexis Nexis, Charlottesville

Levine S (1984) Groundwater: louisiana's quasi-fictional and truly fugacious mineral. La L Rev 44:1123

Lukas T (1982) When the well runs dry: a proposal for the change in the common law of groundwater rights in massachusetts. BC Envtl Aff L Rev 10:445

Maharashtra Water Resources Regulatory Act 2005
Meyers C (1971) A historical and functional analysis of the appropriation system. National Water Commission, Arlington
Panagariya A (2008) India: the emerging giant. Oxford University Press, New York
Richardson J (2014) Water and economic development in Indiana: modernizing the state's approach to a critical resource (Unpublished, on file with author)
Richardson J (2015) Agricultural preferences in eastern water allocation. Nat Res J 55:329
Singh M (2005) Of oxford, economics, empire, and freedom, The Hindu, 2 October. http://www.thehindu.com/2005/07/10/stories/2005071002301000.htm. Accessed 16 Oct 2016
Thompson B, Leshy J, Abrams R (2013) Local control of water resources: cases and materials, 5th edn. West, Eagan

Cases

Acton v. Blundell (1843) 152 Eng Rep 1223 (Ex Cham)
Basavana Gowd v. Narayan Reddi (1931) AIR Mad 284
Boquillas Land & Cattle Company v. Curtis (1909) 213 US 339
Bradford v. Pickles (1895) AC 587 (HL)
Coffin v. Left Hand Ditch Co. (1882) 6 Colo 443
Cooper v. Hall (1832) 5 Ohio 320
Costello v. Frederick County Sanitation Authority (1999) 49 Va Cir 41 (Fred Co Cir Ct)
Foster v. Commonwealth (1898) 96 Va 306
Frazier v. Brown (1861) 12 Ohio St 294
Greenleaf v. Francis (1836) 35 Mass (Pick 18) 117
Hindustan Coca-Cola Beverages (P) Ltd. v. Perumatty Grama Panchayat (2005) (2) KLT 554
Jones v. Adams (1885) 6 P 442
Karathigundi Keshava v. Sunnanguli Krishna Bhatta (1946) AIR (33) Mad 334
Katx v. Walkinshaw (1903) 74 P 766
Mahomedans of Lonar v. Hindus of Lonar (1945) AIR Nag 106
Malayam Patel Basavana Gowd v. Lakka Narayana Reddi (1921) AIR Mad 284
Miller v. Black Rock Springs Improvement Co. (1901) 99 Va 747
Perumatty Grama Panchayat v. State of Kerala (2004) (1) KLT 731
State of Bombay v. Laxman Sakharam Pimparkar (1960) 62 BOMLR 106
Stephens v. Anglian Water Authority (1987) 3 All ER 379 (CA)
Sukry Kurdepa v. Goondakull (1872) 6 Mad HC 71
Sury v. Pigot (1625) 79 Eng Rep 1263 (KB)
Vansickle v. Haines (1872) 7 Nev 249
Weishaupt v. Commonwealth (1984) 227 Va 389

Conflicting Interests and Intelligible Utilisation of Common Property Resources: A Study of a Tropical Wetland in South India

P.J. Christabell

Human beings are at the centre of concerns for sustainable development. They are entitled to a healthy and productive life in harmony with nature.
(Declaration of Principles, The Rio Summit of 1992).

1 Introduction

Planning, in a broad sense, may be considered as an attempt by the society to consciously regulate the economic process through collective decisions so that equitable and sustainable economic growth is achieved. A missing feature of Indian economic planning has been that lack of sufficient concern for the environmental dimension of development. Environmental planning would imply planned exploitation, utilisation, conservation and development of the living and non-living components of the world's environmental assets—plants, animals and people as well as land, water and air—to achieve certain short-term as well as long-term objectives (Nambiar 1995). The relationship between people, resources, environment and development is in fact very complex, and therefore, the prospects for the success of sustainable management and development depend upon the correct identification of the crucial dimensions of the development process—economic, human, environmental and technological—at micro levels.

Sound environmental management is the optimal allocation of finite resources between different possible uses. Environment management is a difficult, delicate and complex task. The factors, such as social, technical, political, legal, ecological and economic, acting singly or in any combination of these make it difficult to

P.J. Christabell (✉)
Department of Futures Studies, University of Kerala,
Thiruvananthapuram 695581, Kerala, India
e-mail: christabell@keralauniversity.ac.in; christabell@fastmail.fm

S. Pellissery et al. (eds.), *Land Policies in India*, India Studies in Business and Economics, DOI 10.1007/978-981-10-4208-9_4

manage (Khoshoo 1991). Environmental criteria and economic considerations favour that such allocation should be efficient. Simultaneously, the available resources should be protected from degradation and scarce and diminishing resources should be conserved. The cornerstones of environmental management are: environmental planning, environmental status evaluation, environmental impact assessment, environmental legislation and administration.

The environmental planning concept is rooted in the integration of environmental considerations in the economic development planning process as hitherto practised. For management of a system, a system status evaluation is a must. In the case of a complex dynamic system like the environment, this task is not only extremely difficult, but also fraught with several uncertainties. There is no single parameter or index of the status in such cases. Under these circumstances, one possible approach would be to attempt evaluation of status of subsystem like air, water, land, flora, fauna, etc. Environmental impact assessment is a procedure for bringing out the potential effect of human activities on environmental systems. Environmental legislation supported by well drafted regulations and meticulous enforcement systems and administrative machinery is an essential component of environmental management.

When conventional methods of development fail to yield any significant results, there is need for some rethinking about the socio-economic institutions that link resource, people and government. These institutions are the backbone of economic models of development. In a system of planned development, conventional wisdom generally prompts the introduction of government as an alternative agent to 'people' in the process of taking and implementing decisions. While macroeconomic decisions, actions and policies regarding flow of resources, financial management, trade prospects, price formulations, etc., are well within the realm of the government, its role in bringing about sustainable development at the rural grassroot level is becoming increasingly doubtful. Various alternative formulations of rural development programmes have been attempted. Community development programmes, Panchayat Raj institutions, integrated area and rural development programmes, national rural employment guarantee programmes, block development models, etc. are instances of different ideological approaches opted for, at different points in time in India, in the process or rural development aimed at 'people' at the grassroot level (Chopra et al. 1990). The solutions of India's rural problems and eco-management require one key change: the right of the people as a village community to manage their village environment and to care it in the way they want. In short, the resource management of the land, water and forest should be a local task and responsibility. The Panchayat Raj system being organised throughout the country ought to serve the purpose of putting on the ground such a system throughout the country. It is ultimately a strong connection between people and natural resources that make local people the best and most effective protectors of the environment (Katiyar 1997).

2 Common Property Resources

In the traditional rural societies, the poor have often been found to depend upon what is called as 'Common Property Resources' (CPRs). They are in general defined as resources accessible to the whole community to which no individual has exclusive property rights. Common properties are not one's property or state property or private property. The importance of CPRs is not only economic; CPRs are also central to many cultural and social activities of poor rural women and men. CPRs are a central part of poor women and men's coping and adaptive strategies, contributing to sustainable livelihoods, and playing a major role in poverty reduction. They play an imperative role in the rural economy and benefit its population in a number of ways. The fuelwood and shrubs available from CPRs are used for cooking and heating; grass, leaves and shrubs are used as animal fodder, bamboo, small timber and palm leaves for housing and a variety of fruits, vegetables and fish, for sustenance, particularly during the lean seasons. CPRs also contribute significantly to private property-based farming as well as to the household enterprises. These provide irrigation water, mulch and manure for cultivation, raw materials and common pastures for grazing.

Despite their significant contributions to the economy of rural people, these CPRs have seldom received enough attention of planners. The important reason is that the rural development planning has largely emphasised private property resource (PPR)-centred activities. In rural areas, inadequate understanding of the survival mechanisms used by the poor as well as the complementarities between CPRs and PPR-based activities are a major issue and the contributions of CPRs are not only numerous and varied but also they are often available as a matter of routine (Jodha 1986). All over the world, especially in the rural settings of India, it is observed that overtime the size of CPRs has been declining because of various factors, resulting in the deteriorating status—quantity—of resources. The decline and deterioration of CPRs have raised the questions regarding the health of both, the ecological balance and the poor rural households that depend upon the resources in question. It is a known fact that the decline and degradation of common lands and natural resources can be attributed directly to changes in how communities think about the commons and in the institutional arrangements underlying the management of these resources.

Land, water and forest were treated as resources held in common. All these resources are owned by government. But the local communities play the most critical role in the protection and use of these resources. It is wide held notion that CPRs can be efficiently managed by the local community because CPRs and communities are totally interdependent and one cannot survive without the other. So there is need for institutional arrangement to transform the theory of CPR into a reality. These institutional arrangements can link people and resources, translating interests into claims, claims into rights. In short, common property regimes are forms of management grounded in a set of accepted social norms and rules for the sustainable interdependent use of collective goods such as forests, grazing grounds, fisheries and water resources, etc. (Jodha 1986). The CPRs are usually managed by community organisations (traditional, modern or elected) for the use of the members of community under certain rules, regulations and restrictions. Customary regulations and communal control may provide 'social boundaries' to the use and abuse of nature collective action can emerge, in some circumstances, as an efficient alternative to privatisation and nationalisation (Bon 2000). The governance of natural resources used by many individuals in common is an issue of increasing concern to policy analysts. Both state control and privatisation of resources have been advocated, but neither the state nor the markets have been uniformly successful in solving the problems related to CPRs. In contrast to the proposition of the tragedy of the common argument, common pool problems sometimes are solved by voluntary organisations rather than by a coercive state (Ostrom 1990).

From the history of traditional community organisations in India who were by and large concerned with common property resources, one can easily identify three minimal preconditions for such a group to emerge. First, the community organisations should be able to reinforce the existing structures of authority. As pointed out by Wade (1987), as long as tradition and authority are upheld, the concept is acceptable. Second, the community should feel empowered, and be independent of outsider's (including government) intervention. Third, the set of rules and norms of cooperation should be such as to meet the felt needs of the people (Chopra et al. 1989). While people have maintained over time a set of customary regulations upon village resource use patterns, these regulations are on the verge of extinction as people are neither legally entitled to, nor encouraged to implement them. One salient feature of these regulations is that, from the point of view of social legitimacy, the purpose of resource utilisation is as important as the claim to use it (Bon 2000). Indigenous institutions for CPR management are under strain due to modernization and globalisation pressures, and conflicts amongst users are apparent. The extent of influence of the poor on such institutions is, limited (Beck and Nesmith 2001).

Panchayat Raj is the only system available for CPR management all over India. The democratic structure of Panchayat Raj ensures people's participation to a great extent. Some of the resources which are common for more than one village panchayats have to be jointly managed. The bigger resources, like irrigation channels, forests, roads, mines, river beds, can be managed by District Panchayat or Block Panchayat (Ragupathy 1999). Common property resource management involves costs and benefits and in turn it affects resource management too. They vary according to the temporal, spatial, tangibility, and distribution dimensions. The local institutions will be most effective in management if the benefits of resource management accrue quickly, locally, visibly and individually or collectively. The opposite is true if the benefits are delayed, remote, hard to identify and do not accrue to the investors of efforts. The management of the natural resources also depends upon the characteristics of resources. The less renewable a resource is the more risk there is that poor management will have drastic consequences, and the more reason one can offer for some form of government involvement (Gurung 2005).

3 Methodology and Data Sources

This study mainly depends on the secondary sources of data. Semi-structured interviews are conducted with people in all walks of life like people's representatives, local people, farmers, fishermen, office bearers of farmers' committee (*Karshaka Samithi*), environmentalists and scientists. The physical features of the Vellayani Lake are compiled from the secondary data of various experts who had worked on the various aspects of the lake before.

4 Vellayani Lake—A Tropical Wetland

In Kerala, the fresh water resources consist of the 44 rivers originating from Western Ghats, 29 manmade reservoirs, ten fresh water lakes, countless number of village ponds, household ponds and temple tanks. The average rainfall in Kerala is 2615 mm with a range of 3500 mm in the north to 900 mm in the south. Of the total annual rainfall, 60% is accounted by the south-west monsoon (June–September), and 30% by the north-east monsoon (October–December), while another 10% of the rainfall is estimated to come during the hot pre-monsoon period (Aziz 1989). The 580 km coastal tract of Kerala is renowned for the occurrence of several small and large lakes.

Kerala has a steep terrain. The distance between the highest spot in Kerala, i.e., Anamalai and Arabian Sea is only 150 km. So the rain which falls in the Western Ghats will reach the sea within 42 h. Only a very little water is stored in the natural and artificial reservoirs. Though Kerala is endowed with a large number of fresh water sources and two monsoons, during summer water becomes a scarce commodity. Lakes have a natural role of storing the precious rain water and maintain the ground water table, recharging the innumerable number of wells in the adjoining areas. The fresh water lakes have a predominant place in Kerala's natural wealth. Kerala has three big fresh water lakes. They are Vellayani Lake in Thiruvananthapuram District, Sasthamcottah Lake in Kollam District and Pookot Lake in Wayanad District (GoK 1993). One of the development challenges Kerala now faces is the destruction of fragile ecosystem, depletion of resources and pollution of natural resources. So the renowned Kerala model is increasingly become unsustainable (Issac and Harilal 1997).

Lake Vellayani is the only fresh water lake situated in Thiruvananthapuram District. It is the Common Property Resource of four Grama Panchayats—Nemom, Venganoor, Kalliyoor and Thiruvallam. The lake is a source of irrigation and drinking water to these adjoining panchayats. So it becomes the responsibility of these Grama Panchayats to manage this CPR efficiently. The Vellayani Lake, now a fully freshwater system 11 km south of Thiruvananthapuram city is the only natural fresh water lake in the Thiruvananthapuram District. Lying between latitude 8° 24′ 90″ and 8° 26′ 30″ north and longitude 76° 59′ 08″ and 76° 59′ 47″ east, the lake is bordered by the Thiruvallam and Nemom villages of the Neyyattinkara Taluk (Aziz 1989). Nair et al. (1988) have traced the geological evolution of Vellayani Lake. During the past, tidal water had reached much inward along the lower basin of River Karamana and also along the basin of its then existing tributary from the south. Protected all around by steep hills, the areas of the tributary basin had been locally submerged. Subsequent to the regression of the sea water, the deeper portion of the tributary became Vellayani Lake.

Vellayani Lake is the type of lake which set far back in the coastal land away from the modern shoreline and presently devoid of any connection of the sea. The freshwater supply to this lake is from internal drainage and underground sources (Nair and Thrivikramji 1996). Contradictory reports from different agencies are available on the extent of the lake. According to Revenue Department, the original extent of the lake is 441.98 acres. The total extent of the lake, according to Irrigation Department is 490 ha. The lake begins to swell up after the receipt of the south-west monsoon and attains its full volume and glory during December after the north-east monsoon is over. The lake is only 3 m deep even at the deepest part. However, the local residents claim that the lake was over 3 m deep in the past (Sanjeev 1994).

The width of the Vellayani Lake is 600 m in the north, tapering towards the south (200 m). The lake is surrounded by laterite ridges on eastern, southern and western sides. The northern part of the lake is having gentle slope towards the Karamana River (Nalinakumar and Nair 1998). The elevation from the mean sea level (msl) is more in the western part compared to southern and eastern parts. The maximum elevation is in the western parts, 60 m from the msl. The ridges are flat topped and having moderate slope in east, south and western portions. The flood plains are mostly associated with water body of the lake and the northern portion of the lake is draining into the Karamana River. According to Sanjeev (1994), Vellayani Lake is undergoing rapid transformation through changes in land use around the lake, indiscriminate cultivation practices, encroachment and reclamation coupled with high soil erosion around the lake.

5 Stakeholders Are Multiple and Varied

One common feature of any common property resource is that the stakeholders are multiple and varied. In the case of Vellayani Lake also, the same can be observed. Some of the stakeholders identified in the study and the benefits accrued by them are discussed.

5.1 Kerala Water Authority and Drinking Water Source

Thiruvananthapuram is the district which receives the minimum rainfall in Kerala and that itself is decreased over the years. During the drought periods, the Kerala

Water Authority (KWA) spends lakhs of rupees to supply water in the adjoining areas of Thiruvananthapuram city. Even during the monsoon seasons, the KWA supplies water to the different parts of the Thiruvananthapuram city. In this context, the importance of Vellayani Lake is highlighted by KWA. The only perennial source in the Greater Trivandrum Water Supply Scheme (South zone) area apart from Karamana River is Vellayani Lake. Almost all the Water Supply Schemes in Thiruvananthapuram Taluk solely depended on Karamana River as source. Since the Scheme area is on the tail end of Karamana River, there is a possibility of intrusion of sea water to the intake point during tidal times (KWA 1997a).

The Vellayani Lake is gigantic with peculiar features. The water in the lake has an ideal quality. The water spread area of the lake is of the order of 5.55 km^2. About a third of the land area forming the central lake is government property. The remaining land area comprising about 1000 acres of peripheral land belongs to private land owners. This area is also mostly under water logged conditions throughout the year. The agricultural practices inside the lake are no longer in vogue now. The water in the lake cannot be pumped out now, as it will result in deprival of water at the intake of the drinking water supply schemes. Besides the private land owners, the Agricultural College Authorities have also stopped cultivation in the lake area. So the Investigation, Planning and Design (IPD) division of KWA recommended that the Vellayani lake area comprising water spread area of 5.55 km^2 of which 1.73 km^2 is Government land and the remaining area mostly water logged private land be declared as a lake preservation scheme for use primarily as source of drinking water supply schemes to the south-zone areas of Thiruvananthapuram city and also for developing the lake for other secondary uses like tourism and recreation. The private land may be acquired by the Government after providing suitable compensation (KWA 1997b).

The water of the lake was found to be directly used for drinking purpose in the Agriculture College which is situated at the banks of the lake. No special treatment except with lime and bleaching power is done. So the lake should be viewed as a dependable source of potable water in the future. If the lake is destroyed ruthlessly, it will be a total loss to the adjoining areas. Thousands of people residing around the lake are devoid of water during summer season. So the water resource in this fresh water lake should be reserved for the domestic use of the people. Vellayani Lake is only an aerial distance of 6 km from the city limit. It is a replenishable lake with 64 rivulets. The lake is situated in the urban fringe, and there is not much difficulty in the planning and using it for the future needs. But some kind of engineering planning and administrative measures will be needed. Then the water can be supplied to the adjoining panchayats as well as to the other parts of the Thiruvananthapuram city. Freshwater resources need special care and attention to take it available sustainably for the present and future generations. Scientific measures have to be adopted to prevent further siltation and encroachment of Vellayani Lake.

5.2 Panchayats and Tourism Potential

The Development Reports (*Vikasana Rekha*) prepared by the panchayats adjoining to lake give adequate importance to the Vellayani Lake. They studied extensively the problems, issues, solutions and the possibilities of the lake. They also suggest remedial measures in their Development Strategy (*Vikasana Thanthram*). Of the four Grama Panchayats, the Kalliyoor Panchayat—having the longest stretch of the lake—gives more importance to the lake, in its Report. It explains the origin of the lake, its importance and their commitment towards its conservation. The report also looks into the possibilities of tourism in the lake. The Vellayani Lake was the principal tourist resort during the period of the erstwhile rulers of Travancore. The Koikal Moola Palace is one of the resting bungalows of the royal family situated on the western bank of the lake. Later in 1953, this Palace was converted into the Kerala Agriculture College. The world famous tourist spot, Kovalam is about 5 km away from the lake. The Thiruvananthapuram international airport is 10 km away from the spot. These places are well knit by road network.

If the lake is developed as a tourist spot, the tourists coming to Kovalam can visit the Royal Palaces, gardens of Kerala Agriculture College and the beautiful lake. They can go to Kanyakumari via N.H.47 through Vedivachankovil. A local club organises a boat race for 'Ayyankali Trophy' in the Vellayani Lake during the Onam season. This can be made more attractive and be held with a festive mood to attract tourists to this spot. But not much attention is paid in this regard. It is done only as a local programme. The tourists can make trip in the lake for about 30 km. For that, necessary infrastructure should be made. Apart from that a ring road can be constructed to connect the banks of the lake. Facilities such as picnic park, children's park, honey moon cottage also can be constructed. The tourists can be provided with cycle boating and pedal-boating services. The mechanised boating which will cause pollution by the leakage of the oil can be thus avoided. Big houseboats can be introduced to attract tourists. Restaurants can also be put up. Without affecting the purity of lake, a public water transport system can also be launched. The tourism development will definitely fetch more income for the adjoining Panchayats.

5.3 Fishermen and Their Livelihood

Although the lake was the major source of freshwater fishes in Thiruvananthapuram city a few decades ago, now the lake cannot claim that reputation. When the size of the lake has dwindled as a result of reclamation of lake land for paddy cultivation, the habitat available for the fish population also decreased. This has inflicted a severe blow to the fish and prawn resources of the lake. The annual dewatering of the lake caused catastrophic damage to the entire aquatic resources of the lake. Now because of the action taken to ban the dewatering, the fish population has increased.

But it is reported that the size of many fishes has decreased. A lot of people had depended on the lake for fishing. But scientific and eco-friendly aquaculture has not been done in this lake.

5.4 Farmers and Agricultural Activities

When the Second World War was going on Sir C.P. Ramaswamy Iyer, the then Dewan (Prime Minister) of Travancore, launched the 'Grow More Food Campaign' to get relief from the poverty. As a part of that programme, the banks of Vellayani Lake were dewatered and paddy was cultivated. A second wave of the Campaign which was launched by the Chief Minister of Travancore–Kochi region Mr. Pattom Thanu Pillai in 1952–53 was more successful. Thus a lot of farming lands (called *Padashekharams*)—Mankilikari, Nilamelkari, Chittakathukari, Pandarakari, Thamarakari, Punchakari, Valiavilakalhukari, Kulangarakari, and Palapoorukari—were made. The remaining lands were given to different people on lease. An old farmer remembered that some people came from the northern part of Travancore to cultivate in these lands. They dewatered the lands and gave it to various local farmers and appropriated the profits.

Later, the government gave 350 acres of land from these '*Padashekharams*' to poor farmers for group farming. For that purpose, a Farming Society was formed in 1957. But it failed to achieve its objective. Inefficiency and exploitation of intermediaries hastened the fall of the society. Later, the government liquidated the society and handed over the land to the Vellayani Agriculture College (Nemom Grama Panchayat 1996). Some people, as the part of the Campaign got the land on lease system. They influenced the different governments that came to power from time to time and got the land rights and changed it as their private property.

The Kerala Agriculture College established on the banks of lake in 1953. During the summer season, the college authorities used to drain the lake and cultivate paddy. It was the time of the Green Revolution the spirit of which was in the veins of the people and scientists. Many hazardous pesticides were experimented in the fields. This polluted the lake. The shallow areas of lake lands in Kerala are reclaimed for the cultivation of paddy. Lake reclamation programmes were launched in Vellayani Lake even before independence. But, the last three decades have witnessed missive development programme involving extensive reclamation of lake lands for agricultural operations.

The coir industry was also in the Kalliyoor Grama Panchayat some years back. When the lake lands were reclaimed, the employment opportunities of many people were lost. When the lake was used for cultivation, a lot of people lost their livelihood, especially, the fishermen and the duck-raisers. It was projected that about 1000 families were directly benefited out of the paddy cultivation besides indirect benefits to another 1000 families around the lake. Apart from the production aspect, the cultivation provided employment and livelihood to the people in the vicinity. Every year 25,000–30,000 man days were employed for the cultivation of the lake lands during a paddy season. The paddy cultivation in the lake was usually done during summer season when the water level falls. They dewatered the remaining water and sowed the seeds. The farmers remembered that they had not even wanted to plough the land. Because of the fertile loose sediments, they only had to sow the seeds directly into the land.

As the College authorities do not dewater the lake nowadays, the lands of private individuals inside the lake are under water. They become useless for people as they cannot either do the farming or sell the property. The land value has declined considerably. To add to this problem, there are not much takers also. The farmers who are unable to do cultivation in the lake land have to face a lot of other problems. The stoppage of cultivation made them buy additional grains from outside. Non-availability of fodder for their cattle affects the dairy farming production. Above all, it becomes a social problem. Many people, who got the land as their family inheritance and as gift cannot either sell or cultivate it. Some of the farmers are ready to give up the lands, if the government will remunerate adequately.

5.5 Real Estate and Alternate Land Use

There is a growing tendency to retire from the city to have some dwellings in the side of the lake. A lot of people including bureaucrats and high officials have settled here. Some of them even use the lake for sewage purposes. They also set up farm houses in the banks of the lake after reclamation. Many famous contractors of Thiruvananthapuram city own lands in the lake. In meantime, the land value of the area had increased. So it becomes a tendency to reclaim the lake land for building purpose. Tonnes of soil dumped into the lake. These actions lead to the shrinking of the water body.

5.6 Scientists and Conservation Measures

The launching of the ‘Grow More food Campaign’ and other developmental activities witnessed unprecedented degree of anthropogenic interference on the ecosystem of the lake. The inflow of water into the lake causes siltation. Nearly 64 rivulets drain into the lake bringing along with it considerable amount of silt. Some of these get washed on when lake overflows but silt outflow does not always match the inflow and the silt settles at the bottom of the lake making it progressively shallow. Absence of scientific soil conservation measures in the adjoining uplands and hillocks having red loams soils contributes to a great extent for the unabated siltation of the lake.

Pollution from urban and agricultural sources, coupled with poor management and protection measures, has contributed to a steady deterioration in the water quality of the Vellayani Lake in Thiruvananthapuram. The Vellayani Lake is undergoing a steady deterioration in water quality and the report observes that human intervention and pollution from urban and agricultural sources are well registered in the Vellayani Lake. The nitrate content was found to be higher in the surface, bottom, and interstitial waters of the lake. Fertiliser-intensive farming in the adjoining paddy fields and the exponential rise in the quantity of NPK fertiliser use in Thiruvananthapuram district from 1961 to 2010 are cited as reasons. A substantial portion of the unused nutrients in the catchment area would reach the lake through surface and groundwater pathways, especially during monsoon. It calls for steps to mitigate the adverse impact of unscientific human interventions on the lake systems (Krishnakumar 1996).

5.7 *Environmentalists and Uniqueness of Wetland*

The Vellayani Lake is a typical example of man's intervention on nature, particularly on the wetlands of the developing countries tropics, which are undergoing rapid transformation through indiscriminate encroachment. In their excitement for development, people tend to forget the lakes, tanks and similar such water bodies play a natural role in storing rain water, in maintaining the recharge of ground water, and as an aquifer for the dug-wells in the neighbourhood. They collect and store large quantities of water during the monsoon period and serve a very useful purpose in the conservation of water, more especially in the topographical situation such as the one existing in the state of Kerala. The wetlands should not be considered as unimportant, useless or derelict areas, but should be treated as very valuable components of the ecosystem, serving specific functions. Steps should therefore, be taken towards the conservation of water bodies such as Vellayani Lake.

6 Proposals to Conserve

As the stakeholders are varied, the proposals put forward by each one of them are of wide ranging in nature. Some of the prominent proposals put forward on various aspects by the stakeholders are discussed.
Fishery resources: In order to ensure sustainability of fisheries of the lake, the government should develop an integrated lake conservation plan which includes prevention of encroachment, ecosystem protection and adoption of co-management of lake's resources with the involvement of local fishermen. The involvement of local fishermen in conservation activities would help, as they currently keep a vigil against sand mining. They also say reinstalling the connectivity of the lake with Karamana River would help the movement of migratory fish such as eels.

Water resource: Vellayani Lake is a community well. So it should be maintained with utmost care. No compromise with any interest groups should be made. There is a famous saying. 'The land you cultivate and water you drink are not inherited properties. These are the properties we borrow from the future generation'. So it becomes the duty to give it to the future generation for their use without causing any damage.

Audit is necessary: At least 100 m from the boundary of Vellayani freshwater lake should be declared as the land regulation zone and all human interference be prohibited by suitable management. The government should acquire the lands of the private individuals by giving adequate remuneration for the preservation of the lake. The government should take bold steps to preserve the lake as protected area. Apart from that, a continuous ecological audit, economic audit and social audit should be done regarding the current state of the lake.

Prevent encroachment: A lot of encroachment has taken place by the private parties. So it is better to demarcate the government lands from the private land owners who own the proper property rights. The government should take over the lands which were encroached into the already declined area of Vellayani.

Strict laws and legislations: All over the world, the natural resources are protected with utmost care. Here also, the 780 ha lake is the property of the government. This type of ecological fragile area is to be considered with utmost care using strict laws and legislations.

Prevent soil erosion: The average depth of the lake is only 3 m. For the better storage and drainage of the water, the rivulets can be cleared and desilted. The dredging of the soil in the lake can be done under the auspice of panchayats. Only a little amount has to be spent and the panchayats can sell the soil. So the panchayats can earn some profit from this. Scientific measures should be adopted to prevent further soil erosion into the lake. Crops around the lake should not be competitive in nature. For the cultivation of high-yielding crops, the soil will be highly disturbed. The lake is surrounded by high Thiruvallam hills. So an overhead tank can be constructed and using the particular geomorphological conditions of Thiruvananthapuram city the water can be made to flow effectively to the city.

7 Underlying Conflicts

It is common to have conflicts when there is a lot of stakeholders try to find a bite in the cake. The stakeholders range from proponents of drinking water to conservationist of the unique tropical wetland. The conflicts prevailing in the study area are discussed in brief.

Drinking water versus paddy cultivation: The Vellayani Lake is not only the source of drinking water scheme, but also a unique non-renewable ecosystem. So it should be an irrecoverable mistake from the part of the people to use this land for cultivation. Another aspect of the problem is that there is no guarantee that this land would be used for paddy cultivation itself in the future. The claims of private land owners for cultivation are only a bogus one. Everyone knows that the paddy cultivation is not lucrative in Kerala. So the land under paddy cultivation in Kerala which was about nine lakh hectares in 1990 has come down to 4.6 lakh hectares. It is very easy to find alternative arrangements for paddy cultivation. We can import rice from other states at a reasonable price. But we cannot get water from any other place. A family needs only 2–3 kg of rice per day. But a person needs more than 100 l of water per day. A person can survive without food up to 3–4 days. But he cannot survive without water after 6 or 7 h. We should think of this situation in the context of ever increasing demand of water. During summer the demand for water will rise.

When the lake lands are reclaimed, the water table falls down and a lot of environmental problems arise. The intensive cultivation of paddy (*Punja*—summer cultivation) lands necessitated the application of chemical fertilisers, insecticides and pesticides in a big way. These types of modern agricultural practices pollute the lake highly. So it becomes hazardous to use the water for drinking purposes. Another danger is that it may lead to the growth of weeds (eutrophication) in the water and thereby made the ecosystem in the lake in danger.

The farmers' committee (Karshaka Samithi) points out that many of the farmers and their families who are depending on these lands for their livelihood is now in poverty. The fodder for the cattle is also not available. More than thousand families are directly affected by this action. The Karshaka Samithi threatens to resort the militant ways of strikes. The Samithi even announced that the farmers are going to retting the coconut husk in the lake. Now the Samithi has emerges as a very strong pressure group. The Samithi tried to persuade the Government to give the permission to cultivate. On the other hand, The panchayat representatives criticise the Karshaka Samithi in a strong way. Even if the paddy cultivation in the lake is a business involving a lot of risk and financial loss, some vested interests are working under a banner try to destroy the lake. If this type of aggression is allowed, the lake will become a small pond in the near future.

Conflicts in ownership and conservation of CPR: The problems regarding fresh water lakes were came into the attention of the Kerala government. So an Environment Committee (Paristhithi Samithi) was set up by the Kerala Legislative Assembly in 1992 under Mr. K.P. Nuruddin. The committee pointed out that the administrative control of the freshwater lakes in Kerala have not handed over to any particular department of agency. According to the Kerala Panchayat Act of 1960, the responsibility of conserving the lakes was entrusted with the panchayats. But it did not do any good. The reason was that panchayats have a lot of economic and administrative constraints to take over the responsibilities such as conservation and pollution control of the lakes. So the committee recommended that it is good to vest the administrative control of the lakes on any department or agency. In the case of Vellayani Lake, the committee recommended to give the administrative control to the Irrigation Department.

All the panchayats around the lake failed to prepare any project to conserve their common property resource. This is because some panchayat Committees have the representation from the various interest groups and they argue for their temporary gains. The Vellayani Lake has its boundary in the Block Panchayats-Athiyanoor and Nemom. The Block Panchayats have also given some references about the lake in their Development Reports (*Vikasana Rekha*). But they also failed to prepare any project in the first annual plans. This may be due to the other pressing problems which they have to attend in the day to day course. They cannot give adequate attention to the preservation of lake. In the District Panchayat level, problem of the lake has not at all got its place. No project for the conservation of the lake either directly or indirectly has been made in the Thiruvananthapuram District Panchayat Plan also.

Conservation versus tourism: The environmentalists argue that one should never think of tourism activities inside the lake because tourism means commercialisation. It will bring pollutants such as more plastics, dirt, sewages, etc. It is argued that the non-motorised boats can be used. But it should be remembered that once boating is allowed the other types of motorised boats will come in due course. So it should be better not to lease the lake to commercial interests. Environmental protection and commercialisation cannot go side by side.

Market interest versus scenic beauty: A wide range of migratory birds also come to the lake and its surrounding areas in every season. Wide varieties of plants and animals can be seen in the lake. This makes the lake a diverse ecosystem. The Environment Committee found that one-third of the Vellayani Lake was under private people doing paddy cultivation. Apart from that illegal trespassing of government lands and of Kerala Agricultural College lands are going on. Lake is a precious resource not only for the people of adjoining areas but also for whole humanity. It is the abode of many birds, aquatic animals, local flora, medicinal plants, etc. The lake can be used as a common property resource for the fishermen around the lake. No charge except the licence fees should be charged.

8 Management of CPRs: A Tough Task to Accomplish

Sustainable development is the basic principle which has to govern and guide developmental policies and programmes in all sectors of the economy. The concept implies systematic and planned utilisation of all resources, especially, the natural resources in a most optimal manner. It is very much true in the case of CPRs which are in turn accessible to and collectively owned/held/managed by an identifiable community and on which no individual has exclusive property rights. Many environmental resources are not privately owned, being characterised by either common property regimes or open access in which ownership is either ill-defined or non-existent. In these circumstances, there are several sources of inefficiency in the use of the resource. The major problem arises from the fact that stewardship of the asset is likely to be poor where users cannot expect to receive the fruits of investment of the resource (Perman et al. 1999). The case of management of water resources by a local body, whether formal or informal, has been referred to as community management of common water sources. In India, apart from local self-government (like panchayat) and formal local organisations (like cooperative, Pani Panchayat, Sinchai Samitis and other farmers associations), totally informal but functionally effective local-level organisations for managing common water resources are commonly found in a large number of villages (NSSO 1999).

Conversely to those arrangements existing in many villages in India, the case study discussed in the present paper is a typical example of how the varied stakeholders take different stands on a common property resource which makes it's management impossible. Even though scores of suggestions and proposals had been suggested to conserve the lake by the people from different walks of life, in reality, no effective management regime which satisfies all stake holders has come up in the view. The major reason for the same is that the suggestions and proposals are from multiple angles and they are also conflicting to one another. For example, while the environmentalist and Kerala Water Authority are in the lobby of protecting the lake and its surroundings in the way it is there, while the farmers and the real estate lobby would like to dewater the same and use it for their respective economic activities. It is due to conflicting situation, in actual practice, an effective environment management practice is not taking place in the lake and its surroundings. Hence the lake is under immense pressure which leads to slow deterioration and the decline of the CPR. The role and activities of environmentalists is high to create awareness among the people. But it is observed that neither a holistic conservation of the lake nor an assurance of sustainable livelihood to the stakeholders around the lake is visible in the near future.

The case study reminds us of the fact that there are a number of similar cases in the state of Kerala and in other parts of India. The political will of the local leadership is sometimes not enough to tide over the problems in the local settings. While discussing with the representatives of panchayats around the lake it is found that they are very interested in the conservation of the lake. They have extensively studied the problems and issues concerning the lake; they too have interacted with the local people. On the official side, they had reported the same in their Development Reports of the respective panchayats. But they could not translate that information into any conservation projects as it is a sensitive issue in the local area. If the political representatives are taking the side of one of the stakeholders, the other stakeholders create troubles in the local settings which the same representatives are to solve. Hence, they cannot take any specific side as it is very tricky and complex as far as CPRs are concerned. Even though the literature repeatedly emphasises the fact that panchayats or any other local bodies could manage the CPRs, here in this specific case, the interesting observation which one reaches is that it is very difficult to manage the lake by the Grama Panchayats around it. This is expressed from the fact that they have not framed even a single project to conserve the lake directly or indirectly so far. Yet another reason cited is that the resources of panchayats are limited, even if they have the will, they are unable to accomplish the task of management at the current settings.

The literature of management of CPRs clearly states that whether taking the form of 'participatory conservation/development', 'community-based conservation', or 'natural resource co-management', all common property management involves multiple individuals and groups beyond the social group that holds the resource in common. Stakeholders may include national government ministries, district government officials, commercial extraction interests, local communities or international NGOs. These groups have different powers and interests with respect to the CPR (Turner 2007). The study tried to make an enquiry in that direction too. The tiers which are above the Grama Panchayat level, i.e. Block Panchayat and District Panchayat have very little commitment towards the lake. They are dealing with many pressing local problems. So they do not give adequate importance to the lake. The same is the case with the State Government. Hence, an efficient management regime imposed from the top level is not likely.

Conflict over CPRs is central to poor households' experience of poverty. A well-defined social group with rights to a clearly defined resource; ability to exclude others from using the resource; set of use rules that limit the seasonality, extent, or ways in which the resource is extracted by individuals are the features of successful CPR management (Turner 2007). The present case study exhibits the feature that neither of the social groups involved in the conflict have a clearly defined right nor are able to exclude others from using the resource. For example, those who are arguing for the conservation of lake—environmentalists, experts, common people and panchayat representatives—are not organised. On the other hand, the farmers' committee (Karshaka Samithi) which is campaigning for the reclamation of the lake lands is well organised and has political affiliations and support. So the latter group got more weight. When the issues went out of control, at last the state government had to intervene into the scene. It is going to delegate only a small area inside the lake for conservation. The revenue department has started to encircle the regions constituted the innermost part of the lake stating that it is state property. The rest of the area inside the lake is unattended and the conflicts are unresolved due to complexities attached to the whole issue.

Despite scores of illustrated benefits, wetlands are the first targets of human interference and are among the most threatened of all natural resources. Around 50% of the earth's wetland area is estimated to already have disappeared over the last 100 years through conversion to industrial, agricultural and residential developments. Even in current scenario, when the ecosystem services provided by wetlands are better understood, degradation and conversion of wetlands continues. This is largely due to the fact that the 'full value' of ecosystem functions is often ignored in policy-making, plans and corporate evaluations of development projects (SAC 2010). The study showed that the experts and researchers warn against the destruction of this natural reservoir. It is a unique water body which can provide one of the basic needs of human beings, water, in the coming years. The indiscriminate destruction of the lake by way of reclamation and pollution will harm the people in the adjoining areas. So the conservation of this fragile ecosystem becomes necessary. But as the stakeholders and actors are wide and varied, their interests are also conflicting to each other. No consensus is arrived till date to have a common management of this fragile ecosystem.

For 'equity' and 'sustainable' management of common lands to be a reality, their management by the community of users is necessary and desirable

(Damodaran 1991). In this case study, it is noted that the stakeholders are multiple and varied. There were no clearly defined rights for each and every stakeholder which in turn leads to conflicts in the locality. Community based conservation and co-management of natural resource are not taking place in an efficient manner. Proper management by all the stakeholders who depend upon the common property resources is the need of the hour of many of these kinds of resources in the rural scenario of India. The management must be efficient and sustainable, then only it would lead to an intelligible utilisation of the natural resources available in the developing parts of the world.

References

Aziz APK (1989) The Vellayani Freshwater Lake, Thiruvananthapuram, Kerala—a status report. Kerala State Committee on Science, Technology and Environment, Government of Kerala, Thiruvananthapuram

Beck T, Nesmith C (2001) Building on poor people's capacities: the case of common property resources in India and West Africa. World Dev 29(1):119–133

Bon E (2000) Common pool resources and communal control: two case studies in Himachal Pradesh, India. In: Proceedings of the 8th IASCP conference Bloomington, Indiana, USA, 31 May–4 June 2000

Chopra K et al (1989) People's participation and common property resources. EPW 24(51–52): A189–A195

Chopra K et al (eds) (1990) Participatory development: people and common properly resources. Sage, New Delhi

Damodaran A (1991) Tragedy of the commons and comedy of common property resources. Econ Polit Wkly 26(38):2213–2215

Government of Kerala (1993) Environment Committee (1992–94): first report, fresh water lakes in Kerala, submitted on 2nd Feb 1993 under the Chairmanship of Mr. K.P. Nuruddin. Kerala Legislative Secretariat, Thiruvananthapuram

Gurung Om (2005) Concepts and methods of common property resource management. Dhaulagiri 1:33–41

Issac TM, Harilal KN (1997) Planning for empowerment: people's campaign for decentralised planning in Kerala. EPW 32(1–2):53–58

Jodha NS (1986) Common property resources and the rural poor in dry regions of India. EPW 21 (27):169–181

Katiyar VS (1997) Environmental concerns, depleting resources and sustainable development. Pointer Publishers, Jaipur

Kerala Water Authority (1997a) Greater Thiruvananthapuram Water Supply Scheme (South Zone), Preliminary Engineering Report, prepared by Investigation, Planning and Design Division, Thiruvananthapuram

Kerala Water Authority (1997b) Proposal for Conservation of Vellayani Lake for Drinking Water Supply Schemes, prepared by Investigation, Planning and Design Division, Thiruvananthapuram

Khoshoo TN (1991) Environmental concerns and strategies. Ashish Publishing House, New Delhi

Krishnakumar A (1996) Textural and Geochemical Studies of the Vellayani freshwater lake sediments, Kerala. M.Sc. project report, Department of Marine Geology and Geophysics, School of Marine Sciences, Cochin University of Science and Technology, Kochi

Nair ASK, Thrivikramji KP (1996) Classification of Kayals in the coastal zone of Kerala. In: Proceedings of the eighth Kerala Science Congress, Kochi, 27–29 Jan 1996
Nair NJK et al (1988) Environmental Geomorphic Atlas of Kerala Coastal Zone. Centre for Earth Science Studies, Thiruvananthapuram
Nalinakumar S, Nair ASK (1998) Environmental degradation of Vellayani Kayal using IRS-LISS II data. In: Proceedings of the tenth Kerala Science Congress, Kozhikode, 2–4 Jan 1998
Nambiar KV (1995) Sustainable economic development: need for holistic approach. In: Pillai PP, Nair RP (eds) Understanding ecologically sustainable development. Institute of Planning and Applied Economic Research, John Mathai Foundation, John Mathai Centre, Thrissur
National Sample Survey Organisation (NSSO) (1999) Common property resources in India. (NSSO Report No. 452 (54/31/4) 54th round, Jan–June 1998). Government of India, New Delhi
Nemom Grama Panchayat (1996) Development report (Mal.). Nemom, Thiruvananthapuram
Ostrom E (1990) Governing the commons: the evolution of institutions for collective action. Cambridge University Press
Perman R, Ma Y, McGilvary J, Common M (1999) Natural resource and environmental economics, 2nd edn. Longman, London
Ragupathy V (1999) Common property resource management in Panchayat Raj. In: Palanithurai G (ed) Empowering people: issues and solutions. Kanishka Publishers, New Delhi
Sanjeev V (1994) Pedological investigations on the ecosystem of Vellayani Lake. M.Sc. project report, Department of Social Sciences and Agricultural Chemistry, College of Agriculture, Thiruvananthapuram
Space Application Centre (SAC) (2010) National wetland atlas. Indian Space Research Organisation, Ahmedabad
Turner M (2007) Ecological complexity and the management of common property resources. Tenure brief. University of Wisconsin, Madison
Wade R (1987) The management of common property resources: collective action as an alternative to privatisation or state regulation. Camb J Econ 11:95–106

Land Transfer Tax Policy Regime and Its Influence on Property Markets: Analysing the Land Transfer Tax Policy of Kerala in the Last Decade

V.P. Nirmal Roy

1 Introduction

While markets are institutional arrangements facilitating exchange, government has been considered as a crucial institution supporting markets by ensuring and enforcing the rules of the game. Market supporting institutions can be classified into as market creating, market regulating, market stabilising and market legitimising institutions (Rodrik 2013). It has been noted that government plays a key role in the distribution, regulation and in the efficient functioning of property rights institutions. Property rights institutions have been shaped in such a way that government provides legality/security to land rights and transactions through the establishment of other institutions (Deininger and Feder 2009). Whereas in the case of land and property markets, the government acts as both market developing as well as market regulating institutions, our emphasis here is to analyse the role of governments as market regulating institution. The present land and property markets are the result of many past market-creating institutional activities such as property rights development, property rights distribution such as land reforms and any current institutional analyses that have to be on market regulating institutions.

Land regulation in the Indian federal system, is a state subject; i.e. property rights, tenures, taxes, transaction, etc., comes under state domain.[1] And, therefore the system and structure of land administration in each state is different. Apart from this, the institutional structure of land administration within states is also multi-faceted with different agencies administering various departments such as

[1]Seventh schedule (Article 246) of the Indian constitution defines the powers of the centre and states into three lists; the union list, the state list and the concurrent list.

V.P. Nirmal Roy (✉)
Madras Institute Development Studies, 79 - 2nd Main Road, Gandhinagar, Adyar, Chennai 600020, India
e-mail: vpnirmalroy@mids.ac.in; nirmalroyvp@gmail.com

S. Pellissery et al. (eds.), *Land Policies in India*, India Studies in Business and Economics, DOI 10.1007/978-981-10-4208-9_5

revenue, survey, registration, etc. It has been noted that interconnectivity among these different agencies is nearly absent (Morris and Pandey 2009). While the land tax is collected by the revenue department, property tax is collected by the local bodies. The registration department collects stamp duties and registration fees for administering land and property transfers. While property registration can be considered as a way in which government intervenes/participates in the land markets, institutions such as this essentially records property rights and its transfers. Though Indian land registration system is presumptive in nature calling for modernisation, land transfer taxes (hereafter LTT) are increasingly seen as a revenue generating mechanism along with intervening in land markets (Deininger et al. 2016).

Land and real estate markets are of increased importance in developed as well as developing countries due to its importance in household wealth. Globally, land and real property constitutes an important share in household wealth composition, whereas in the case of developing countries its prevalence is much higher (Davies et al. 2008). The fluctuating land values and innumerable crises associated with it also brought out the fact that land markets are prone to crises (Gaffney 1994; Foldvary 1998). As a store of wealth, the question of land has got importance in the contemporary global scenario, where land and allied assets are increasingly becoming assets of trade and speculation. Also, its role in the generation of black money is also increasingly debated in recent times in India. It is a common knowledge that land and real estate transactions involve under-reporting of actual market values so as to evade land transfer taxes. While tax evasion is pervasive in land markets, there is virtually a paucity of research that has attempted to understand the problem and its causes and implications.

2 Review of Land Transfer Taxes (LTTs)

Land registration and revenue collection Land registration is seen as means of taxation revenue for the government. Dachis et al. (2012) note that most of the developed countries have imposed tax on land transfers. Land transfer tax (LTT) or stamp duty tax ranges from around 2% in the United States (US), about 6.75% in Australia, around 1–4% in the United Kingdom (UK) and about 4.8% in France. On the revenue side, LTT contributed around 2–22% of the total revenue in various American States, about 1.25% of revenue in UK and around 3% of budget in France. However, considering the pervasive nature of taxing the land transaction, it has been noted that the impact of LTT has been least studied (Dachis 2012). As reviewed, land registration policies can have the objectives of controlling market behaviour as well as maximising revenue from the market. However, there are some drawbacks to LTT policies.

Land transfer taxes to control Speculation Land taxes are widely used measures curbing land speculation. Case (1992) distinguishes taxes used for controlling speculation in asset markets into two major types as (1) taxes levied on the transfer of assets, and (2) taxes levied on the holding of assets. Whereas in the case of land sale transactions, taxes levied in the first category includes (a) Japan's real property gains tax, (b) Taiwan's 'Land Value Increment Tax' and (c) Vermont's 'Land Gains Tax'. The second type of tax on land is a market value based property tax, which is a major source of revenue in developed economies. Taxes levied on the holding of assets are intended to curb hording of land anticipating more gains in a scenario of high land demand.

The former kind of taxes is generally aimed at controlling short-term trade based excessive speculation in land known as 'bandwagon speculation'. These taxes vary with holding period and with the size of the gain. In the Japanese case, Case (1992) notes that taxes on the transfer of real property held for less than 10 years are levied at the greatest of 40 or 110% of taxpayer's top marginal rate. If the property is held less than 2 years, the rates are 50 or 120% of the taxpayer's top rate. Also a taxpayer in the top marginal bracket (50%) in Japan would pay a rate of 60% on property gains from holding periods under 2 years. Long-term gains are taxed at lower rates. Similarly, Vermont tax is aimed short-term transactions. Here all gains earned during a holding period of less than 4 months are taxed at 60%. If the gain exceeds 100% of the basis, the tax is 70%, and if the gain exceeds 200% of the basis, the tax is 80%. However, here in Vermont tax, land held for over 6 years is not taxed at all. Similar tax rates in Taiwan are based on a gain basis ratio. The rate is between 40 and 60% depending on the gain basis ratio. While taxing the capital gains from land is often considered as the remedy to curb land speculation, the effectiveness of these kinds of public policy measures is also considered doubtful (Case 1992; Brown 1927). However, Case (1992) refers to a study by Yinger et al. (1988) which has provided a long-term impact of property taxes on asset volatility. ***Land transfer taxes and its adverse impacts*** As mentioned earlier, impact of land transfer taxes is rarely studied. However, there are few studies that have analysed the welfare losses associated with LTTs. Dachis et al. (2012) have studied the welfare lose associated with the imposition of LTTs on Toronto's single-family homes during 2008. While their estimation brought out that 1.1% tax caused a 15% decline in the number of real estate sales and a decline in asset prices about equal to the tax, the associated welfare loss is also found to be substantial, about $1 for every $8 in tax revenue. In a follow-up commentary, Dachis et al. (2012) again noted that Toronto's LTTs had reduced single-family transactions to the tune of 16% as well significantly reducing asset prices

Land transfer taxes can have distortionary effects. As evidence suggests, introduction of new or increased LTTs can reduce future consumption resulting in the reduction of the market activity and ultimately the revenue. In a time when the government expenditure is increasing, fall in the revenue from any source can be counterproductive. Inactive asset markets can have adverse impacts on the investors as money invested cannot be withdrawn in unprofitable scenarios resulting in deadweight welfare loss to the investing households. Also, in case if the transactions are taking place, high LTTs can also precipitate under-reporting of actual market values at the time of registration process so as to evade the taxes if proper regulatory mechanisms are not implemented. Therefore institutional mechanisms to regulate land real estate and its implications have scope for study in the current scenario of increasing land and real estate prices.

This paper studies government's land registration taxation policies of a state in India. As land is a state subject, state specific studies can only bring out the impact land governance issues in Indian context. For understanding the problems of land administration in India, Deininger et al. (2016) studied land administration of Andhra Pradesh, Bihar, Jharkhand, Karnataka, Odisha and West Bengal while analysing a set of land development issues. While very few studies have analysed the LTTs in the Indian context (Mukherjee 2013; Wadhwa 2013; Naresh 2003), there are hardly any studies that have analysed the introduction of fair value land tax or capital gains land tax. Kerala, which is renowned in development discourses for notable interventions in land, of late has experienced changes in the LTT tax regime is considered for the study.

3 Background

Kerala, a state in India reputed for its land reforms however presents an interesting case in the realm of land reforms and is the focal point of this study. At present, Kerala reveals land governance issues precipitated by a dynamic land market. Latest debates on land in Kerala have recognised the changed status of land to that of a scarce asset and used for speculative purposes (Harilal 2008). While this is supported by the increased land market activity in the last decade, latest data also reveals the boom and bust cycles in Kerala's land market scenario and the revenue from it (Govt of Kerala (GoK)). Kerala is also unique for studying the impact of land tax policy as it has frequently initiated changes in land transfer tax policies. Realising the revenue potential of land markets, lot of changes were introduced in land registration as well as the tax rates. Also, in order to control the speculative nature of the market, changes were introduced in the land transfer tax structure in the last decade. This paper attempts to analyse the land transfer tax regime of Kerala in the last decade so as to understand the LTTs and its role in the land and real estate market.

4 Methodology and Data

The major enquiry of this paper is to understand government's interventions in the asset market through its tax arm and its implications. Verifying the ways in which government intervenes in the land markets through taxation policy would be ideal for answering the objective. Information pertaining to changes in the land transfer tax regime was collected from the budget documents, finance bills and finance acts of the GoK in the last decade. For analysing the implications of the changing LTTs, appropriate proxy for land transfer data and revenue mobilised in monthly frequencies has been collected from the office of the Inspector General of Registrations of GoK.

5 Analysis

A closer look at the LTTs in the Kerala case reveals the two distinct ways through which it is imposed and regulated. LTTs are maintained through changes in the rates as well as the structure. In the paper, an analysis of changes in the rates and structure of LTTs is attempted to understand government interventions in land markets and its impacts. The paper is divided into the following sections for analysis.

5.1 Changes in land transfer tax rates.
5.2 Changes in land transfer tax structure.
5.3 Influence of tax policy changes on land markets.

5.1 Changes in Rates

Stamp Duty, Surcharge and Registration Fees Transfer (or conveyance) of land and real estate (immovable property) in Kerala is based on the Indian Registration Act of 1908 and the Kerala Stamp Act of 1959. Indian Registration Act of 1908 stipulates that all transactions of the immovable properties have to be registered with the registration department. Sale transaction deed has to be prepared on stamp paper carrying fixed percentage of the value of the property which is being transferred. The rate of stamp duty is fixed by the state government during the annual budget preparation.[2] Until 2009–10, surcharge on the stamp duty was also collected for conveyances involving immovable properties. Registration fees are also collected apart from the stamp duty at the registrar's office. All these taxes fixed by the government on the reported value of the property have to be paid at the sub-registrar's office at the time of the registration of the sale deed. Information pertaining to rates prescribed for the stamp duty, surcharge and registration fee charged on conveyances in Kerala in the last decade is provided in Table 1.

The above table detailing the tax on conveyances in Kerala can be best described as having two halves. While the first half, from 2005–06 to 2009–10, display high levels of tax burden, the second half, from 2010 to 2011, exhibit drastic reductions. The crucial break in 2010–11 was due to the withdrawal of surcharge on stamp

[2]The stamp duty rates used to vary across Panchayath, Municipality and Corporation areas in Kerala until 2013.

Table 1 Percentage of stamp duty, surcharge and registration fees charged in Kerala in the last decade

Year	Stamp duty* (1)			Surcharge on stamp duty* (2)			Registration fee* (3)			Cumulative tax burden* (1 + 2+3)		
	Panchayath	Municipality	Corporation	Panchayath	Municipality	Corporation	Panchayath	Municipality	Corporation	Panchayath	Municipality	Corporation
2004–05	2	3	4	2	2	2	2	2	2	6	7	8
2005–06	6	8.5	8.5	4	4	5	2	2	2	12	14.5	15.5
2006–07	6	8.5	8.5	4	4	5	2	2	2	12	14.5	15.5
2007–08	6	8.5	8.5	4	4	5	2	2	2	12	14.5	15.5
2008–09	6	8.5	8.5	4	4	5	2	2	2	12	14.5	15.5
2009–10	6	8.5	8.5	4	4	5	2	2	2	12	14.5	15.5
2010–11	7	8	9	–	–	–	2	2	2	9	10	11
2011–12	7	8	9	–	–	–	2	2	2	9	10	11
2012–13	7	8	9	–	–	–	2	2	2	9	10	11
2013–14	5	6	7	–	–	–	2	2	2	7	8	9
2014–15	6	6	6	–	–	–	2	2	2	8	8	8

* Figures denote percentage to the reported values of the property in the transfer deed

Source Government of Kerala (Budget speeches, financial bills and financial acts of GoK 2004–05 to 2014–15)

duties and the introduction of ***fair value land taxation***.[3] It can also be seen that during 2013–14 the transfer tax rates were coming down again. This was owing to the introduction of ***capital gains tax*** on the short-term transactions. In sum, there has been a decline in the tax rates charged on conveyances in Kerala in the last decade and the two main new features replacing higher tax rates have been the introduction of fair value taxation and capital gain tax. Now let us look into these two relatively new revenue streams which came into existence as a result of the change in the tax structure.

5.2 *Changes in the Structure*

Here, the analysis is on those government interventions that restructure land conveyance tax regime to increase revenue from land transfers by preventing under-reporting of market prices of the property at the time of documentation and record current market prices. Fair value land taxation and capital gains taxation were the new tax policy changes in this regard.

5.2.1 Fair Value Land Taxation

While fair value is used to refer the rational estimate of the market value of an asset whose actual market value cannot be ascertained, fair value land taxation intends to collect conveyance tax based on a predetermined fair market price of the asset transacted. It is assumed that this fair market price will be closer to the actual market price of the asset, and in Kerala's case it is assumed to be about 50% of the market price.[4] The need for fixing fair value of land in Kerala arises out of the conviction that actual land prices are usually under-reported in the conveyance deed so as to avoid the tax burden during the deed registration process. The first proposal for fair value of land was announced in 2004–05 (Budget speech 2004–05). Anticipating fair value notification, the government by an ordinance in December 2003 itself had reduced the stamp duties.[5] This, however, was not implemented at all and therefore, the duties for conveyance were increased back to higher rates in the next year.[6] The succeeding government in 2005–06 again proposed the

[3]In fact the low rate during 2004–05 was on the expectation of a possible introduction of fair value land taxation which however was not materialised.

[4]In the 2010–11 Budget speech where the fair value land taxation was notified, the finance minister Sri T.M. Thomas Isaac mentions that it was insisted that the fair value should not exceed 50% of the market value.

[5]As per this, stamp duty was fixed to 2% at Panchayath level, 3% at Municipalities and 4% at Corporation premises for immovable property conveyances. Surcharge of 2% of stamp duty was also included for all the regions.

[6]See the previous section for details regarding increased rates during 2004–05.

implementation of fair value land taxation (Budget Speech 2005–06). However, this got delayed further. While notification process was started during 2008–09, the fair value was fixed as on 1 April 2010 (Budget Speech 2008–09, 2010–11). In the recent budget, it has been announced to review the fair value of land on a periodical basis of 5 years at a fixed percentage (Kerala Finance Bill 2014, no. 281).

5.2.2 Short-Term Capital Gains Tax

Capital gains tax is the tax on capital gains or profits realised on the re-sale of capital assets such as stocks, bonds or property in the short term.[7] By 2013, capital gains tax on transactions involving the re-sale of land purchased within a short term was proposed for countering the speculative tendencies and the hike the land prices. Re-sale of a land purchased, within a period of 3 months from the date of registration of the purchase deed shall be subjected to double the stamp duty of the previous conveyance deed (Budget speech 2013–14).

5.3 Influence of Tax Policy Changes on Land Markets

Now let us graphically examine the impact of tax policy changes on the land markets (represented by total deeds registered in the state) and the revenue mobilisation scenario. While, number of total transactions is plotted in graph 1, revenue collected through stamp duty and registration fee in real terms is provided in graph 2. The graphs depict changes in these variables to changes in policies pertaining to stamp duty and registration fees during the last decade. The intersecting dotted line breaks are used to show the significant policy interventions with respect to tax instruments such as the stamp duty, registration fee, fair value taxation and capital gains tax. As marked in the graph, the changing policy shifts and its impacts on land markets registered are explained in Fig. 1.

The dotted line breaks shown in the graph represent some of the major tax policy changes in land conveyance scenario. The line breaks are used to represent:

1. Increase in stamp duty and surcharge on stamp duty.
2. Rate of stamp duty payable on powers of attorney executed for transacting immovable property hiked.
3. Notification for fair value of land issued.

---

[7]Capital assets are distinguishable on the basis of the period of holding. This can vary across taxing institutions. For example, Kelkar in the Report of the Task force on Direct Tax (2002) considers any transactions involving capital assets more than 3 years as long term. In the case of equity, more than one year is considered as long term.

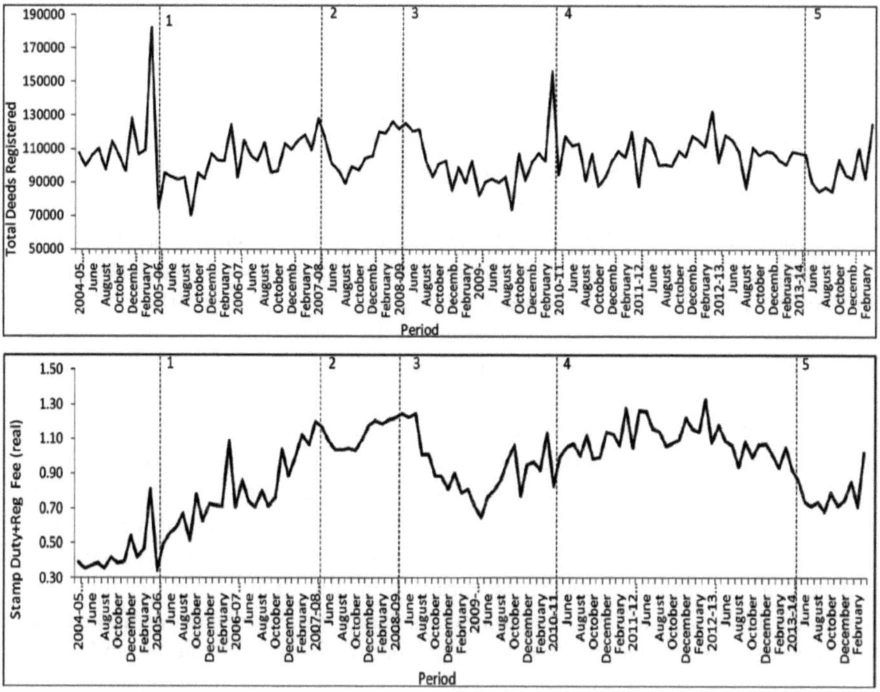

Fig. 1 Tax policy interventions on land market transactions and revenue collection through stamp duty and registration fee. *Source* Data collected from Inspector General of Registration, GoK

4. Surcharge on stamp duty abolished. Stamp duty also reduced. Fair value prices of land fixed.
5. Capital Gains tax introduced.

The first significant policy shift shown in the graph relates to an increase in the stamp duty.[8] The effective rates on conveyances were thus almost doubled comparing to the previous year.[9] The result is well seen in the graph. Anticipating rise in the new financial year in April, there was significant spike in transactions registered in the last months of the previous financial year and a subsequent fall in April 2005. The second policy intervention was introduced after a couple of years. This was through the hiking of the rate of stamp duty payable on powers of attorney executed

[8]Stamp duties were increased to 6, 8 and 8.5% respectively at Panchayath, Municipality and the Corporation. Surcharge on the stamp duty were at the rate of 4% at Panchayath and Municipality and 5% at Corporation (Budget Speech 2005–06).

[9]Please see Table 1 for a comparative picture.

for transacting immovable property from Rs. 150 to 6% of its value.[10] It can be seen that in the new financial year, this change has resulted in a decline in the number of transactions in the forthcoming months. This was at a time when speculative property transactions based on power of attorney was said to be raging in Kerala. The third policy regime change was the announcement of land transaction tax to be based on fair value land price in the budget speech of 2008–09. This fair value was supposed to be based on the existing land prices of 2008. Incidentally, this was also the period characterised by the commencing of global financial recession. Due to these reasons, both the land market transactions experienced deceleration in the subsequent periods. The forth break represents one of the significant tax policy interventions. During 2010–11, surcharge on the stamp duty was fully abolished.[11] This was in anticipation with the introduction of fair value based conveyance taxation. Fair value prices of properties in Kerala were fixed from the 1 April 2010.[12] The final tax policy shift shown in the graph was introduced in 2013–14. Capital gains tax on short-term transactions announced in the 2013–14 budget. This was with respect to the short-term land transactions which were speculative in nature.[13] Also, the existing rates of stamp duty were reduced by 2–5, 6 and 7%, respectively in Panchayaths, Municipalities and Corporations. These twin measures are seen to have a decelerating effect on land transactions indicating a negative impact of these measures. However, it can be equally considered that short-term capital gains tax was successful in combating short-term speculation in the land markets and therefore the decline is the numbers registered. But importantly, all the impacts baring the one during the recession are seen to have short-term repercussions only.

5.4 *Impacts*

The above exercise has provided a simpler picture of how tax policy influences land markets. While the above analysis provides enough directions regarding the impacts of tax policy interventions on market behaviour, it also brings out interesting facts

[10]Regarding providing power of attorney to a promoter or developer for construction or development of a property or sale or transfer, stamp duty has to be paid on the value of the property par with conveyance rate prescribed in respective locations. Stamp duty if paid earlier for such agreements regarding the construction shall be deducted from the stamp duty payable for the conveyance (Budget speech 2007–08).

[11]The effective rate of stamp duty, surcharge and registration fee in Corporation areas was brought down from 15.5 to 11%; in Municipality/Township/Cantonment areas from 14.5 to 10%; and in Grama Panchayathh from 12 to 9%.

[12]However, it was insisted that the fair value of land should not exceed 50% of market value (Budget Speech 2010–11).

[13]As per this, re-sale of a land purchased within a period of 3 months from the date of registration of the purchase deed shall be subjected to double the stamp duty of the previous conveyance deed and for those after 3 and before 6 months of purchase to warrant one and half times the stamp duty of the previous conveyance (Budget Speech 2013–14).

regarding land market behaviour and revenue from it. ***First***, the spike in transactions and revenue during the last months of the financial year and the fall during the initial months of the financial year indicates seasonality behaviour of the land markets. This suggests that the timing of land sales responds significantly in anticipation of the tax policy shifts in the future. In other words, the decline in market activity during the initial months of the financial year can be attributed to changes (possibly hike) in the tax rates or structure introduced in the beginning of the previous financial year, while the increase in market activity can be reasoned the anticipation of future hike in the taxes in the forthcoming financial year. Land sales will be mostly operationalised in the period up to financial year while anticipating the forthcoming tax policy shifts as adverse in nature. Tax policy changes are normally announced during the budget speech, which is usually done during the last week of February on Kerala. Changes are assumed to come in place at the beginning of every financial year, i.e. April. The reason why the dotted line breaks are placed at the month of April of each year with tax policy changes is due to this. Anticipating changes in the forthcoming financial year, there is a spike in the last month of the financial year, i.e. March, indicating more transactions before the new tax change comes into practice in April. This is common for the revenue also as more transactions lead to higher revenue. However, there is a fall in April and subsequent couple of months. This may be due to lower number of transactions resulting from the introduction of new tax policies.

Second, there are no long-term strong impacts of tax changes on either land markets or revenue. These changes have short-term impacts leading to a few months on both the variables under analysis, i.e. number of transactions and revenue from stamp duty and registration fee. The variables stabilise in the long term and arche back to local maxima by the end of the financial year.[14] ***Third***, the implication of tax waivers (represented by the surge in revenue shortly after 2009–10 caused without a corresponding increase in land transfers) is also very much visible in the analysis. This has brought out the importance of tax waivers in increasing the revenue potential from land transfers taxation often blinded by under-reporting of land values.

6 Concluding Observations

This paper addresses the changed land transfer tax regime in the light of spiralling land prices in a state in India. While Indian land governance scenario is grappling with complex land administrative framework, the study provides a chance to

---

[14]But the revenue curve represented here in real variable did not maintain the momentum shown in the early couple of years, and could not recover after the fall during 2008–09 unlike the previous acceleration. This may be due to the fact that after the introduction of fair value taxation and subsequently short-term capital gains taxation, the rates of stamp duty and registration fees were normalised to lower rates. Though these measures have increased revenue in nominal terms it has actually brought lower real revenue.

understand how the Indian state responds to rise in land prices and land market activity. As mentioned in the literature, the multitude of layers of land administrative system in India is posing serious challenges to the rapidly growing and urbanising Indian landscape (Morris and Pandey 2009; Deininger et al. 2016). Among the impediments is the absence of proper of land records, digitalised records, maps, etc., which is coupled with high transaction taxes. It has been argued that higher transfer taxes encourage scope for under-reporting of actual values for lowering the tax amounts. Though the high stamp duties and registration fees were progressively brought down, the state has embarked on fair value land taxation and capital gains tax as new institutions in the land transfer tax system. This was however in light of the stupendous rise in land values across kerala and the under-reporting of land values coupled with speculative land purchases.

As mentioned in the literature, the introduction of new property transactions taxes was in light of the speculative spiralling of the land prices. The abnormal increase in land prices and the land market activity has unequal welfare implications on the society. While the owners of land stand to gain from land price hike and also through under-reporting of actual values at the time of sale, there are also negative impacts on the land revenue mobilisation by the government. Also speculative spiralling of land values reduces the chances of landless sections to access land; it also impacts the landowners in times of bust in the land market through abnormal fall in the land values. These situations necessitated the need for land transfer taxes such as capital gains tax and fair value land tax. In this background, this study based on the changes in the land transfer regime of a state in India offers some interesting inputs with respect to revenue optimisation from land markets.

The interventions by way of *fair value* land taxation and *capital gains* tax during times of speculative land price hike can be considered as utilitarian in nature. Apart from the policy requirement of maximising revenue from favourable conditions, it also aims for reduction in the speculative land price movements and land market behaviour. While LTTs intended for legalising the transfer contract of property rights, it is advocated that higher rates will be burdensome and therefore can lead to evasions. However, fair value and capital gains taxation is welfare generating overall considering the wider social implications even though are high compared to the pre-taxation taxes for the property traders. Similarly, it can also be argued that these newer forms of tax interventions are also having an egalitarian side as it is same for all the participants in the land market.

Now considering the findings which point towards the fact that LTTs are not market distorting in the Kerala case during the period considered for analysis. While literature on land transfer taxes considers high land transfer taxes as market distorting, it advocates the trimming down of the rates (Bird and Slack 2002). Careful analysis has depicted that land transfer tax policy regime in Kerala has followed pro-market norms in reducing land transfer rates. However, capital gains taxes on land sales were also considered market distorting (Pietola et al. 2011). In this aspect, the analysis of 12 months of data since capital gains tax were introduced reveals that the land markets were not distorted as a result. Though 12 data points may not be enough to prove this point, the previous finding on the short-term nature of policy impacts brings home our point that capital gains taxation was not market depressing for the land markets of Kerala. Since the data pertaining to the period after the recent hike in tax rates as well as capital gains taxes is not accessible, analysis was not attempted for this change. However, market signals report the latest changes in LTTs as market distorting.

However, the short-term nature of tax policy impact is significant in two aspects. First, tax policy interventions are not counterproductive. In the case of the land market, the distortions caused by tax interventions are clearly seen as short term with the market recovering within a year. Though, the deviations are high during certain occasions, it is recovering shortly indicating that government regulations as having lesser impacts on the land market activity. Similarly, revenue is also exhibiting short-term policy impacts, as explained in previously. Second, it can be argued that since revenue from the market is also not affected in the long term, there lies scope for introducing revenue maximising interventions or maintaining the higher levels of tax rates as in the previous periods.[15]

As results have indicated frequent changes in tax rates (higher) and anticipation towards higher rates distorts market activity leading to a fall in the revenue. However, changes in tax structure seem to have shorter impacts on the market activity. Reviewing the tax structure periodically is needed to optimise revenue without distorting the markets. This point can be further supported on the following grounds. One, even with fair value taxation in practice, the current aim is to target only 50% of the actual market value as fair value without initiating any steps to prevent under-reporting of land values and thereby tax evasion. And the recently announced periodical revision is slated once in 5 years which is really a too long term in economics standards. In fact, the analysis of real revenue has clearly showed that revenue earned in real terms is very meagre which clearly calls for periodic revision of fair value prices, while bringing the tax rates to very lower levels. Of course this might involve significant administrate efforts and costs, but considering the modern state's growing fund requirements, optimising revenue streams from land, especially land registration taxes are going to be a necessity for developing countries where land is still under-taxed.

To conclude, as the Indian landscape is moving into the ambit of growth and urbanisation much integrated with the global business conditions, the current land governance scenario calls for modernisation in the records, mapping and the taxation policies. The current multi-layered taxation structure has to make way for taxation based on much robust utilitarian and egalitarian ethos. Findings from the case of Kerala indicate that intervention of new taxes has not distorted the land markets and this points to the fact that lower rates of taxes based on actual market values can be introduced for better results.

---

[15]Tax rates on transfers were normalised to lower rates in the recent years with the introduction of fair value and short-term capital gains tax policies.

References

Bird RM, Slack E (2002) Land and property taxation: a review. Available at http://www1.worldbank.org/publicsector/decentralization/June2003Seminar/LandPropertyTaxation.pdf

Brown HG (1927) Land speculation and land-value taxation. J Polit Econ 35(3):390–402. Available at http://www.jstor.org/stable/1822055. Accessed on 18 May 2009

Case KE (1992) Taxes and speculative behavior in land and real estate markets. Rev Urban Reg Develop Stud (4)

Dachis B (2012) Stuck in Place: The Effect of Land Transfer Taxes on Housing Transactions. Commentary No. 364, C D Howe Institute

Dachis B, Duranton G, Turner MA (2012) The effects of land transfer taxes on real estate markets: evidence from a natural experiment in Toronto. J Econ Geogr 12(2012):327–354

Davies JB et al (2008) The world distribution of household wealth. Discussion paper 2008/003. UNU-WIDER, Helsinki

Deininger K, Feder G (2009) Land registration, governance, and development: evidence and implications for policy. World Bank Res Observer 24(2). Available at http://wbro.oxfordjournals.org

Deininger KW, Hilhorst D, Huberta M, Narayanan S, Bahadur D (2016) India—land governance assessment: national synthesis report. World Bank Group, Washington, D.C. http://documents.worldbank.org/curated/en/643361468038336423/India-Land-governance-assessment-national-synthesis-report

Foldvary F (1998) Market-hampering land speculation: fiscal and monetary origins and remedies. Am J Econ Sociol 57(4):615–637 Available at https://www.jstor.org/. Accessed on 21 July 2008

Gaffney M (1994) Land as a distinctive factor of production. Wealth and want. Available at http://www.wealthandwant.com/docs/Gaffney_LaaDFoP.htm. Accessed on 1 Nov 2008

Government of Kerala Various Issues. Economic Review. Kerala State Planning Board, Thiruvananthapuram

Government of Kerala Various Issues. 'Administrative Reports.' Inspector General of Registration. Thiruvananthapuram

Government of Kerala Budget Speeches 2004–05 to 13–14. Available at http://www.niyamasabha.org/Budget. Accessed on 1 Oct 2014

Government of Kerala. Kerala Finance Bills. Various Issues. Available at http://niyamasabha.org/bills/13kla/published. Accessed on 1 Dec 2014

Harilal KN (2008) Bhooprasnam muthal bhooprasnam vare. Madyamam Online, March 11th to 18th. Available at http://www.madhyamamonline.com/news_archive. Accessed on 2 April 2008

Kelkar V (2002) Report of the task force on direct tax. Consultation paper to Government of India. Available at http://www.prsindia.org/uploads/media/DTC%20Bill/kelkar%20direct%20taxes.pdf. Accessed on 26 June 2014

Morris S, Pandey A (2009) Land markets in India: distortions and issues. India Infrastructure Report

Mukherjee V (2013) Determinants of stamp duty revenue in Indian states. South Asian J Macroeconomics Public Finance 2(1):33–58

Naresh G (2003) Property taxation in India. In: Bird RM, Slack E (eds) International handbook of land and property taxation. Edward Elgar

Pietola K, Myyrä S, Pouta E (2011) The effects of changes in capital gains taxes on land sales: empirical evidence from Finland. Land Econ 87(4):582–594

Rodrik D (2013) The institutional organisation of the market economy. Available at http://isites.harvard.edu/fs/docs/icb.topic1220470.files/The%20Institutional%20Organization%20of%20the%20Market%20Economy-2.ppt. Accesed on 27 Mar 2014

Sreekumar TT (1993) Urban process in Kerala. Centre for Development Studies, Thiruvananthapuram (Occasional Paper series)
Wadhwa A (2013) Distortionary impact of stamp duty evasion in Haryana a case study of Gurgaon city. PhD thesis submitted to the Maharishi Dayanand University. Accessed from http://hdl.handle.net/10603/7867
Yinger J, Mills ES, Börsch-Supan A, Bloom HS (1988) Property taxes and house values. Academic Press

Development or Disaster? Land Acquisition and Dispossession in the Mining Belts and Coastal Zones of Rural Odisha, India

Sarmistha Pattanaik

1 Introduction

> What is good for the rich, it seems, is also good for the poor. The overwhelming justification for economic growth at any cost during the past two decades is not that it suits the interests of the wealthy elite and the middle classes but that it addresses in the best possible way the long standing challenge of mass poverty. It enlarges the national pie which can then be distributed more lavishly between rich and the poor alike. (Shrivastava and Kothari 2012).

Based on the above statement, there often has been the critics of neo-liberalism in India on the issue of growth and distribution being the major aims of neo-liberal economic policy that this doctrine should be criticised not only for its effects on trade, investment and finance, but also the consequences it has for social welfare, environmental sustainability, control of the economy and labour. Ironically all the developmental strategies since independence till the globalising era have made a small amount of progress on the conditions of the poor and marginalised although alleviation of poverty has continued to be the major goal of the state through its various development programmes. The poverty map has not changed perceptively yet in spite of various development strategies of the government (Saxena and Haragopal 2014). The economic growth was uneven and bypassed the bottom level of social hierarchy.

Allied with this, the issue of land acquisition and dispossession through its many revised acts and policies in India has made the problem more complex as it has not only compelled the local people through the coercive measures to sacrifice their land and livelihoods but also has caused a series of devastation and trauma to their

S. Pattanaik (✉)
Department of Humanities & Social Sciences, IIT Bombay, Mumbai, India
e-mail: spattanaik@iitb.ac.in

S. Pellissery et al. (eds.), *Land Policies in India*, India Studies in Business and Economics, DOI 10.1007/978-981-10-4208-9_6

lives after displacing them. Amy Chua, professor at Yale Law School, in her book '*The World on fire*' (2002), writes, "the neo-liberal capital is the reincarnation of colonialism, where a global capital displaces local people, misappropriates local assets and livelihood, marginalises local capital, and reduces the vast chunk of humanity into proletariats working hours together to earn respectable lives as consumers". The book reveals the true nature of globalisation. The author here discusses different reasons for the market dominance of different groups and through various citations the book projects a World, where real development in terms of ecological sustainability, quality of intellectual and emotional life, leisure activities, social bonding, family ties does not happen.

Flagging out this particular paragraph is perhaps a repetition of the Marxian doctrine of how capital, which naturally faces a falling rate of profits, expands into monopoly power in order to secure its profits and in this way snatches away every other source of production which lay with the community and proletarizes the people. Displacement, in the Marxian scheme, is therefore an obvious and inevitable fallout of development (Somayaji and Dasgupta 2013). Ironically, since vast areas of lands are available in the remote rural areas of India, any kind of development project in the name of justifying national interest, have made the rural people victims who since bear the brunt of acquisition over the last more than a century. Based on this backdrop, this paper discusses precisely what have been changed in the political economy of land dispossession with the transition to neo-liberalism in India by taking a case study approach in the Odisha state as a specific context. The paper is also an attempt to bring insights from the conflicts and resistances that take place by the local communities against the land acquisition and dispossession in the state of Odisha. Mining activities in these areas have various impacts on the natural environment, most prominent of all the clearing of patches of tropical forest, land alienations, water pollution resulting and livelihoods loss. The study attempts to link the 'land acquisition' issue or dispossession of land with a theoretical framework of 'political economy' approach; and linking the conflicts erupting from the consequences of acquisition of land through the absolute power of the state that challenges the democratic ethos, principles of equity and social justice in India and its people. It also uses a 'political ecology' framework to link the nexus of 'land acquisition', 'displacement' and 'social conflict' in the context of India in general and in the state of Odisha in particular. Against this backdrop, the paper addresses very crucial strategic questions: How far the issues of displacement under '*eminent domain*' doctrine still exists in India and in what form? How does the question of 'land' in its new Bill of 2011 and 2013 address the issues evident in the political theory framework—state's relationship with its citizens through a 'political economy' discourse? How the land acquisition in India is understood in the context of development induced dispossession and displacement (through a theoretical framework of understanding of primitive accumulation and the theory of 'by dispossession'—in order to understand the inter-linkage between the role of the state, economic development, agrarian change, rural politics, access and control of resources, social and ecological conflict through people's resistance)?

The paper is divided into three sections apart from introduction and conclusion. Section 2 delineates a brief theoretical analysis of the Political economy and Political ecology of framework in order to understand the complexity of 'land accumulation', dispossession, displacement, conflict and resistance. Section 3 documents the methodology, study area, the land as commons and as a commodity in the lives of different actors involved in the whole debate of politicised environment in the field location with narratives. Section 4 details the contemporary trends in the changing pattern of livelihoods, displacement and alienation of the indigenous communities from CPR due to endangered mining in the districts of Keonjhar and Sundergarh through land acquisition projects and due to other FDI projects in the district of Jagatsingpur district. The paper also reflects with a note on the issues related to the protest and resistance of the grassroots communities in their local indigenous cultures as a consequence of the marginalisation and dispossession due to the land acquisition and forceful displacement through a socio-ecological lens.

2 Theoretical Background

2.1 Political Economy Discourse of Land Reforms and Land Acquisition

The issues and problems of land acquisition and land grabs have now become a major global issue and attracting significant scholarly attention in Africa,[1] Southeast Asia[2] and Latin America.[3]

The land acquisition issue in India has become more controversial and conflicting over more than a decade since its amendment. Scholars have argued that in its 117 years of existence, the Land Acquisition Act 1894 (LAA 1894) has influenced the expansion of the power of the State to acquire and take over land. It has helped institutionalise involuntary acquisition. Premised on the doctrine of 'eminent domain', it presumes a priority to the requirements of the State which, by definition, is for the general good of the public, over the interests of landowners and users. The doctrine of eminent domain invests power in the state to acquire private land for public purpose on payment of compensation (Ramanathan 2011: 10). The Land Acquisition Act (LAA) 1894 bears the testimony to the power of the state to acquire land. In 1984, when the LAA 1894 went through elaborate amendment, the role that the State had taken on in acquiring land for companies was reinforced. Walter Fernandes has given a wider analysis of data sources on the displaced Populations under Eminent Domain principle since independence (Fernandes 2008). The LAA

[1]Woodhouse (2012).

[2]Li (2007), Dwyer (2013).

[3]2012 special issue on 'land grabbing in Latin America'. *Canadian J. of Development Studies*, 33 (4).

1894 was comprehensively amended in 1984, nearly after a century, by introducing some transitional provisions with regard to compensation paid to the population settled on the land which mainly includes poor tribals and lower castes (Majumdar 2013: 63). In 1996, the Draft National Policy for Rehabilitation of persons of the Ministry of Rural Development, Govt of India, acknowledged that cash compensation was not an acceptable proposition for the tribal people who inhabit the tribal regions with full of mineral resources. In 2003, the national policy on Resettlement and Rehabilitation project for affected families was passed which was replaced by the National Policy on R&R, 2007. The government abandoned the idea of having separate laws, one for land acquisition and the other for rehabilitation and resettlement. Instead, it integrated the two in the proposed new Bill on Land Acquisition, 2011 renamed as the Draft National Land Acquisition and Resettlement and Rehabilitation Bill, 2011. There have been various salient features of the draft Bill mentioning the definition of public purpose, the justification for introducing, amending and implementing the new law, definition of affected family, various approaches towards defining compensation and so on.[4]

In 2013, the 1894 law governing land acquisition made two significant changes. First, it openly allowed the government to acquire land for the private sector and thereby extended its powers beyond public interest. But what it added alongside are some processes which included seeking the consent of landholders and carrying out social impact assessments so that compensation for all livelihood-dependent people can be ascertained. However, the public discourse on this policy raised many controversies and how does its contents have hurt the affected communities on several points mentioned in the Bill. There has been controversies on various aspects of this Bill—at the level of framing of concepts to operational, structural and governance aspects. Nonetheless, this subject brings to light a very important question of inquiry—what is the role of the state with its citizens? In this context argues Fernandes, "for several decades, development projects in India have expropriated and forcibly displaced scores of people, and much more worst has been done under the doctrine of '*Eminent Domain*'". Further, "India's land laws ensure the land alienation of subalterns communities from CPRs because these lands are governed by the colonial principle of 'eminent domain', which conceives of land as only a commodity and a place for cultivation and building" (Fernandes 2009).

[4]Ministry of Rural Development (MoRD), The Draft National Land Acquisition and Resettlement and Rehabilitation Bill, 2011, August 2011. For a more detailed understanding of the new Bill visit the website: http://rural.nic.in/sites/downloads/policies/Final.pdf.

2.2 *Political Economy of Dispossession: How the Question of Land Is Understood?*

2.2.1 Marx's Theory of Primitive Accumulation

In the final chapters of Vol I of *Das Capital*, Marx explained as to how the origins of capitalist relations lay in the historical process of divorcing the producer from the means of production (1977: 875). Basing his analysis, Marx argued that the violent process of expelling peasants from the land generated the preconditions for capitalism by effecting the 'two transformations', whereby the social means of subsistence and production are turned into capital and the immediate producers are turned into wage labourers.[5] In a process stretching over several centuries and of the eighteenth century, the English common lands (along with state and church lands) were turned into sheep walks and capitalist farms while commoners were turned into a proletariat. Based on this theoretical perspective I have tried to look at the problem of Land Grabbing as Primitive Accumulation in India with a specific context in rural Odisha.

2.2.2 Accumulation by Dispossession (David Harvey)

In addition to Marx's theory of primitive accumulation, by looking at the agrarian transitions over more than two decades in India, I have tried to understand the current phase of agrarian transitions and land grabs for capitalist development during the phase of globalisation, neo-liberal state and dispossession in India as well as in Odisha. Attempt has been made to link the issue of land grab with the question of dispossession through the formulation of the concept of '*Accumulation by Dispossession*' of David Harvey. Harvey's theory of Accumulation by Dispossession is taken in order to understand the issue of global capitalism.

David Harvey's concept of 'Accumulation by Dispossession' defines the neo-liberal capitalist policies in many western nations, from the 1970s and to the present day, as resulting in a centralization of wealth and power in the hands of a few by dispossessing the public of their wealth or land.[6] In his work '*A brief history of Neo-liberalism*' (2005) he provides an historical examination of the theory and divergent practices of neo-liberalism since the mid-1970s. This work conceptualises the neoliberalised global political economy as a system that benefits few at the expense of many, and which has resulted in the (re)creation of class distinction through what Harvey calls 'accumulation by dispossession'. Harvey's examples of accumulation by dispossession include the expropriation of land and natural resources from peasant populations, the conversion of common or state property

---

[5]Ibid.

[6]Harvey (2004).

into private property, the extraction of rents from intellectual property rights. More so, Harvey's theory of 'accumulation by dispossession', describes the ways capitalism uses force and theft to rob the world of value—both human beings and nature—in its insatiable quest for profit. As Harvey writes in *A Brief History of Neoliberalism*, the theory is a critical extension of Marx's writings on primitive accumulation. In Indian context this theory has been largely used and marks a significant advancement on primitive accumulation precisely in its ability to capture diverse contemporary dispossessions that take sector-specific and geographically dispersed forms and whose significance for capital lies more in the expropriated asset (the Land) than in the labour power of the dispossessed owner (Levien 2015: 148).

3 Empirical Background

3.1 Study Area

This research, although conducted in different phases during 2009–2013, is still relevant in that it illuminates the dark backyard of shining India through the detrimental effects of the forceful land acquisition policy for big industrialisation projects and capitalist development in the state of Odisha.

The population of Odisha stands about at 41 million, making it the 11th most populated state in India (Census 2011). It holds a key position as a mineral producer state. The scheduled tribe (ST) population of the state is about 8,145,081 and this constitutes 22.1% of the total population of the state and 9.7% of the total population of the country. The mineral resource base in Odisha is mainly spread in the tribal community dominated districts. Mineral-intensive growth is known to create significant environmental externalities and this is clearly observed in the two major mineral-rich districts of the state—Keonjhar and Sundergarh. This study has sought to explore the impact of mining on these two districts through the land acquisition policy in the surrounding environment and on the most vulnerable sections of the society who are called as 'indigenous communities' in those two districts.

Keonjhar district covers a geographical area of 8303 km^2 or 830,300 ha, it lies between 21° 1′ and 22° 10′N latitudes and 85° 11′ and 86° 22′E longitudes. The district occupies an important place in the mineral resource map of eastern India. High quality of iron and manganese ore deposits are found to be located under large tracts of forestland, rich in bio-diversity and water catchment areas of Baitarani river one of the large river of state. The forest land of Keonjhar constitutes one of the major parts of forest resource of Orissa. Apart from this, it is home to a sizeable tribal population; including some of the most primitive tribes called as indigenous, those who are totally dependent on forests and agriculture for their livelihoods and survival. The total population of the district is 1,802,777 (Census of India 2011) and tribes constitute the total population of 818,878 (their percentage is 45.42% of the total population of Keonjhar district). The district presents a panorama of millennium, from the geographical and anthropology point of view. Anthropologically, one of its unique tribes (PTG) called as Juangs carry a distinct and primitive past.

Sundergarh, another district of Odisha out of 30 districts of the state, located in the northern extremity of Odisha, lies between 21° 32′ and 22° 32′N latitudes and 83° 32′ and 85° 22′E longitudes. Total geographical area of Sundergarh district is 971,200 ha. The population of the district is 2,080,664 and of this population, tribals constitute around 51% (Census of India 2011).

Field visit was conducted in Keonjhar district in the Bansapala block of Ganasika hill range and Panchayat. The randomly selected blocks were—Jhumpura, Bansapala, Gonasika, Suakathi and Keonjhar Sadar. The communities studied were mainly Juangs, though few of them were from Munda, Dehury and Gond tribe. In the Sundergarh district the study was conducted in the Khandadhar hill region surrounding the Khandadhar water fall, the biggest waterfall of Odisha state and the PTG group called as Paudi Bhuyan.

Jagatsingpur district, the coastal belt of Odisha, was earlier a part of the erstwhile Cuttack district, is surrounded by Bay of Bengal in the East, Cuttack district in the West, Kendrapada district in the North and Puri district in the South. Having a geographical area of 1759 km^2, the Jagatsinghpur district is the smallest district in Odisha in terms of territorial locations. There are 8 blocks, 8 tahasils, 1320 villages, 194 gram panchayats and 13 police stations functioning in the district.[7] The district became a centre of discussion in the global map by the activists, environmentalists, human rights groups and social scientists during 2005 while the region witnessed a strong people's movement against a steel plant and captive port proposed by POSCO-India, a subsidiary of South Korean steel major POSCO, which was initiated during 2005 and continued till 2014 as it became a landmark of reference for the current resistances against neo-liberal state and globalisation projects in contemporary India. The project was the single largest infusion of Foreign Direct Investment (FDI) since Indian economy liberalised in 1991. Estimated at US $12 billion (Rs. 52,000 crores), the project was claimed by Orissa government to "bring prosperity and wellbeing to its people" by embarking on major industrialization based upon exploitation of its natural resources. However, this project has faced strong resistance from a vigorous people's movement on the ground, comprising of villagers apprehensive of losing lands and livelihoods.[8]

For the purpose of my study I had conducted the field visits in the Ersama block of the district and the affected villages were taken from 3 village panchyats—Dhinkia, Nuagaon, Balitutha, Govindpur and Gadakujannga were visited from 2010 to 2014 at different phases. My observations were based on finding out the Changing pattern of livelihoods, displacement and alienation of the people who

[7]Available at http://ordistricts.nic.in/district_profile/aboutus.php.

[8]*Iron and Steel: The POSCO-India Story,* Mining Zone Peoples Solidarity Group. http://miningzone.org/October 20, 2010.

already have lost and were in the process of loosing their land from CPR due to the proposed project in the plant and port site. The study analyses the various issues collected through the data in the original field setting from the victims, activists and through interview transcriptions, field notes, news articles, posters, flyers, websites and social networking sites to identify key themes.

3.1.1 Methods

In all the three districts along with field survey data that had been collected for the purpose of the study, an ethnographic study through participant observation method was also made particularly in the Jagatsingour district in order to observe the intense of the resistance in the movement's site and to know the current implications of this struggles and the relevance of commons that have been degraded in the name of economic development in local.

4 Political Economy of Land Acquisition

4.1 Discourses in Odisha

Several studies discuss about the land distribution system in Odisha through land revenue system, land fragmentation and land tenancy (Mishar, n.d.). The survey of the legislative framework of Odisha confirms that 'land reform policies have been based on the principle of redistributive justice and on arguments regarding efficiency (land to the tiller, fixation of ceilings, prevention of fragmentation, etc.)' (UNDP Status Report 2008). Since Independence, nearly 3.01 million hectares has been declared as ceiling surplus in the country. Of this nearly 2.31 million hectares has been taken over by the government and 1.76 million hectares distributed among 5 million beneficiaries, half of whom are Scheduled Castes and Scheduled Tribes Besides, 7.26 lakh acres of government wasteland have been provided to the landless in the state. In addition, 5.80 lakh acres of *Bhoodan* land (donated land)[9] have been distributed to the poor in Orissa (ibid). Despite all these efforts, access to land still remains a distant dream for the vast majority of the poor. This particular fact reveals various issues concerning implementation of land reforms in Odisha where land that has been given to the landless by the state government under

[9]The *Bhoodan* movement was initiated by Acharya Vinoba Bhave in 1951 with the objective of bridging the gap between the landed peasantry and the landless by invoking a sense of altruism for redistribution of land for social justice. Since then land was received as donation from benevolent land owners and the same were distributed among the landless persons under the *Bhoodan* Act, 1953 and Rules 1954 which was later replaced by the *Bhoodan* Act, 1970 and Rules 1972.

various schemes such as Bhoodan, and some other schemes, viz, Vasundhara Yojana and distribution of land pass book,[10] tries to assess to what extent the allottees are in actual possession of the land so distributed.

In addition to this, the FRA 2006 has created more complicacy to the tribes and schedule castes in the scheduled areas of Odisha. This act does not define forests, it defines forest land as land of any description falling within any forest area and includes most types of forests (ibid). The law provides for recognition and vesting of forest rights to Scheduled Tribes in occupation of forest land prior to 13 December 2005 and to other traditional forest dwellers who have been in occupation of forest land, up to a maximum of four hectares, for at least three generations, i.e. 75 years. These rights are heritable but not alienable or transferable.

4.1.1 Losing Land to Mining Due to Land Acquisition

Tribal land acquisition in the scheduled areas of Odisha has been going on rampantly as it has been claimed by the state that rapid expansion of capital intensive mining and industry can enhance economic growth and improve rural people's livelihoods. There are about three major mineral belts in the state covering an area of 6000 km^2 and covering the major tribal-dominated districts of Odisha. As per 1999–2000 records, the mining leases themselves are only 7% of the total leases in India but the area under lease is around 16% of the total lease area of the country (ibid). In Odisha, mining activities are concentrated in some of the districts with Keonjhar and Sundergarh accounting for about 50% of the area under lease in the state. An overwhelming majority of mines in Orissa are open cast mines naturally effecting displacement and environmental pollution including land degradation.

The following table mentions the area under acquisition and the number of families displaced in some mining and industrial ventures in the state (Table 1).

4.2 Agricultural Land Grab Through Extraction of Mining: Alienation and Dispossession in the Districts of Keonjhar and Sundergarh

Studies have witnessed of how for several decades, development projects in India have expropriated and forcibly displaced scores of people without giving them the protection that a formal policy on development-caused displacement should give to these vulnerable communities (Fernandes 2008; Mathur 2006; Mehta 2009). In

[10]Ibid: 14, available at http://www.undp.org/content/dam/india/docs/land_rights_ownership_in_orissa.pdf.

Table 1 Land acquisition and displacement in some high profile mining/industrial ventures in Odisha

Name	Area of families affected (acres)	Families expected to be displaced	Affected villages	Remark
POSCO Steel Plant	4100	3700	11	POSCO would displace nearly 22,000 people from Dhinkia, Nuagaon and Gadakujang Gram Panchayats
Kalinga Nagar Complex	13,000	1150	–	The Government had acquired the land at Kalinga Nagar during 1990 and 1996 and paid compensation of Rs. 35.14 crore for 6895 acres of private land at an average cost of Rs. 51,000 per acre
Mahanadi Coal Field Ltd, Talcher	13,610	–	77	–
Arcelor-Mittal Steel plant	8000	3000	–	15,000–17,000 people are expected to be displaced in Keonjhar district.

Source UNDP Status Report (2008: 35)

addition to this, the available literatures have also witnessed the far-reaching social, economic and cultural impacts of such forced displacement on the indigenous communities (Banerjee et al. 2005; Parasuraman 1999; Cernea 1997, 1998). The state of Odisha, being not an exception, has a fairly long history of dispossession for 'development'. The field work observations in the two districts of Odisha witnessed a continuous Changing pattern of livelihoods, displacement and alienation of juangs and Paudi Bhuyans, popularly known as PTGs (primitive tribal groups) from CPR due to endangered mining in the region. The following section briefly discusses this point.

Mortgage and sale of patta land is the most common form of land alienation, especially in the scheduled areas of Odisha. The normal procedure is mortgage and sale without any valid document causing alienation of *patta* (no records of legal ownership) land. Driven by poverty and indebtedness, people have no choice but to sell or mortgage the land they have received from the government. The fundamental reason for tribal land alienation is the fragile, constantly shrinking economic base of the tribals. Their non-monetised self-sufficient economy crumbled and the tribals became exposed to barter or cash transactions for the fulfilment of their basic needs. Their traditional skills lay in the gathering of forest produce. With the introduction of state ownership of forests, however, from owner gatherers, the tribals were reduced to wage earners or encroachers (Ambagudia 2010). Again, alienation of land from tribals has also occurred directly as a result of the developmental policies of the government. Statistical figures of the Planning Commission indicate that more than 40% of the displaced families due to developmental projects in Orissa are tribals and they lost control over their source of livelihood.

4.2.1 Change in the Ownership Right Due to Mega Industrialization Projects and Mining Leases

The traditional and sustainable use of resource base and the livelihoods pattern of Juang and Pauri Bhuiyan community have undergone a dramatic change in the area over the past more than two decades, particularly in between 1985 and 2000 due to the liberalisation of Indian economy that has brought in a large number of investors, including multinational companies to the mineral sector in the state. According to it Orissa State Pollution Control Board (OSPCB), zone 1 includes districts like Keonjhar and Sundergarh, which are rich in iron ore and manganese ore and face extensive pollution of rivers and rivulets. Environmental impacts due to iron ore mining in these areas comprise cumulative environmental impacts of several contiguous small, medium-sized iron ore mines as well as environmental impacts of large mechanised iron ore mining projects. In different study areas environmental impacts of these clusters of mines on forest growth and natural water sources are of prime concern. Large-scale deforestations are going on for development of infrastructure and other mining activities. No significant effort (barring only a few mines) has been made to rehabilitate mined out areas through plantation. During the rainy season, the water in rivers turns red and the level of total suspended solids goes up to 1000 mg/1 (CSE 2008). Orissa produced more than 46 million tones of iron ore in 2004–05 of which at least 3 quarters came from Keonjhar alone. Out of the 3 major mining districts of Orissa (Keonjhar, Sundergarh and Mayurbhanj) almost one-third (32%) of the land under mining is located in Keonjhar district alone. Almost all of it was and still is carted away in nearly 30,000 trucks from the 119 mines of Keonjhar district (Frontline 2007). The trucks move north from Joda, to the Jharkhand border where they supply iron ore to Jharkhand's rapidly expanding steel industry and northwest to Haldia port. But, the majority move south through Keonjhar town towards Cuttack and cut through to Paradip port, from where the ore is shipped in containers to one of the few countries that have a bigger appetite for steel than India, i.e., China. Till today, as many as 64 sponge iron units in Keonjhar and Sundergarh districts have destroyed drinking water sources and agricultural fields (Das 2005). Poverty is further exacerbating along the lines of social groupings. The marginalised sections of the area, specifically tribal's, scheduled castes and other forest dwellers suffer from some of the worst indicators in terms of poverty levels and incomes, access to productive assets, education, heath, etc. The presence of iron ore mines and sponge/steel industries have put serious impacts on the local community of the upper catchments of Baitarani river basin, disrupting their social structures and production system (Pattanaik 2012).[11]

4.2.2 Alienation from CPR Due to Endangered Mining

Simultaneously, there has been a strong case in point regarding the alienation of Juang community's communal lands by the state against leasing to the MNCs for mining projects in the Bansapala block in *Kadalibadi* village. It has been found from the study villages that the livelihoods and lives of primitive tribal groups, the Juangs are being destroyed in the name of development, in violation of Schedule V of the constitution and the laws framed by the State itself to protect tribal groups. Juangs, an autochthonous primitive tribal group (PTGs), who are the earliest inhabitants of these regions, and who consider the whole Juangpirh as their ancestral home. The Juangs of Kadalibadi have enjoyed customary communal ownership over the village area since times immemorial, though legally they have but access to one-tenth of its area (Vasundhara 2005).[12]

All Juangs in Kadalibadi practice shifting cultivation either fully or partly. The Juangs have customarily depended on swidden cultivation. Several studies confirm the relationship of shifting cultivation to tribal nutritional security and its role in combating hunger, apart from its customary cultural and social importance. The hill slopes are cultivated in three-year sequence, first year sesame, second year upland paddy and third year sesame. Then the patch is left fallow for four to five years (Panda 1999; Vasundhara 2005). However, due to the shifting of various important patches of land from the Kadalibadi village to the forest department by the revenue authorities recently and the land has been converted into a plantation under compensatory plantation scheme by the state, the alienation of the Juang communities from their ancestral land has become a clear picture of marginalisation and the structural injustice imposed by the state on its tribal people through the very system of formal land tenure. Due to the series of plantations and conversion of major part of their communal lands into plantations by forest department (1970s–2005)

[11]The data collected through field survey in Keonjhar district have been analysed and highlighted in the paper about the community's response about the environmental problems related to water and forest and how the situation has ben changed over time. Here, in this paper, I have summarized briefly the analysis of those data from the perspective of socio-economic and human health aspects of the tribal communities of the region due to iron-ore mining (see Pattanaik 2012, pp. 324–328).

[12]This is the title of the report published by Vasundhara on Juangs. Notes on Alienation of Juang communal Lands by the State in Juangpirh, Orissa: A case study of Kadalibadi Village 2005, Land Rights Team, Vasundhara, available at http://vasundharaodisha.org/DiscussionPaper_eng/Kadalibari%20Case%20Study-15.pdf, 11/01/15.

'Vasundhara' (http://www.vasundharaorissa.org) is a research and policy advocacy group located in Bhubaneswar, that works on environmental conservation and sustainable livelihood issues. It is a non-governmental organisation working as a support group to support community forestry initiatives in Orissa for policy and institutional support for strengthening community-based natural resource management.

(Rath 2005) deprived them of the access to these *swidden* (shifting cultivation) lands and has pushed them to starvation levels.

Paudi Bhuyans are the worst off among the tribes who live in Khandadhar waterfall area in Bonai subdivision. Being designated as particularly vulnerable tribal group, they are not only backward in their per capita income but also in literacy and other human development indicators which is much lower than Odisha's average per capita income and literacy rate. The Central government has set up the Paudi Bhuyan Development Agency but it only works in 22 of the 49 Paudi Bhuyan villages in the district (Action aid).[13] The other major hurdle is that few families have any rights over the land; after the Forest Rights Act, 2005 (FRA), many Paudi Bhuyan families filed individual and community claims, although few of the families who had applied got land titles. However, the land they have got was far less than their legitimate claim of up to 10 acres of land as per the FRA.

The current socio-economic status of the Paudi Bhuyans of Khandadhar area is doubly in jeopardy due to the Khandadhar mines, one already ongoing over the past three decades or more, and the one proposed by the Odisha government recommends for Prospecting License (PL) in favour of POSCO-India to excavate minerals from Khandadhar mines in Sundergarh district.

Currently, Orissa Mining Corporation (OMC) is already operating in the area. Khandadhar mines has two leases in favour of OMC: one is Kurmitar block with lease area of 1212 and 1208 ha is forest land operation since 29/04/1965, the other is Rantha block operating within the forest land since 1968 in area of 408 ha.[14] OMC is drawing water from the upper head of the Khandadhar water fall, which has resulted in drastic fall in water flow of the mountain to the Talabahali villagers. The situation will again become more acute and the region will suffer from a huge water crisis if an additional mining operation will be started by POSCO. The MoU between POSCO and the Orissa government requires the latter to grant prospecting licenses and mining leases for the next 30 years for POSCO to extract a total of 600 million tonnes of iron ore for use in its proposed steel plant in the area, and further obliges it to assist POSCO in acquiring another 400 million tonnes of iron ore for its steel plants in South Korea (Mining Zone People's solidarity group report 2010).[15] As a result of this Mou in December 2006, the state government recommended to the central government that POSCO be allocated prospecting license for 6204.352 ha of Khandadhar mines—even though 225 other applicants had put in applications for these mines, many of them before POSCO had even appeared on the scene.

The major issue that brings more attention is what will happen to Khanadhar region and more specifically to the life and livelihoods of Paudi Bhuyan community if POSCO will be granted license for mining in the area? Because many of

---

[13]As per Action Aid India report which works on Paudi Bhuyans in Sundergarh, Available at http://actionaid.org/india/what-we-do/odisha/working-paudi-bhuyan-tribes-sundargarh, 11/01/15.

[14]Source collected through RTI, IBM, Regional office, Bhubaneswar.

[15]Available at http://miningzone.org/October 20.

important ecological issues are missed in the EIA regarding what the impact of the mining by POSCO will bring to the environment, economy and livelihoods of the many thousands of local tribals in the region. A brief field visit to the area was conducted with a small team of two independent observers, during June 2010 for an enquiry about the proposed issues. With the interactive association of the local people and activists some of the facts have been brought into notice which has not yet been done by MoEF or any environmental impact assessment (EIA) study yet since mining lease has not yet been awarded to POSCO.

In the MoU, it has been recommended that POSCO will be granted license over an area of 2500 ha in village Kensara, Bhutuda, Rantha, Batagaon, Sareikala, Lusi and Raisuan under Bonai subdivision in the district of Sundergarh for the purpose of iron ore. However, as per local community's view and the activist as well as the president of Vana Suraksya Samiti Mandal, a local NGO operating in Khanadhar by Aswini Mahanta, "around 16–20 villages of seven GPs namely Talbahali, Bhutuda, Saskela, Phuljhar, Mahulpada, Dalaisara and Haldikuda of this area critically depend upon this water for drinking, bathing and irrigation purposes".[16] Hence, along with all these GPs, the local economy of the whole area, which is regulated by agricultural activity, will be drastically affected if the water catchment area is permitted for mining for POSCO. Mining activities in the Khandadhar hill will result in the death of all these streams, thus directly affecting the local livelihood.

The formulation of the new policies of FRA 2005 and 2006 has led to the severe loss of traditional livelihood practice of tribals. The Fifth Schedule envisages that the rights of the tribals or PTGs over their land must be protected. However, the provisions in Fifth schedule are being directly contravened in by denying the rights of tribal on land customarily owned by them and vital for their subsistence and livelihoods due to the FRA 2006 Act. Time and again, these communities have suffered great hardships, rather, at the hands of forest officials who enforced the restrictions with great severity, so that even a minor breach of regulation is treated as a 'crime' (Munshi 2012). The POSCO-affected area in the scheduled areas of Sundergarh and Keonjhar have witnessed this contradiction. Recently, violating the recommendations of committees set up by FRA and ignoring the regulations of the National Green Tribunal, the MOEF gave environmental clearance to the POSCO project in January 2014 (Kumar 2014). However, unfortunately for the Bhuiyans, Khandadhar hills are repositories of good quality iron ore deposit with 69% iron content, being eyed by many of iron and steel producers till recently when the State government announced that it is likely to clear the prospective mining license to POSCO for mining 600 million tones of iron ore (Asher 2009).

[16]Based on the direct interview with Aswini Mahanta during the field visit, June 2010 and an informal meet at Bhubaneswar in 2012.

4.2.3 Another Cry of Khandadhar

A report has been published today in *Down to Earth* (31/March/2016)[17] on ecologically rich Khandhar hills which have been again handed over to the state's mining body for mining, the hilly region which was being rescued from the Korean giant POSCO just one year before in 2014. As already has been discussed elsewhere in the draft about Odisha Mining Corporation Ltd (OMCL) that has already been mining in the region for the past five decades and has damaged the ecologically sensitive area beyond repair, now if the entire region is mined, it will have a major detrimental effect to the whole ecosystem—villages, forests and water resources within the 10 km radius of the mountain will be wiped out. The Pauri Bhuiyan community, once used to grow 18 varieties of crops but now due to the existing mine waste in most of their fields, they are bound to work in the mines as labourers. This current issue again reflects an important aspect of development and dispossession in the state of Odisha through 'land acquisition'.

4.3 The Neo-liberal State, Resistance and Dispossession in Odisha: Narratives of the Story of POSCO *Through Revisiting Political Ecology Discourse*

Thus, there is a new emerging nexus between the agrarian economy of Odisha through land acquisition and the corporate capital that are being mediated through the redefinition of 'development' based on the extractive force, that is the process of industrialisation. This force is being used to extract the mineral resources for industrialization projects that has been witnessed in the two mineral-rich districts in the state for Iron ore mining in this study. In the neo-liberal federal order that has been unfolding in India, State governments have been competing against each other to attract private capital. An essential feature of this development has been the use of state power to facilitate the establishment mining and mineral-based industries. The POSCO-affected villages in coastal Orissa in Jagatsingour and Khandadhar hills in northern Orissa have been the epicentres of this conflict.

The POSCO project had three components:

- Captive iron ore mines in three areas of Keonjhar District and Sundergarh District. Mining lease on 6204 ha in Sundergarh District recommended to be approved by the Supreme Court.
- Steel plant: in Jagatsinghpur District, coastal area.
- Private port: at the mouth of the river Jatadhari, close to steel plant area; the MoU only makes reference to the possibility of a 'minor port' being created.

---

[17]Available at http://www.downtoearth.org.in/news/fight-for-khandadhar-53257, accessed on 31st March 2016.

In addition to that, the Orissa government recommended the POSCO steel plant and port for a 'Special Economic Zone' (SEZ) status to the central government, as it had promised to do in the MoU, and the central government gave it the in-principle approval in October 2005 pending land acquisition to give it the final approval. The in-principle approval was extended twice in 2007 and 2008, since POSCO failed to acquire land. In 2009, as there was no process in place for giving it a third extension, POSCO had to submit a de novo (fresh) application for SEZ status, which has also been approved (Mining Zone People's solidarity group report 2010).

4.3.1 Displacement Under Eminent Domain in the Region: Does the Land Bill of 2011 and 2013 Address the Local Problems or Further Impoverishes the Poor?

Under the clause of 'Eminent Domain' and 'Public Purpose' the state is empowered to acquire privately owned land. Till now with minor amendments in 1984 this Act is being followed by the State of Orissa as well as Government of India in the matter of land acquisition and distribution of compensation to the land owner. The mode of compensation is based on the market value of land only. The legal holders are only entitled to get the compensation on the basis of a land valuation fixed by the government taking note into the sale deeds of that area. The valuation as fixed by the LAA fails to take into consideration the future returns of land and which is usually less than the replacement cost of land. Another important dimension of land acquisition is that those people having land record of rights are accounted and people having no title to land rights and dependants on Common Property Resources (CPRs) are discounted from the purview of the act (Behera, n.d.).

The livelihoods in Jagatsingpur area demonstrated a vast area of proposed displacement due to the POSCO project. During my field visit in 2009, 2010 and again 2013, I came across various consequences of the proposed project, few already had happened and more were proposed. There were environmental impacts such as Impact on Availability and Quality of Water, Impact on Coastal Topography and Continued Viability of the Paradeep Port, Impact on Forest Cover and Resulting Effects on the Lives of Local Adivasis. Impacts on Marine Life and Wildlife, Impacts on Public Health Due to Mining and Violation of CRZ Notification at Jatadhari river mouth. In the mater of livelihoods, the people of the POSCO-affected area cultivate "*Paan, dhan, macch* (beetle, paddy and fish)—the trinity is the essence of their life". The 4004 acres of land earmarked for the steel plant includes fertile agricultural land on which paddy, betel nut, cashew and other crops are grown, and coastal riverine zones where extensive prawn and fish farming is done. In addition, some of the forest areas that the villagers depend on for forest produce are also slated to be clear cut and the land handed over to POSCO.

However, in spite of many such efforts by the state and its allies POSCO project was not being able to move on. The project affected people of Jagatsingpir were no longer prepared to suffer displacement along with its concomitant attributes like occupational degeneration, social disorientation, pauperization, loss in dignity and often getting cheated of the compensation amount, which serve to make the experience a trauma. This had given rise to protest movements, the anti-POSCO movement started gearing up against land acquisition from the beginning of 2005 and continued till 2014. The strong people's resistance demonstrated the protest at plant, port and mining sites. Their voices in protest against the project, barring those families that have agreed to sell their land. Official statistics show that only 438 acres of the 4000 acres required for the POSCO site are private land, the rest being government land, recorded as 'under forest' or '*anabadi*'. Government records do not show that most of this land has been under betel, cashew and other cultivation for generations. The local people have submitted applications for title claims several times but the government failed to initiate any regularisation and settlement of the betel vine lands (Asher 2009).

Finally, POSCO's ambition to set up a 12-million-tonne-capacity plant in India with an investment of Rs. 51,000 crore plant in Odisha in the Jagatsingpur district has finally given up due to the above strong people's protest in the region finally in 2014 and also due to the current government's intervention of the mining leases of the region that needs to be put to auction based on Mines and Minerals (Development and Regulation) Act, MMDRA 2015. The MoU expired in 2010 and was never renewed.

4.3.2 Land Acquisition as 'Accumulation by Dispossession'—POSCO Project

'Accumulation by dispossession marks a significant advancement on primitive accumulation precisely in its ability to capture diverse contemporary dispossessions that take sector-specific and geographically dispersed forms and whose significance for capital lies more in the expropriated asset (the Land) than in the labour power of the dispossessed owner (Levien 2015: 148)'. My argument in the case of POSCO in Odisha demonstrates the nexus between land dispossession and capitalism (drawing Harvey's framewok of ABD), prevails through the continuation and proliferation of accumulation practices which Marx had treated of as 'primitive' or 'original' during the rise of capitalism. Those practices include the commodification and privatisation of land and the forceful expulsion of local farmers populations, into exclusive private property suppression of rights to the commons (through the new Land acquisition act of 2011 and 2013); commodification of labour power and the suppression of alternative (traditional/indigenous) forms of production and consumption; colonial, neo-colonial, and imperial processes of appropriation of assets (including natural resources); monetization of exchange and taxation, particularly of land, the use of the credit system as a radical means of accumulation by dispossession.

So, when the state acts as the facilitator of the land transfer process, its partiality towards large corporations is exposed (Levien 2011: 71). Such a 'land broker' state is different from the old developmental state (Polanyi 1944).

POSCO was in need of some 4004 acres, of which ten percent belong to the cultivators. The rest of the land required belongs to the government, and this has been recorded as 'under forest' in official documentation. Government records do not show that the vast majority of this land has been under cultivation by the people living in these areas for generations. But this is not new. B.K. Roy Burman in his article "What Has Driven the Tribals of Central India to Political Extremism?" (*Mainstream*, 17 October 2009) sets out the reality: "as against involuntary displacement, in many predominantly tribal areas the tribal people are deliberately dispossessed of their lands and resources thereon in a meticulously planned manner. This is a serious charge. But this is true".[18]

4.3.3 Resistance Against POSCO: A Successful Story

By drawing the concepts from political ecology and resistance theory, I have attempted to show the resistance in these three districts whether against POSCO, or other mining projects in Khandadhar and Sundergarh regions, these series of strugglers have been called as 'Land Wars' or Land Wars due to global capitalism.

Political ecology approaches help explore how governments and their line agencies—often in conjunction with external advisers and producers of 'expert' knowledge—employ a variety of strategies to 'governmentalise nature' (Whitehead et al. 2007) and territorialise peripheral and marginal areas (for example, Peluso and Vandergeest 2011), thereby enhancing control over both natural resources and rural/indigenous people. Claiming and classifying forestland and forest resources as 'state property' has been a common strategy for ordering and appropriating nature in most southeast Asian countries (for example, Forsyth and Walker 2008). In his seminal work *Seeing like a State*, Scott (1998) identifies the administrative and simplified ordering of nature and society by the state as one major reason for failed planning that ignores local realities and knowledge systems beyond simplification and territorialisation.[19]

The resistance to POSCO's projects in Orissa has been centred mostly against the forcible acquisition of land by the government of Orissa for POSCO-India. The focus has been on the impact of the project on the homes, farms and livelihoods of the people-resistance against POSCO—has been seen through the lens of everyday politics as the preferred resistance strategy of peasants, as postulated by Scott (1985), the farmers of Jagatsingpur district in Dhinkia, Gada Kujanga and Govindpur have responded to dispossession and displacement by employing a myriad of resistance strategies, ranging from road blockades, open confrontations

[18]Drawn from POSCO: Tribal Dispossession, Environmental Destruction and Imperialism by Analytical Monthly Review.

Analytical Monthly Review, published in Kharagpur, West Bengal, India, is a sister edition of Monthly Review. Its February 2010 issue features the following editorial. Ed., available at http://mrzine.monthlyreview.org/2010/amr250210.html, accessed on 28/05/15.

[19]Similar argument on 'Everyday resistance' by Scott (1985).

with district collector, police security guards and military personnel, demonstration marches and petitions. The movement against the POSCO project is the frontline of the most critical global struggle of our time; to preserve an environment in which the next generations can thrive, against the primary enemy of humanity, imperialist capitalism (Analytical Monthly Review 2010).

5 Conclusion

To quote T.K. Oommen, "it is no accident that the 'temples of modern India' got de-sacralised and the 'destructive development' pursued by the Indian state came to be intensely interrogated by late 1970s" (Oommen 2008). The Land Acquisition (Amendment) Bill and the Resettlement and Rehabilitation Bill (2011 and subsequent modifications in 2013) openly allowed the government to acquire land for the private sector and thereby extended its powers beyond public interest strengthens the power of the State. These bills are attempts to overcome the contradiction for capital generated by the increased demand for land driven by neoliberal policies and the inelastic supply rooted in farmers' unwillingness to sell (Levien 2011). The observations in the context of Orissa point out that the trans-border/global dimensions of land grabbing provide valuable clues to uncover the role of state in this dispossession-through-coercion. The State presents development as a solution but it results in their marginalisation and the vicious circle of a transition away from their sustainable culture. The POSCO project in the plant, port and mining sites shows the need for a search for alternatives till 2014, but the anti-POSCO movement and resistance serves as a frontline of the most critical global struggle of our time being a success story; to preserve an environment in which the next generations can thrive, against the primary enemy of humanity, imperialist capitalism. It also sends a message that the laws of the current land acquisition policy should look at solving the problem of the local people, not the capital and the Land Acquisition Act (Amendment) Bill and Resettlement and Rehabilitation Bill should be substantially altered for bringing justice to the local people and maintaining sustainability.

References

Ambagudia J (2010) Tribal rights, dispossession and the state in Odisha. Econ Polit Wkly XLV 33:60–67

Asher M (2009) Striking while the iron is hot: a case study of the Pohang Steel Company's (POSCO) proposed project in Orissa. National Centre for Advocacy Studies, Pune. https://stoposco.files.wordpress.com/2009/09/striking-while-the-iron-is-hot_posco-case-study.pdf. Accessed 11 Jan 2015

Banerjee P, Chaudhury SBR, Das SK (2005) Internal displacement in South Asia: the relevance of the UN's guiding principles. Sage, New Delhi

Behera NK (n.d.) Land acquisition and displacement in Western Odisha, an overview. http://humanistvoice.in/join-hv/item/253-land-acquisition.html. Accessed on 26 Mar 2016
Centre for Science and Environment (2008) Rich lands, poor people: is sustainable mining possible. In: The State of India's environment: the 6th citizen report. Centre for Science and Environment, New Delhi
Cernea M (1997) The risks and reconstruction model for resettling displaced populations. World Dev 25(10):1569–1587
Cernea M (1998) Impoverishment or social justice? A model for planning resettlement. In: Mathur HM and Marsden D (eds.) Development projects and impoverishment risks: resettling project-affected people in India. Oxford, Delhi
Chua A (2002) World on fire: how exporting free market democracy breeds ethnic hatred and global instability. Doubleday, New York
Das P (2005) Industrialization will harm Orissa's ecology greatly. In: The Hindu businesslike. The Hindu Group, Chennai. Accessed on 7 June
Dwyer M (2013) Building the politics machine: tools for resolving the global land grab. Dev Change 44(2):309–333
Fernandes W (2008) Sixty years of development-induced displacement in India. In: Mathur HM (ed) India social development report 2008: development and displacement. Oxford University Press, New Delhi, pp 89–102
Fernandes W (2009) Displacement and alienation from common property resources. In: Mehta L (ed) Displaced by development: confronting marginalisation and gender injustice. Sage, New Delhi, pp 105–129
Forsyth T, Walker A (2008) Forest guardians, forest destroyers: the politics of environmental knowledge in Northern Thailand. University of Washington Press, Seattle
Harvey D (2004) The 'new' imperialism: accumulation by dispossession. Soc Reg 40:63–87
Harvey D (2005) A brief history of neoliberalism. Oxford University Press, Oxford
Kumar K (2014) Confronting extractive capital social and environmental movements in Odisha. Econ Polit Wkly XLIX(14):66–73
Levien M (2011) Special economic zones and accumulation by dispossession in India. J Agrarian Change 11(4):454–483
Levien M (2015) From primitive accumulation to regimes of dispossession. Econ Polit Wkly L 22:146–157
Li TM (2007) The will to improve: governmentality, development and the practice of politics. Duke University Press, Durham
Majumdar B (2013) State-led development-induced dispossession and displacement. In: Dasgupta SS (ed) Sociology of displacement: policies and practice. Rawat Publications, New Delhi, pp 57–80
Marx K (1977) Capital, vol I. Vintage, New York
Mathur HM (2006) Development projects and displacement of tribal peoples. Adivasi Dev Displac Rehabil 46(2):50–57
Mehta L (ed) (2009) Displaced by development: confronting marginalisation and gender injustice. Sage, New Delhi
Munshi I (ed) (2012) The Adivasi question: issues of land, forest and livelihood. Orient Blackswan, Hyderabad
Oommen TK (2008) Protest against displacement by development projects: the Indian case. Indian Soc Dev Rep. CSD, Oxford University Press, New Delhi
Panda S (1999) Towards a sustainable natural resource management of tribal communities: findings from a study of swidden and wetland cultivation in remote hill regions of eastern India environmental management. Environ Manag 23(2):205–216
Parasuraman S (1999) The development dilemma: displacement in India. Macmillan Press Lt, London
Pattanaik S (2012) Impact of mining on water and human health: a case study of Baitarani river ecosystem in Orissa. In: Prakash A, Saravanan VS, Chorey J (eds) Interlacing water and human health: case studies from South Asia. Sage, New Delhi, pp 311–332

Peluso N, Vandergeest P (2011) Taking the jungle out of the forest: counter insurgency and the making of national natures. In: Peet R, Robbins P, Watts M (eds) Global political ecology. Routledge, New York, pp 254–284

Polanyi K (1944) The Great transformation: the political-economic origins of our time. Beacon Press, Boston

Ramanathan U (2011) Land acquisition, eminent domain and the 2011 Bill. Econ Polit Wkly XLVI 44&45:10–14

Rath B (2005) Vulnerable tribal livelihoods and shifting cultivation: the situation in Orissa with a case study in Bhuyan_Juang Pirh of Keonjhar district. Vasundhara, Bhubaneswar, Available at http://www.google.co.in/url?url=http://vasundharaodisha.org/Research%2520Reports/VulnerableTribalLivelihoodandShiftingCultivation.pdf&rct=j&frm=1&q=&esrc=s&sa=U&ei=YVyyVIWYHoyJuASlv4GABQ&ved=0CBMQFjAA&sig2=km6gaR9olP0isAgbF5012Q&usg=AFQjCNFNClFtt_VrSYQjGKz4jeso5gLtzg. Accessed on 11 Jan 2015

Saxena KB, Haragopal G (2014) Introduction. In: Saxena KB, Haragopal G (eds) Marginalization, development and resistance: essays in tribute to R. Sankaran, vol 1. Aakar Books, Delhi, pp xiii–lx

Scott JC (1985) Weapons of the weak: everyday forms of peasant resistance. Yale University Press, New Haven

Scott JC (1998) Seeing like a state: how certain schemes to improve the human condition Have Failed. Yale University Press, New Haven

Shrivastava A, Kothari A (2012) Churning the earth: the making of global India. Penguin, New Delhi

Somayaji S, Dasgupta S (eds) (2013) Sociology of displacement: policies and practice. Rawat Publications, New Delhi

Vasundhara (2005) http://vasundharaodisha.org/DiscussionPaper_eng/Kadalibari%20Case%20Study-15.pdf

United Nations Development Programme: Land Rights and Ownership in Orissa, Status Report, 2008. Available at http://www.undp.org/content/dam/india/docs/land_rights_ownership_in_orissa.pdf. Accessed on 22 Mar 2016

Whitehead M, Jones R, Jones M (2007) The Nature of the state: excavating the political ecologies of the modern state. Oxford University Press, New York

Woodhouse P (2012) New investment, old challenges: land deals and the water constraints in African agriculture. J Peasant Stud 39(3–4):777–794

The "Public Purpose" That Is Not Inclusive

Shruti Yerramilli

1 Introduction

Eminent domain is the power of the government to take away private property for "public purpose" (as defined under concerned laws in India) against just compensation. There exist differences in the treatment of the concept in some other countries, like the Fifth Amendment to the US Constitution subjects the invocation of eminent domain only for "public use" (Wex, Legal Information Institute). In the Indian context, the monument of eminent domain greatly depends on the foundation laid down by the interpretation of the phrase "public purpose." How does a government justify taking away private property, when these transactions, in most cases, allow almost no bargaining power to the affected parties? What must be the nature of this "public purpose" to justify expropriation by the government? How public-oriented must this purpose be? One may be tempted to take up the Shakespearean argument, but nomenclature of legal concepts bear the burden of interpretation. The interpretation and scope of the term could have been significantly different if it was penned down as public "benefit," "welfare" or as encoded in the US Constitution, as public "use."

In the Indian context, the most recent definition of "public purpose" comes from The Right to Fair Compensation & Transparency in Land Acquisition, Rehabilitation & Resettlement Act, 2013 (hereafter LARR 2013, for brevity), within Section 2(l)(a-f). To quote the Act, Section 2(1) "*The provisions of this Act relating to land acquisition, compensation, rehabilitation and resettlement, shall apply, when the appropriate Government acquires land for its own use, hold and control, including for public sector undertakings and for public purpose and shall include the following purposes…*" The *purposes* list out different kinds of projects that qualify as satisfying public purpose, like projects for strategic purposes relating to the defence forces or State Police (Section 2(1)a); infrastructure projects

S. Yerramilli (✉)
Indian Institute of Management Bangalore, Bengaluru 560076, India
e-mail: shrutii002@gmail.com

S. Pellissery et al. (eds.), *Land Policies in India*, India Studies in Business and Economics, DOI 10.1007/978-981-10-4208-9_7

involving agro-processing, cold storage, or other projects concerning agriculture, projects for industrial corridors, for water harvesting and conservation structures, etc., for government-aided education institutions and for tourism, sports, and health among others (Section 2(1)b(i-vii)); projects for project affected families (Section 2 (1)c); for housing for prescribed income groups (Section 2(1)d); for planned development of village sites (Section 2(1)e); and for residential purposes to the poor or landless (Section 2(1)f). This is of course not the exhaustive list from the actual Act, but serves as a reasonable indicator. The full form of the definition is lengthy to be quoted in its entirety. In its current form, Section 2(2)(a-b) also states the conditions under which the concerned government may acquire private property for public–private partnership projects or a private entity. It is clear that the definition encompasses a large variety of projects from those involving rehabilitation or resettlement infrastructure for the deprived, to projects for tourism. It stretches the notions of public purpose enough such that problems of misinterpretation or moral hazard become inbuilt in the system of acquisition.

It is not the objective of the paper to derive an exhaustive definition of the phrase. However, the expression represents the fundamental philosophy behind the act and guides the manner in which it is implemented. "Public purpose" should mean *for* the public. It will not be far-fetched to believe that for the public must also be in the interest of the public. However, the poor implementation of rehabilitation and resettlement (R&R) policies for most of the land acquisition cases in India and the superficial calculation of compensation amounts, even within the new LARR 2013, does not support our previous understanding. Any R&R policy needs to identify all if its beneficiaries to be successful. In the absence of proper land titling, property rights can neither be recognized nor be guaranteed effectively. The new land acquisition act recognizes the right to compensation however properties rights enjoy the same demoted status since they ceased to be Fundamental rights in 1978 (Wahi 2015). "The *right* to compensation has preceded the idea of right to property in India…" (Yerramilli 2016).

In the light of several implementation issues around the land acquisition process in India, it is hard to justify any acquisition as intended towards a public purpose. As early as the 1960s, the judicial interpretation of the phrase "public purpose" accepted acquisitions made for companies or private entities as justifiable as long as some part of the compensation was borne by the state or concerned government, as if to indicate their presence. One such strange case was that of *Indrajit C Parekh Vs State of Gujarat* AIR 1975 SC 1182. The Supreme Court upheld the claim by Gujarat government that a contribution of even a rupee by the government was enough to show that the acquisition for the private company was justified under the clause of "public purpose."

The paper does not question the merit of eminent domain in the absolute sense. Shavell (2010) suggests eminent domain becomes important where high transaction costs, due to market failure issues like holdup problems, do not encourage private investment. While the author acknowledges the existence of such cases of market failure, eminent domain may not be the best way to address them. Government intervention, in itself, distorts the markets, and lowers bargaining power of the affected parties. The primary question the paper asks is who the beneficiaries of an acquisition by the government are? In other words, how is the notion of public purpose realized through eminent domain, in practice? In answering these questions, we can understand better what informs the government's priority and goals while dislocating people for perceived greater benefits. The paper will discuss the issues with the current definition of the phrase "public purpose" and the problems created by the limited interpretation of the term.

2 Cost of Achieving "Public Purpose"

Expropriation of land by the government results in large-scale displacements of both the resident population and people who draw their livelihood from the acquired land. The acquisition could be for a government project or a private company, as long as the project can be shown to justify the cause of public purpose (LARR 2013, Section 1 and 2). Section 2(1) (a-f) of LARR 2013 specifies the projects that satisfy the definition of public purpose. The section includes infrastructure projects including projects for industrial corridors and any infrastructure activity that is notified by the Central government after the same is tabled in the Parliament. The loose phrasing of the section allows a multitude of projects to be recognized as being pursuant to some public purpose, effectively giving "*very broad discretionary powers to the state*" in interpreting and deciding the scope of the phrase (Raghuram and Sunny 2015).

The cost of allowing such projects to come to life are twofold: (i) the actual cost to be borne by the government, company or both, of running the project and the cost of acquiring the piece of land against just compensation; and (ii) the cost borne by the affected parties, in terms of loss of livelihood, displacement, loss of social structure, and impoverishment. The benefits of most projects accrue to an entirely different section of the society, not including the displaced. Since they do not share the benefits, the least that can be done is to compensate them for their losses. However, compensation amounts cover only the loss in value of the property and a solatium due to nonvoluntary nature of the sale. It is not enough to restore the state of their lives, even if it cannot make it any better.

2.1 Costs Beyond the Price of Land

The costs of acquisition borne by the affected parties include not only loss of bargaining power but also a loss of participation in the decision-making process. Forced eviction is understood to be the only way to implement an acquisition. That need not be the case as we will discuss in a later section. The forced nature of these changes uproots the residents or beneficiaries of the property, with not much room to re-design their lives to accommodate the large shifts that come with displacement. Displacement leads to loss of livelihood and social security. Most of the affected persons belong to the economically weak strata of society and draw their living from the land they occupy. Displaced farmers are constrained by their skills to move into other industries. Skills are not an easily gained attribute. Skill differences become a major hurdle in the process of labor movement and one of the main causes of impoverishment.

One such story of destruction was the creation of Korba Super Thermal Power Plant, located at Jamanipali in Korba district, Chhattisgarh. The construction of the reservoir severely affected 59 tribal villages, 20 of which were fully submerged in the process of construction, along with damage to almost 100 km^2 of forest area. "*No one consulted with or even informed the 2721 families of these 59 villages, who had been condemned to be internal refugees to the cause of "national development," about the project*..." (Hemadri et al. 1999). The loss of say in the process deprived the affected families of any chance to negotiate the fate of their futures. Hemadri et al. (1999) point out that almost 85% of the affected families were either Dalits or tribals. Uprooted from their ancestral homes, these families migrated in search of livelihood and shelter. The protests around the construction that caused large-scale involuntary displacement forced the government to make some rehabilitation arrangements albeit much delayed.

This is a story from the times of the draconian Land Acquisition Act of 1984. However, the inclusion of R&R process in the new law has not improved its implementation much. It is worth reiterating that land acquisition procedures were in the name of public purpose even in the older law. It is strange that even as millions are displaced and pushed further down the social pyramid, due to these acquisitions, they are continued to be treated like sacrificial commodities in the name of greater social good. Several scholars have studied the issue of displacement in India. Swain (2014) comments on the magnitude of displacement and laments the lack of proper accounting of the same. Ratnakar (2014) quotes other studies to point out that "*country's development programmes have caused the displacement of approximately 20 million people*" in just the first four decades of independence. However, not even a third of them were rehabilitated. As a country, we witness enough forced migration and movement due to several reasons like conflicts, natural calamities, even without accounting for the so-called development efforts (Dutta 2014). It is, therefore, not expected from a welfare state to push rehabilitation and resettlement of project affected people at the bottom of priority list.

There is also the problem of multiple displacement. Pandey and Rout (2004) discuss the case of the projected affected families due to acquisitions for Rihand dam. The families were first displaced on the 1960s due to acquisition for the Dam, only to be displaced again in 1970s due to certain coal mining projects and more than once in 1980s due to other industrial projects. They note that with each displacement "*...they were progressively pauperized.*" These cases say a lot about the poor planning process that concerned governments utilize to decide the merit of a proposed acquisition. Gendered responses to the forced rehabilitation process also are a part of the cost that the project affected parties must bear. Individuals depend on their families as families depend on their communities. These social structures are the basis for survival, well-being, and identity of families, especially in tribal and rural areas. The social strings form mutual support systems for the families. At the heart of families are the women and children. Women and children make up almost 70% of the total internally displaced population, not limited to displacement due to development projects (Ghimire 2011). Once displaced, these women lose the comfort of their support systems. Social adversities as a result of forced displacements are well documented.

2.2 The Unequal Weight of Social Costs of Displacement

The problems faced by displaced women are only exacerbated by the preexisting gender inequalities in the Indian society and family systems (Pandey and Rout 2004). Resettlement forces affected families to move to alien communities and changes or even diminishes their access to basic common resources. It may adversely affect their access to adequate shelter, sanitation, and livelihood opportunities. Torn away from their "extended families" women may lose their sense of security (Asthana 2012). The enforced movement changes the women's roles in labor markets. They are forced into markets to become wage earners to support their dwindling economies. Lack of specialized skills, in most cases, necessitates that they take up whatever work they find. It may force them to work in subhuman conditions. The new act, LARR 2013, makes an effort to correct the historical bias against women, with respect to property rights. The act recognizes widows, divorcees, and women abandoned by their families, as separate entities. They are entitled to be treated as distinct entities for the purpose of allotting compensation and R&R facilities. Although a step in the right direction, our discussions have shown that the biggest hurdle in the implementation of the acquisition laws tends to be the poor political will or administrative slack.

One of the many problems associated with the cost-benefit analysis of land acquisition projects is the accounting of social costs. The method in itself is beset with problems of general equalization of costs and benefits. What it means is that a project would be considered viable if the total costs of acquisition and displacement associated with it are exceeded by the benefits that it will generate. First, the costs and benefits are associated with different groups of people. The displaced families are almost never stakeholders in the project. They bear the cost of loss of home, jobs, social security, and identity, but the cash compensations cannot equalize the costs they bear. Let us take the case of the Srisailam Dam project. This project was also supposed to have an aligned irrigation project. It took 20 years to build the multipurpose dam, the work on which began in 1960. Huge returns were expected from the project, and they may have been used to justify the displacement of more than 20,000 households. We will discuss the benefit justification for the project in the next section.

The point is that the expected benefits should have been able to cover the compensation expenses, even if they could not support the complete rehabilitation of the affected families. However, that is not the case. Three and a half decades have passed since the completion of the project, and yet affected families are still waiting for their compensation. "*The state government in 1986 issued orders (GO Ms No. 98) sanctioning monetary compensation, besides a government job for one member in each of the families displaced.*" (Times of India 2015). Out of nearly 11,000 families that the state government identified only 2000 were found to have eligible candidates for government jobs, of which only 33 were given permanent jobs. Even if we assume for a moment that state did not lack in will but in actual funds to support their promises, their cost calculations must have been significantly off the mark to be able to support only 0.3% of identified affected families. If the state, however, did lack in will, their failure became a realized cost for the displaced.

3 Social Benefits and Public Purpose

There are merits for invoking eminent domain, though in limited scenarios, like in the case of severe holdup problems. However, the bigger question is if such forced appropriation of private property, and thereby its reallocation, can generate sufficient social benefits. Government's intervention in the property market, either through the administration of prices or forced acquisition of property, causes market failure. Any insistence on expropriation of property can only be justified if the government recognizes an alternate use of the same to generate greater social value. Even if a superior alternate purpose exists, for which the property can be allocated, the government should be able to do so, such that the net social value of the land/property (after adjusting for just compensation) is greater than expected private value (Shavell 2010).

The accounting net profits that the proposed project will generate can be quantified with relative ease. The real problem arises in recognizing the social costs involved in the expropriation of property. The LARR 2013 describes the components of cost of acquisition in Section 3(i) as including the amount of compensation (including solatium and interest payments), demurrage to be paid for damage to land or standing property on land, cost of rehabilitation, and resettlement (R&R) including cost of necessary infrastructure and amenities, administrative costs, and costs of conducting a Social Impact Assessment study. The amount of compensation is dependent on the market value of the land along with any standing property on it. It does not include the cost of rebuilding livelihood and damages due to sudden loss of community and access to common resources. The notion that demanding such sacrifices from the people in the name of "public purpose" is justifiable, by uprooting their social structures and taking away their livelihood, is highly contestable.

3.1 Regressive Benefits

In practice, compensation values turn out to be regressive in nature, with affected parties of higher valued properties getting higher compensation and vice versa (Singh 2015). Since compensation values depend on market values, it is only natural for them to be affected by the distortions in land pricing. It is an open secret that most property transactions in India, especially those concerning land, tend to be undervalued, to save on taxes (Bose 2013). Most property transactions use circle rates as reference points. Circle rate is the minimum value at which a property or plot of land may be sold in the market. This rate is decided by the State government, and stamp duties are charged on this rate or the actual value of the transaction, whichever is higher. It is not difficult to see why there is no incentive to declare the actual value of a property. Circle rates must serve as good indicators of the direction of property prices in the market, except they are not as dynamic. Since they are not revised as often, they are usually lower than the actual market rate. Remember that these rates are the state government's perception of property value in an area. Actual market rates are established by forces of demand and supply. In remote or rural areas, the government established rates may not even come close to reflecting the actual tradable value of the land depending on its features, resources (or even productivity). This means that even if compensation is decided at four times the market value of the land (in rural areas), as per LARR 2013, it may still fall short of the actual value of the property. This is where the *use* and *exchange* values of the same piece of land start differing. Davy (2016) describes this as the existence of polyrationality, such that "*...no one can claim what the 'true' meaning of land value (is).*" Where the tradable value of land in question is too low, its price may not fully reflect value realized by the occupants of the land, who depend on it for sustenance. This issue is separate from mere under-reporting of land value. Compensation values can therefore not depend on merely prescribing seemingly high multiples of existing market value of land, without taking into account both the actual and implicit values of the same.

Where undervalued compensation denies the affected families a portion of the benefit, such large multiples may also unduly increase the cost of acquisition. We are not concerned with the disbursal of artificially high values of compensation to the affected families. Net social benefit by definition must also include minimum, efficient expenditure by the government. Large cash transfers to the affected families, in the name of compensation, seldom benefit them. Compensation in cash is like a windfall gain. Hemadri et al. (1999) point out in their study that "*cash compensation is depleted by oustees in short periods, by fraud, for repayment of old debts, in liquor and conspicuous consumption.*" They are not helpful in rebuilding the lives of the displaced. A higher value of cash compensation cannot be viewed as more just or fair (Bell and Parchomovsky 2010). Calculating private benefit does not pose a major challenge. However, the calculation of social benefits can be subject to several assumptions (due to incomplete/asymmetric information) and evaluator's discretion regarding the components of both costs and benefits.

3.2 *The Idea of Benefit and Public Purpose*

Social Impact Assessment report (LARR 2013, Chapter II Section 4(4)) is required to evaluate if the acquisition is necessary and favorable alternate use of resource;

if the project serves a public purpose; and the extent of damage it will inflict on life, land, and property. Unfortunately, the report does not inform decisions regarding compensation (nature and size), rehabilitation, and resettlement or even income restoration. The act requires that the specific provisions be made to address the problems that the report highlights. However, implementation of the same has remained a hope.

What “purpose” does an acquisition serve? Who benefits from the large-scale development projects that are designed on the backs of the evicted communities? The creation of irrigation projects or industrial corridors creates positive value; however, the benefits and costs are not shared by the same set of people. The equation seems balanced on the whole, but there is gross injustice built into the mechanics of it. Assocham conducted a survey covering nearly 2000 people in more than ten districts of West Bengal, to understand how people perceive the fiasco around the Tata’s Nano car project in Singur. The survey had the most interesting results. Nearly 80% people believed that the issue had been over politicized and that Tata should have continued with its project. The project would have created jobs and boosted the state’s manufacturing sector. About 50% of the respondents believed that given the expanse of the project and the productivity of the agricultural land, the affected families should have been offered higher compensation amounts (Times of India 2008). It is interesting how the same project served national interest for some people while it was unjust to others. It is worth noting that there is a natural divide between the experiences of those who hope to reap the benefits of such projects and those who did not expect to play any role in the process.

The survey does indicate an interesting fact. Many of these large-scale projects are equipped to generate positive spillovers and even direct gains. The problem is that the oustees do not share the benefits pie. A scheme which allows prospective oustees to participate in the value generation process, from the project, would reduce the friction between the government/private company and the vulnerable communities. Truly, the development project should bring an opportunity to these communities to enhance their standard of living. In cases where displacement is inevitable, it must be ensured that the project benefits can secure at least their existing state of living so that they may not be worse off as an aftermath of the project. It is possible to treat these projects as “*development opportunity and allows planners to manage impoverishment risks and turn the people dispossessed or displaces into project beneficiaries, particularly the poor and vulnerable, who may be disproportionately affected by resettlement losses*” (ABD n.d.).

As discussed, some parts of the LARR 2013 Act, like the need for Social Impact Assessment (hereafter SIA), do promote greater net social benefit, by trying to reduce the overall social loss. However, protests by various government ministries and even the corporate sector over the requirement of the report cast a shadow over the ability of the Act to make the acquisition procedures more inclusive. It is, of course, true that the 70–80% consent clause (LARR 2013 Section 2(2)(b)(i-ii)) (as the case may be) as well as the SIA report requirements are time-consuming and delay the acquisition process. However, given the stakes, these requirements should be built into the project roadmap, instead of being treated as last-minute hurdles.

Where complete assessment is not feasible, as in the case of large projects, sample surveys must be conducted to gauge the extent of possible impact of the project to see if resettlement and rehabilitation needs can be adequately met; or decide on an alternate project route (ADB 2012). Singh and Panwar (2015) studied 256 cases of land acquisition, where land was acquired without any hindrance or protest, under the Land Acquisition Act of 1984. Even though the process was smooth, they find that "*...in overwhelming number of cases, the government agencies took 1,000 days or more just to make out compensation awards.*" The dismal pace at which the restorative aspects of the projects were handled, in the absence of SIA or rehabilitation requirements, indicate that the protests against the SIA report or consent clause has more to do with the undue munificence that the corporates had come to expect from the system and lax pace at which the government was predisposed to working than any actual harm to the development projects.

Another case of disappearing benefits is the case of Srisailam Project. Hemadri et al. (1999) note that according to the Fact Finding Committee on the project, the methodology of calculation of compensation caused huge losses to the project affected families. The compensation was calculated at market value instead of replacement value. The committee found that the replacement value of land was Rs. 5000 per acre for dry land and Rs. 13,800 for the wetland. The actual compensation paid, including the solatium, was much less than 20% of the value needed to allocate land of the same quality and productivity levels to the project affected families. The benefits also disappeared on account of flawed calculations of the cost-benefit analysis of the project. The Srisailam Project was expected to yield a return rate of 7.98% on capital invested. Part of the project was also building of canal systems for irrigation. Expected returns from the irrigation project were still higher "*...with the two canals likely to produce annual agricultural output at a cost-benefit ratio of 1:1.91 at 10% on capital outlay*" (Shatrugna 1981). The bloated figures for expected benefit or rather shrunk figures for costs, appear as a result of the absence of inclusion of social costs in the equation. The totals also did not take into account the hidden costs and the extent of cost escalations. How does one quantify the loss of habitat, forests, and access to common resources? The project was to displace 100 villages and 20,728 households. The agriculture production levels in these areas were high, a factor which was ignored (Shatrugna 1981).

4 Political Willpower, Administrative Efficiency, and Judicial Pro-activism

The new land acquisition act of 2013 has, on paper, tried to rectify several deficiencies of the former act. However, it faced several oppositions, from government ministries and private corporations alike, since some of its provisions make the acquisition process more "cumbersome." The consent clause and the need for Social Impact Assessment report demand certain accountability, to which neither is willing to commit. It is true that efficiency is an important criterion and undue expense or delay in the execution of a development project is not a desirable situation. It is, however, unjust and irrational to ignore obvious social aspects of an expropriation process, to hasten its implementation. A consent clause causes most problems since the prospective displaced have no share in the expected benefits that the concerned development project will generate. This issue will be addressed in greater detail in the next section. If our land records were adequately documented and land surveys were duly updated, the process of assessing the next best use of land, the allocative efficiency of the project and the estimation of the number of affected parties would have been easier. A case in point is that we digress when we propose to discard the need for SIA report or adequate consent to reduce project cost and implementation timeline.

The need for emerging economies like India, to attract capital and accelerate growth, is so strong that social issues like displacement become nothing more than politicized coffee table discussions. They do not get the priority they deserve. "*The people affected by land appropriation get media attention only when they resist and agitate against governmental land acquisition*" (Guha 2014). Sadly, there is no official records of the total number of displaced due to large development projects in India. Hemadri et al. (1999) comment on the lack of data, calling it "*painful irony and possible design*" and point out that the figures given by various scholars range between 10 and 50 million (updated till 1999). Even at its most conservative estimate, this nearly two-decade old data brings out an alarming state of affairs. There is a serious lack of proper economic evaluation of the social costs of large development projects.

Referring to a study titled Economic Dimensions of the Sardar Sarovar Project by Alagh et al. (1995), Cernea (1999) points out the serious flaws in the understanding of the economic dimensions of displacement and resettlement. He laments the lack of analysis or even substantial coverage of costs related to displacement and forced migration and the investment needed to restore the incomes and economic statuses of the affected families. Sardar Sarovar Project has garnered criticism for its poor policy and implementation, considering the lack of emphasis on internalization of cost for a project that was estimated to displace nearly 200,000 people. It is not the only case where lack of political will or administrative efficiency has cost several people their livelihood and identity. We will look at the case of three different states as identified in various Reports by the Office of the Comptroller and Auditor General (CAG) of India, namely Odisha, Kerala and Andhra Pradesh. CAG's reports are one of the only authoritative national performance reports covering various aspects of land management, acquisition and allied issue including displacement.

4.1 The Unutilized "Purpose"

CAG Report (2014a) on Land Management by the Government of Kerala with a special focus on land for Aranmula Airport and Smart City Kochi, identified several grounds of failure on the part of the government to monitor and implement land laws.

This has led to several cases of "*alienation of government land, assignment of land to encroachers*." The essence of public purpose lies in the appropriate utilization of the land resource. Mere paper entry of an intention to serve national interest through a project cannot be counted as pursuant to the clause of public purpose. The report suggested that almost 40 private entities that had been allotted land by Kerala Industrial Infrastructure Development Corporation (KINFRA), Kerala State Industrial Development Corporation (KSIDC), and Kerala State Information Technology Infrastructure Limited (KSITIL), in different IT parks, had left their plots unutilized. There were problems in acquisition and allocation of land even for the Smart City Project in Kochi. Smart City Kochi is a Special Economic Zone (SEZ) being set up under the joint venture of Government of Kerala and TECOM Investments, such that government holds only about one-sixth of the total shares. The agreement leaves the state government with barely any representation in the Board of Directors. Given the skewed terms of the venture, it does not come as a surprise that even after 7 years of the signing of the agreement, neither of the promises of the 8.8 million square feet built-up space, or the 90,000 jobs were realized (CAG 2014a).

4.2 The Misappropriated "Purpose"

The CAG reports have been highlighting the opaque and faulty pattern of land allotment in the state of Andhra Pradesh for several years. In their report released in 2011–12, they conducted a performance audit of the same and studied cases over the past five years, from 2006 to 2011. During this period, the state government had made allotments to over 1000 beneficiaries, of a total area of 88,492 acres. The report chose at random 11 districts in the state as their sample, which covered about half the total number of cases of allotments involving 50,285.90 acres of land. The report found that allotments for commercial purposes were not fair or transparent and did not seem to serve any public purpose. The faulty utilization pattern found refuge in the nonexistence of any clear land use policy document or study of the "socioeconomic" needs of the state. Of the total number of commercial allotments, 11 Special Economic Zones and IT parks did not meet their employment generation targets. Four of these SEZs had completely failed to generate any employment, and two could only generate 26,000 jobs over five years. Several allotments that were made in period 2000–2010 had not been utilized, and those that had been, were being used for irregular purposes like hotels and offices. It seemed like the concept of public purpose had been deliberately misunderstanding or ignored.

4.3 The Failed "Purpose"

While the stories of the other two states depict the misuse of the public purpose clause, the case of Odisha reflects the state's apathy and the complete alienation of the term “public’ from “purpose.” The CAG report (2014b) studied the R&R of people affected by Industrial projects in Odisha. The performance audit revealed a stunning lack of responsibility on the part of the government in actualizing the resettlement and rehabilitation schemes for the project affected families. The report revealed several cases where poor planning, inadequate survey, and unsuccessful administration of R&R schemes led to benefits not reaching as many as “*798 project displaced families in respect of 13 industrial projects displaced during 1992–2013.*” Even though a special committee, Rehabilitation and Periphery Development Advisory Committees (RPDAC), was established to monitor the R&R planning, several affected families did not receive adequate resettlement help. Job opportunities were not provided to 588 affected families, as promised, nor were they given any compensation in lieu of the promised employment. Since R&R schemes were not monitored, it was found that resettlement locations lacked most basic infrastructural amenities like piped water supply, healthcare facility, basic navigable roads, and sanitation, even as the allocated funds remained unutilized.

4.4 The Role of Judiciary

The loose phrasing of the clauses in LARR 2013, or even the act (1984) before it, lends itself well to interpretation. The comfortable elbow room has tended to allow for all kinds of interpretative arguments, some in favor of greater emphasis on “public” in the phrase, while others on “purpose.” Kolkata High Court’s judgment and statements were under the spotlight during the Tata Nano-Singur controversy. The people who actively protested against the acquisition argued that expropriation of cultivable agricultural land for progress in the manufacturing sector can not be a good reason to satisfy public interest. The court, of course, realized that public interest was separate from public purpose and ruled that “*what counts as a public purpose, it has noted, is a ‘socio-economic question’ that should be left to local governments to answer*” (Economist 2008).

On the contrary, there have been landmark judgments where the courts have acknowledged the role of their judicial powers, in maintaining consistency and transparency in the interpretation of what constitutes public purpose. In *Habib Ahmed v. State of Uttar Pradesh and Ors.* AIR 1965 All 344, the Allahabad High Court held that a notification could not be dismissed because there is no perceived necessity for the acquisition. “*Whether the land is required for a public purpose or not has to be decided solely by the State Government.*” In *K. Madhava Rao And Ors. vs. State Of A.P. And Ors* 2006 (1) ALD 457, 2006 (1) ALT 562, the Andhra High Court held that “*Prima facie, the Government is the best judge as to whether an acquisition is for a public purpose. But it is not the sole judge.*”

Another connected concept in deciding nature of benefits from a land acquisition process is the concept of compensation. Compensation is akin to the “consideration” that must be exchanged by one party against an offer made by another willing party, for any contract to be void. Yes, the glaring difference lies in the word *willing*. Land acquisition is by no means a duress free process. However, the Supreme Court has recognized compensation as the necessary payment that must be paid and accepted, for the acquisition to be considered valid.

A recent Supreme Court ruling addressed the mist surrounding the phrase "*compensation has not been paid*," as written in Section 24(2) of the LARR 2013. After the enactment of LARR 2013, there existed some confusion around the areas where the matter fell under the shared ambit of the two laws, such as the pending cases under the older land acquisition act of 1984. The Court pronounced, that pursuant to the aforementioned section of LARR 2013, any acquisition proceedings initiated under the older act of 1984 will be considered as lapsed "*where award has been made five years or more prior to the commencement of 2013 Act and possession of the land is not taken or compensation has not been paid*" (The New Indian Express 2014). In a way, the Court sustained the "*retrospective clause*" that land acquisition procedure is void if due compensation has not been made to the affected parties and/or physical possession of the land continues to be in the hands of the affected party (PTI 2014). These judgments add to a series of important precedents that will make the interpretation of the terms contained within the Act, less arbitrary.

5 Alternatives

Several studies show that it is shortsighted to believe that forced displacement through eminent domain is inevitable and, therefore, may be treated as an unfortunate by-product of development processes. At its best, this misguided approach is a result of policy inertia. At its worst, it is indifferent and irresponsible. Eminent domain allows governments to interfere in markets, distort market clearing prices of properties. For such condemnation of land to be considered efficient, the total costs of the project, including the cost of induced price distortions, any administrative costs to execute the appropriation and all associated social costs, must be less than the market cost of acquiring the property and executing the project. Alternatively, the total costs must be less than the cost of utilizing the property for an alternate purpose (Munch 1976). Acquisitions under eminent domain are as much economic decisions as they are political. We must seek different methods of benefit sharing and cost dissipation, for large development projects that can cause significant negative externalities.

5.1 A Stake in Development

No community is averse to the idea of sharing development benefits. It is fair to assume, that most communities would, in their self-interest, be willing to participate in and contribute to the development process. Even though this may seem like a fairly intuitive argument, it eludes most policy designers involved in planning process maps for various large development projects that are likely to cause significant displacement or socio-environment damage. In most cases, resettlement and rehabilitation measures are treated as excess costs on the payers (government or companies). The fact is that financing appropriate R&R schemes seem so expensive because they are treated as stand-alone expenses with no balancing benefits. The affected families contribute to the development process by sharing their resources and accepting (even if under duress) a change in their livelihood and social structure. If their contributions are treated as investments, we can recognize their stake in the project generated benefits. This makes them joint beneficiaries, along with the government and private company, in the process. Internalizing the social cost of resource acquisition will increase the cost efficiency of the project at the same time reduce the unnecessary burden of dealing with delays due to social discord. Perhaps, consenting transactions would reduce the time cost of the project, ceteris paribus.

Cernea (2008) quotes the example of a few countries that recognized the merit of benefits sharing, like Canada and China. Both the countries have invested in several large hydropower projects and multipurpose dams. In the 1960s and 1970s, China made investments in three large dam projects that displaced a total of 90,000 people between them. Unsurprisingly, the displacements led to social unrest and political instability. Realizing the need for a more constructive solution, China brought about a series of changes in its R&R policies. A decade later the Chinese government "... *directed each power plant to allocate RMB 0.001 per kilowatt hour to a development fund for investments in the reservoir area throughout the existence of the power plant itself*" (Cernea 2008). This allowed for sufficient and steady funds to support adequate R&R facilities as well as allowed the displaced to share benefits from the projects.

Canada's case is also similar; except it chose a different model to internalize the social costs of land acquisition. Around the same time as China, in 1971, Canada was also considering the construction of large-scale hydro projects. The project's proposed 20 dams would have adversely affected the habitats of indigenous communities. In response to the protests by the local communities, the Canadian courts stayed the project construction. Consequently, the company involved in the project announced that in recognition of their contribution, regarding resources and land, the indigenous communities would be treated as investors and entered into equity-sharing agreements with the affected persons. These methods are far superior since they also uplift the affected families and share the benefits of development with them.

India too has witnessed such cases, where communities have demanded a share of the gains from such large-scale projects and recognize it as their right. One such case is that of the *Avasari Khurd Industrial Development Pvt. Ltd. in Avasari Khurd village in Ambegaon taluka of Pune district* (Jadhav 2008). More than a thousand farmers came together to form this company and identified barren land worth Rs. 900 crore as the site for Special Economic Zone proposed by them. The farmers realized the benefits of being contributors and resource owners in the process of development, rather than being the victims who could have been ousted by private companies or government for the same opportunity. Since they owned the proposed site for SEZ (as approved by the concerned government), they were able to suitably plan the allocation of land to include industrial and residential zones, along with area earmarked for farming (Jadhav 2008). They did not just accept a share in the benefits; they were able to create the opportunity for its creation.

5.2 *Voluntary Sale & Preemption of Resource Needs and Need for Better Land Use Planning*

It may not always be possible to enter a situation of benefit sharing; but is it always necessary to take the eminent domain route for large development projects? Holdup problems are quite real. However, they usually arise when there is a sudden inelastic demand for a large number of adjacent properties. An example of this could be when a private company aggressively sets out to buy the critical minimum number of adjacent plots needed for its project to be feasible, under a time constraint. The company faces a situation of reduction in bargaining power and price escalation with each subsequent purchase. The sellers realize that given the needs of the project, they can demand a price that is more than the reservation price of the company.

However, preemption of resource needs allows buyers to space out their purchases to avoid holdup problems, at least till a certain stage in resource accumulation process. Many private players have realized the merits of preemptive planning and have been able to avoid taking the land acquisition route through the government. The Hindu (2006) reported the collection of around 4800 acres of land for a SEZ in Kakinada (Andhra Pradesh), through voluntary transactions. Interestingly, this amounts to more than 50% of the total need for land for the project. Practically, it is not possible to avoid the land acquisition route altogether. However, efforts of the promoters of the SEZ effectively reduced the expected number of affected families by more than half. Similar successful efforts were also taken by the developers of Gurgaon SEZ and Navi Mumbai SEZ, respectively (Singh 2012).

If involuntary resettlement is unavoidable, then project plan should try and minimize the social costs of displacement (World Bank 2013). The tradeoff lies between the cost of displacement and project benefits. *Ceteris paribus*, if the cost of scaling the project or the loss due to the same is less than the corresponding social cost of displacement, the former must be considered. If the project benefits outweigh the social cost of displacement, then adequate R&R support must be provided to the affected families. Pearce (1999) explains that if the communities to which the project benefits will accrue are as "*deserving*" or poor as the oustees, then the relative costs of reducing benefits and costs of rehabilitation can be directly compared. The project in all cases must lean towards minimization of social costs.

6 Conclusion

"Public purpose" is a well-meaning but highly misinterpreted term. In our discussions through the various sections, we have seen ample evidence of the social costs of (almost voluntary) misrepresentation of the expression, by the governments and even private companies. The role of judicial interpretation and valuable precedents cannot be stressed enough. Most leeway for poor implementation of the requirements of LARR 2013 for any land acquisition case stems from the loose phrasing of the definition of the term, which allows for enough room for interpretation.

As an emerging nation, it seems, we give precedence to the accelerated pace of growth over inclusive development. The new land acquisition of 2013 faced stiff opposition from industry and even some ministries. The added requirement of minimum consent and Social Impact Assessment report bothered the industry members who expected that the gestation time for each large-scale projects would go up. Time lags and increased compensation requirements could also render projects unviable. While their concerns are not misplaced, the solution to this problem does not lie in the complete removal of both the important clauses. "Public purpose" continues to be treated as profit purpose and social concerns associated with acquisition cases continue to be attributed insignificant priority. We have discussed several cases in the previous sections to support this assertion.

We are not the only country where government and industry alike are pushing at the seams of the expression to extract every possible room for interpretation. The Fifth Amendment to the US Constitution allows a government to take away private property only for "public use" against just compensation. Yes, their choice of words was more restrictive, and that did not last long (Kelly 2006). "Public Use" seems to suggest that the development activity being undertaken, for which private property must be expropriated, should directly benefit the general public and should not be for private benefit. In the famous Case of *Berman v. Parker 1954*, U.S. Supreme Court expanded the scope of eminent domain, such that it could be invoked for any "public purpose" and not just for "public use." Williams (2009) points out that this undue expansion in the government's powers weakened the institution of individual property rights. Following this, another landmark case of *Kelo v. City of New London 2005*, further diluted the meaning of the term public purpose, by allowing for acquisitions that benefited the government (such as creating broaden the tax base), even at the cost of individual harm. As long the benefit could be understood as economic development, it could be allowed under public purpose.

Most development projects that relied on land acquisition instead of direct market transaction have caused significant involuntary displacement. Yet, most of the current debates revolve around the restructuring of the Act to reduce time lags in projects caused by 'unnecessary' procedures like preparation of social impact assessment. The paper is not intended to present a pro-poor argument, but to make a case for more inclusive land policies and laws. We discussed several benefit sharing options that allowed affected parties to share the gains from their resources and reduce social costs of the project. However, if benefit sharing is not an option, "public purpose" demands that better policies for income restoration are designed, that leave the affected families no worse than before. The interpretation of the term has the potential to change the manner in which projects needing land acquisition are approached, to make them more inclusive.

References

Alagh YK, Sardar P (1995) Institute of economic and social research. Economic dimensions of the sardar sarovar project. Har-Anand Publications, New Delhi

Asian Development Bank (ADB) (2012) Involuntary resettlement safeguards. A planning and implementation good practice sourcebook—draft working document. Asian Development Bank, Manila. URL: http://www.adb.org/sites/default/files/institutional-document/32827/files/ir-good-practices-sourcebook-draft.pdf

Asian Development Bank (ADB) (n.d) Cambodia railway resettlement management. Quick reference guide. URL: http://www.adb.org/sites/default/files/projects/162442/cam-rp-reference-guide.pdf

Asthana V (2012) Forced displacement: a gendered analysis of the Tehri Dam project. Econ Polit Wkly 47(47–48):96–102. URL: http://www.indiawaterportal.org/sites/indiawaterportal.org/files/forced_displacement-vandana_asthana_epw_2012.pdf

Bell A, Parchomovsky G (2010) The hidden function of takings compensation. Institute For Law and Economics, University of Pennsylvania Law School. Research Paper No. 10-03. URL: http://ssrn.com/abstract=1569416. Accessed on 03 Mar 2016

Bose P (2013) A land acquisition bill with many faultlines. Econ Polit Wkly 48(26–27). URL: http://www.epw.in/journal/2013/26-27/web-exclusives/land-acquisition-bill-many-faultlines.html

Cernea MM (1999) Why economic analysis is essential to resettlement: a sociologist's view. Special Article, Econ Polit Wkly 2149–2158

Cernea MM (2008) Compensation and benefit sharing: why resettlement policies and practices must be reformed. Water Sci Eng 1(1):89–120. ISSN 1674–2370

Davy B (2016) Land values as the social construction of scarcity. Der öffentliche Sektor—The Public Sector 42(1):131–145. URL: http://oes.tuwien.ac.at/sektor/periodical/pageview/1345558

Dutta P (2014) Reflecting on the role of institutions in the everyday lives of displaced women: the case of ganga-erosion in Malda, West Bengal. Institute for Social and Economic Change. Working Paper 324. URL: http://www.isec.ac.in/WP%20324%20-%20Priyanka%20Dutta%20-%20proof.pdf

Economist (2008) Nano wars: Tata threatens to make the world's cheapest car somewhere else. URL: http://www.economist.com/node/12010079

Ghimire A (2011) Rethinking "women" in forced displacement. Refugee Watch 3:30–43. URL: http://www.mcrg.ac.in/rw%20files/RW37/3.Anita.pdf

Guha A (2014) Generating public consciousness around land acquisition for private industries. Soc Chang 44(2):205–228

Hemadri R, Mander H, Nagaraj V (1999) Dams, displacement, policy and law in India. Prepared for thematic review, 1.3: displacement, resettlement, rehabilitation, reparation and development, World Commission on Dams

Jadhav R (2008) Farmers to set up own SEZ near Pune. The Times of India. URL: http://timesofindia.indiatimes.com/india/Farmers-to-set-up-own-SEZ-near-Pune-/articleshow/2712914.cms?referral=PM

Kelly DB (2006) The public use requirement in eminent domain law: a rationale based on secret purchases and private influence. Cornell Law Rev 92(1)

Munch P (1976) An economic analysis of eminent domain. J Polit Econ 84(3):473–498. The University of Chicago Press. URL: http://www.jstor.org/stable/1829865 Accessed 31 Feb 2016, 13:52 UTC
Pandey B, Rout BK (2004) Development induced displacement in India: impact on women. National Commission for Women, New Delhi
Pearce DW (1999) Methodological issues in the economic analysis for involuntary resettlement operations. In: Cernea MM (ed) The economics of involuntary: resettlement: questions and challenges. World Bank, Washington D.C.
Press Trust of India (PTI) (2014) Supreme court order on land acquisition act has drawn clear lines on implementation: Jairam Ramesh. The Economic Times. URL: http://articles.economictimes.indiatimes.com/2014-04-01/news/48767559_1_land-acquisition-act-retrospective-clause-judgement
Ratnakar M (2014) Displacement: a socio-economic rights perspective. VIKALPA 39(4):11
Raghuram G, Sunny S (2015) Right to fair compensation and transparency in land acquisition, rehabilitation and resettlement ordinance 2014: a process perspective (No. WP2015-07-03). Indian Institute of Management Ahmedabad, Research and Publication Department
Report of Comptroller and Auditor General (CAG) of India (2014a) Land management by the Government of Kerala with special focus on land for Aranmula Aiport and Smart City Kochi. Report No. 6. URL: http://www.cag.gov.in/sites/default/files/audit_report_files/Kerala_Report_6_2014.pdf
Report of the Comptroller and Auditor General (CAG) of India (2014b) General and social sector. Government of Odisha. Report No. 7, p 2. http://www.cag.gov.in/sites/default/files/audit_report_files/Odisha_Report_7_2014.pdf
Report of the Comptroller and Auditor General (CAG) of India (2012) Land allotment. Government of Andhra Pradesh 2011–2012. URL: http://gssaap-cag.nic.in/sites/all/themes/marinelli/Reports/2011-12/Land%20Allotment/English/LandAllotment_Complete_Report_2011-12.pdf
Shatrugna M (1981) Unrehabilitated poor of srisailam project. Econ Polit Wkly 2123–2126
Shavell S (2010) Eminent domain versus government purchase of land given imperfect information about owners' valuations. J Law Econ 53(1): 1–27 (University of Chicago Press, Booth School of Business, University of Chicago, University of Chicago Law School). doi:10.1086/596115
Singh R (2015) Litigation over compensation under land acquisition: actors and outcomes. Seminar delivered, Gokhale Institute of Politics and Economics, Pune
Singh R, Panwar DA (2015) Subverting a progressive law. The Hindu. URL: http://www.thehindu.com/opinion/lead/subverting-a-progressive-law/article7400012.ece
Singh R (2012) Inefficiency and abuse of compulsory land acquisition: an enquiry into the way forward. Working Paper No. 209. Centre for Development Economics, Department of Economics, Delhi School of Economics. URL: http://www.cdedse.org/pdf/work209.pdf
Swain T (2014) Development and displacement in Odisha: a study of anti-POSCO movement in Jagatsinghpur District. Odisha Rev 90–97. URL: http://www.orissa.gov.in/e-magazine/orissareview/2014/Feb-March/engpdf/91-98.pdf
Times of India (2015) 35 years on, compensation eludes Srisailam dam evacuees. Times of India. URL: http://timesofindia.indiatimes.com/city/hyderabad/35-years-on-compensation-eludes-Srisailam-dam-evacuees/articleshow/47169791.cms
Times of India (2008) 85% of Bengalis back nano project. Times of India. URL: http://timesofindia.indiatimes.com/india/85-of-Bengalis-back-Nano-project/articleshow/3438391.cms
The Hindu (2006) SEZ: land acquisition process set in motion. The Hindu, Andhra Pradesh. URL: http://www.thehindu.com/todays-paper/tp-national/tp-andhrapradesh/article3033844.ece
The Land Acquisition Act (1984) As modified up to the 1st Sept 1985. Ministry of Law and Justice. Government of India, New Delhi
The New Indian Express (2014) Land acquisition invalid if compensation not paid to owner: SC. The New Indian Express, New Delhi. URL: http://www.newindianexpress.com/nation/Land-Acquisition-Invalid-if-Compensation-not-Paid-to-Owner-SC/2014/01/28/article2023170.ece

The Right To Fair Compensation And Transparency In Land Acquisition, Rehabilitation And Resettlement Act (2013) The Gazette of India. Ministry Of Law and Justice (Legislative Department). Government of India, New Delhi

Wahi N (2015) The fundamental right to property in the Indian constitution. Available at SSRN: http://ssrn.com/abstract=2661212 or http://dx.doi.org/10.2139/ssrn.2661212

Williams A (2009) Examining the current abuse of the doctrine of eminent domain. Lethbridge Undergrad Res J 4(1)

World Bank (2013) Operational policy 4.12: involuntary resettlement. World Bank, Washington, DC

Wex Legal Dictionary, Legal Information Institute (n.d.). Just compensation clause-fifth amendment. Cornell University Law School

Yerramilli S (2016) The difficulty of justifying eminent domain: The Indian scenario. Der öffentliche Sektor—The Public Sector 42(1):92–99. URL: http://oes.tuwien.ac.at/sektor/periodical/pageview/1345504

The Cyclical Interaction of Institutional Constraints to Formal Affordable Housing Market in Raipur, India

Padmini Ram

Most countries have a housing problem in some form,[1] and all nations, regardless of their orientation towards free markets or central planning, have adopted a variety of housing policies. The production, consumption, financing, distribution, and location of dwellings are controlled, regulated, and subsidised in complex ways. Compared to other economic commodities, housing is perhaps the most tightly regulated of all consumer goods (Hårsman and Quigley 1991).

Even radical proponents of a minimalistic state concede that the market mechanism cannot by itself set all the rules of the game. It does not bring about the preconditions for its own functioning, such as the rule of law, a guarantee of private property, or contract enforcement. Another need for regulation arises because informal consensus about what the 'rules of the game' are, does not guarantee how they are interpreted in specific cases (Berner 2000). Institutions structure behaviours and exchanges in markets, they therefore often serve as a constraint in such markets. However, in addition, they can stimulate actions by providing predictability by creating stable expectations of the behaviour of others. By imposing form and consistency on human activities, institutions both constrain and enable markets.

Raipur, the capital of Chhattisgarh, presents an interesting case for the study of how institutions constrain the market as it is the only state in India to have completely privatised the housing sector. When this failed to create the desired market, public provision of affordable housing (AH) was reinstated.

The State privatised the housing sector and disbanded the state Housing Board in 2002 to stop what was seen as a market distortion and to allow private builders to service the demand. However, the private builders who invested in housing catered

[1]Even if not of the same magnitude or nature, relating specifically to people on low incomes gaining access to adequate housing.

P. Ram (✉)
Department of Land Economy, University of Cambridge, Cambridge, UK
e-mail: padmini.ram@cantab.net

S. Pellissery et al. (eds.), *Land Policies in India*, India Studies in Business and Economics, DOI 10.1007/978-981-10-4208-9_8

for higher income segments.[2] The result was a surplus of higher priced housing while AH was in acutely short supply. In 2004, the state realising the gravity of the problem regarding AH, re-created the Chhattisgarh Housing Board (CGHB) to focus on the housing needs of the urban poor.[3] CGHB (2007) claims to have created more AH stock in three years than was created in the region in the preceding thirty years. Since 2008, CGHB has won several national awards[4] for its performance. However, the housing stock remains grossly inadequate. With 39% of its urban population living in slums, Raipur is listed among the top-ten cities in India with a million-plus population and high proportion of slum households (Census 2011).

The demand for affordable housing aimed at EWS/LIG households is seemingly robust. The number of applications for the government built houses is much more than the number of dwellings available, and the screening for eligibility is a lengthy process. At times, the CGHB has had to call in police to control the restive crowds who had queued up to file their application. The number of eligible applicants is usually many times higher than the number of houses available, and hence, the housing is allotted on a lottery. If a large family (brothers living together with their families) needs, and can afford two adjoining houses, they are not able to buy such housing because of lottery allotment. To understand this better, about 125,000 households are living in slums of Raipur (GTZ ASEM 2010), and as reported by the government officials in their interviews, so far government agencies have been able to build no more than 5000 dwellings a year. So it would take 25 years to house all slum households if the population were to remain constant. Monitor Deloitte, in its industry report on *State of the Low Income Housing Market in India* (2013) claims: As per well-accepted industry (housing and real estate) metrics, a typical household[5] can afford a house up to forty times their monthly income. Using this metric, these segments (LIG/EWS) can afford to buy a house between Rs. 6–10 lacs (USD 11,000–18,000)[6] and Rs. 4–6 lacs (USD 7300–11,000) respectively.

The government is keen on securing private sector participation. Industry reports (Agarwal et al. 2013) concur that affordable housing in India is an economically viable and a potentially large market. "Given current land and construction costs, it is possible for private builders to build houses at these price-points [Rs. 4–6 lacs] and cater to a housing market of 13–15 million units which is potentially worth Rs. 8.5–9.5 lac crore (USD 155–170 Billion)". However, a report (2007) published by Chhattisgarh Housing Board (CGHB) states: "*Private sector builders receive full*

[2]High income group (HIG) and mid income group (MIG).

[3]The Economically weaker sections (EWS) and low income group (LIG) as defined by the government of India are herein referred to as the urban poor.

[4]Assocham Excellence Award 2014 for its Special Contribution to Low Cost housing, HUDCO award for its remarkable work in fields of environmental management and energy efficiency through green building concept, EPC World Award 2012 for Affordable Housing, HUDCO Award for Best Practices to improve the Living Environment 2011–12.

[5]Housing Affordability has to be always measured on a sliding scale as two families with the same income but with different family size might not have the same affordability.

[6]1USD = Rs. 55.

encouragement from the Government. However, it was observed that the private sector, driven by concerns for return on investment, focuses on the top-end of the housing market. They have little or no interest in the low end."

Given the high demand and low supply, why have the private developers stayed out of the affordable housing sector in Raipur? Is it merely a case of economic non-viability? This chapter reports on the institutional constraints to an affordable housing market in Raipur. Employing a theoretical framework of New Institutional Economics (NIE), it uses the concept of institutions, property rights and transaction cost to explain the cyclical interaction of these constraints. The data for this chapter comes from multiple sources, including primary research in Raipur conducted from January to September 2012. It includes surveys of households living in slum areas, interviews with builders/developers and facilitators associated with the provision of housing in Chhattisgarh. Secondary sources include government documents and published reports.

After this brief overview of the case, the following section will discuss the theoretical concepts of institutions, property rights and transaction costs. The third section will discuss the institutional constraints to an affordable housing market in Raipur. The final section will conclude the chapter assessing the effects of these interactions, and will highlight some important points to consider when designing policies for regulating an affordable housing market.

1 Institutions, Property Rights and Transaction Costs

1.1 Institutions

Institutions are viewed in terms of "their capacity to satisfy the functional needs of the community (Knight 1992)". North (1990) says that they reduce uncertainty by establishing a stable (not necessarily efficient)[7] structure to human exchange. Institutions can be both formal and informal. Some institutions get formally institutionalised into written rules and organisations, such as those included in the formal legislation governing the production, exchange and consumption of a product (in this case housing). Informal institutions could be social norms like caste and class divisions which organise a particular society and determine the housing patterns. These are some examples of societal norms which have economic implications and influence economic choices, not necessarily in a 'rational' manner, certainly not in the sense used in mainstream economic theory. Behaviour can sometimes be imitative or habitual (Greif 2006). Even when it is rational, 'rationality' could mean different things to different people (Ensminger 1996).

[7]North here was responding to Demsetz, who posited that institutions evolve so as to produce conditions for steadily increasing economic efficiency. North disagreeing with Demsetz, clarifies that vested interests can prevent movements towards greater economic efficiency.

The interests, even the vested ones, could vary and not be limited to just economic interests. They could be cultural, ideological and/or political.

Formal institutions are easier to change than informal institutions, which are "self-enforced, in the sense that no external authority is available to guarantee that social actors will follow them" (Knight 1992). They are self-stabilised, decentralised and hence deep rooted. If and when the formal institutions are weak (such as ambiguous rules, job descriptions or terms of reference) informal institutions are relied upon to extend that understanding. Ensminger (1997) reveals the reconciliation or 'fit' between formal and informal institutions as the key to the success of public policy. She makes her point by providing evidence from Africa (Kenya) where kinship determined land rights and 'altering property rights meant re-defining social relationships'. Therefore, it is important to understand the context in which institutions operate before making any policy recommendations.

This requires that rules and the policies are in keeping with what the members of the society[8] consider just and fair and that the organisations safeguarding it are trustworthy. However, if the authority is corrupt and policies are implemented ignoring cultural preferences (or, as in some cases, if they are a colonial inheritance), evasion becomes commonplace.[9] A natural outcome to this is a complex regulatory system with high enforcement costs.

1.2 Property Rights

Property rights govern the use of resources (Ensminger 1996). "What is exchanged among parties is a bundle of rights that measures various attributes of the good and services exchanged (North 1986)." It is important to recognise that 'rights' are the product of the 'rules' and thus not equivalent to the rules. Property Rights, as used in NIE is a broad concept. It is wider than the legal concept of property rights and includes social norms (Eggertsson 1990). Categorising[10] it as follows, Eggertsson (1990) provides instances where two or all three of the categories can blend:

1. The rights to use an asset, including the rights to transform physically or even destroy an asset,
2. The rights to earn income from an asset and contract over the terms with other individuals,
3. The right to transfer permanently to another party ownership rights over an asset (e.g. to sell or donate).

[8]There might be considerable dissent among the members of the society.

[9]See Pellissery et al. (2016), for a study on how rent-seeking interests engineered through the nexus of politician-realtor class have legitimised evasion of rules as the norm and driven regulatory changes with regards to planning laws in Bangalore.

[10]Based on the ancient Roman property law principles (usus, fructus, and abusus).

It is the value of the rights that determines the value of what is exchanged (Demsetz 1967) therefore restriction on rights that shrink the set of permissible uses will lower the economic value of an asset (Eggertsson 1990). The value of the right also depends on the enforcement characteristics. The cost of enforcing these rights is reduced when the social norms coincide with the basic structure of the rights that the state seeks to uphold (ibid). The government must play an essential role in enforcing contracts. Therefore, property rights must also include the political process, the state, and the way in which institutional structure specifies and enforces property rights (North 1986).

These rights can be formal (i.e., captured in constitutions, statutes, or regulations) or informal (i.e., norms of behaviour). So long as people respect them, both formal and informal property rights can work effectively.[11] However Boudreaux (2005) cautions that there is a very real risk that reforms enacted in the name of property rights will fail if policy makers employ the rhetoric of property rights (such as giving away titles), but do not weigh how property rights function in the real world.

1.3 Transaction Costs

Allen (2000) after an exhaustive literature review narrows the concept of transaction cost down to two categories: *Transaction Costs #1: The costs of establishing and maintaining property rights*—the costs of policing and enforcing agreements, while implicitly recognising the threat of appropriation or theft. *Transaction Costs #2: The cost resulting from the transfer of property rights*—costs in exchange—because parties to exchange must find one another, communicate and share information. There may be a necessity to inspect and measure goods to be transferred, draw up contracts, consult with lawyers or other experts and transfer title.

Compliance with a complex system of regulations in a bureaucratic set-up with low enforcement increases both kinds of transaction costs (#1&2). This makes the system inaccessible and prohibitive to all but a few privileged groups (Berner 2001). Blaming "an outmoded system of legal property", De Soto (2000) found that grassroots property arrangements "openly contradict the official written law", which his research claims is because the "written law is not in harmony with the way their country actually works". His research in several developing countries established that the obstacles to entering the legal property systems are so daunting and expensive that few could ever make their way through the red tape.

If the cost of the transaction is too high, such that the production costs plus transactions costs are greater than the sale price of the commodity, a market cannot

[11]However, "if private property rights are not viewed as being legitimate or are not enforced adequately, de jure private property becomes de facto open access" (Feder and Feeny 1995).

operate.[12] In housing, slums and squatter settlements represent such a breakdown. Quoting from UNCHS statistics, Berner (2000) mentions that in the large cities of the developing world, between 30 and 70% live in irregular settlements and nearly 85% of the new housing stock is produced in an extra-legal manner. Here we examine how high transaction costs might be affecting the system.

2 The Case Study

This study explores why the formal private sector does not cater to the AH market in Raipur. The usual answer—that it is not sufficiently profitable—ignores the institutional structure of markets and how they affect the market outcomes. Therefore, an alternative theoretical approach was taken: if the institutions were different, it is possible that the market outcomes would be different. Hence, the hypothesis: *Existing institutional arrangements act to prevent the emergence of the affordable housing market in Raipur.*

The sub-headings used in this section refer to the activities which are hindered by the identified institutional constraints.

2.1 Credit for Purchasing the House

The current institutions make it difficult for a low-income household to get formal credit, and its non-availability is undoubtedly one of the biggest[13] demand constraints. Credit for incremental house construction or repairs is more readily available in the informal credit market. However, there are two major problems with informal credit:

1. It is only available in small amounts, so it cannot be used to buy a house in the formal market. Even for major repairs, the person has to borrow from multiple sources to cover the cost.
2. Credit from money lenders usually has a very high-interest[14] rate, which means that households cannot afford long-term loans from them.

Lack of necessary documents for identification, proof of address and of a source of income which can be verified on paper, mean that the EWS/LIG households living in the slums are unable to access loans in the formal credit market. India does

[12]It will begin with several transactions being perceived as 'too costly' that do not take place. Over the years, the system will either revamp itself, or result in a system failure.

[13]The biggest reported constraint being non-availability of affordable housing.

[14]Simple interest of 60% per annum.

not have a unique identification number for its citizen yet. In the absence of such a system, alternative ways of providing a credible identity and proof of address can be considered. The difficulty in getting credit manifests as ineffective demand among low-income households, which was a reported supply constraint.[15]

The Reserve Bank of India (RBI) categorises housing amongst the six priority sectors and has mandated that 40% of a bank's disbursals cater for mortgages. However, in spite of this, lending to the lower segments of the society (loans of up to Rs. 5 lacs) constituted just 22.75% of the total lending to housing sector in 2010 (Cushman and Wakefield 2014), and almost all of the mortgages are likely to have been taken as part of the government housing schemes for the EWS/LIG. This is because most households who need small loans of less than Rs. 5 lacs, and are not formally employed, do not have access to formal credit.

The facilitators were largely of the view that the government could reduce the regulatory guidelines for lending to the EWS/LIG, as it has done on numerous occasions for rural residents. For rural residents, a letter from the head of the village council establishing the identity and proof of residence of the person in the village is accepted by the bank for lending purposes. However, there were a few who were in favour of the present rules to control indiscreet lending. New forms of risk assessment for credit are being advocated by Monitor Group (Deb et al. 2010) in India. In this, the evidence on which the banks rely is collected through a more qualitative field-based approach that involves detailed interviews with the customer and their neighbours, and observing them at their business to get an estimate of the average cash inflow and outflow. The objective is to triangulate and benchmark estimates to build a database of the incomes of informal sector occupations in different localities. The banks themselves, while acknowledging the potential size of a mortgage market for low-income housing, are sceptical about such alternative methods because of high processing costs.

Having the money to pay for their deposit and the monthly instalment, but not having access to formal credit, is fuelling both the informal credit market and, in some ways, an informal land market. Not having access to formal credit and lack of avenues for investment encourages risky investments in the informal land market. People engage in such deals being fully aware that the transaction is not legal; that property claims cannot be challenged in a court of law, nor can disputes be settled legally. This is partly because they see other people in the neighbourhood profiting from such deals, and in part because of the good salesmanship of the broker [*dalal*].[16]

---

[15]For more details on the supply constraints to affordable housing market in Raipur, refer Ram and Needham (2016).

[16]For details of how the informal land and housing market works in Raipur refer Ram and Needham (2016a).

2.2 Trust in Real Estate Dealing

This constraint is rather wide-ranging. The slum households had heard rumours of people being cheated and losing "their entire life savings", and were deterred by such stories. While the informants realised that stories of informal dealing did not necessarily apply to the formal market, they did not have much faith in the formal system either. If the house was not delivered in a state that was promised, they feel that they would not have the wherewithal and the confidence to defend their claims in a court.[17] Possession of a certified document does not always provide them with the necessary sense of security about their investments. However, they have greater confidence in houses built by government agencies and are not averse to buying them.

The builders often construct a model house, set a price for it, and then start taking bookings for the project using the model house as an example. This happens two or three years before the commencement of the actual construction. However, because of delays in approvals,[18] labour shortage, and price rise, they are not able to keep to their promised price, and that gets reflected in either the quality of the house or price escalation, sometimes both. The government builders, because of the subsidy, are in a better position to deal with such cost increases. While the private builders attributed such issues to a challenging business environment, most facilitators tended to agree with the perspective of EWS/LIG, accusing the private builder of less than honest trade practices. This, in their opinion, justified the need for the lengthy approval process and periodic checks even after the approval had been granted. It is hard to assess whether the checks are indeed conducted, or whether they are signed off by accepting bribes without due process, as no builder would admit to his building being signed off without proper inspection. This issue of distrust, on the one hand, deters EWS/LIG living in slums buying from the private builders, and on the other hand, clearly raises transaction costs because of lengthy approvals.

2.3 House Hunting

Most households[19] reported their inability to go house-hunting as one of the demand constraints. Indeed, verifying that a property is free of dispute, fulfils their needs, and is affordable is a time-consuming task. Most of the EWS/LIG

[17]While there is a requirement for builders to meet a certain standard, the monitoring and enforcement of such standards is often times lacking.

[18]Even when the planning permission is granted for the entire project, the building permission is given in stages. For example: the building has 6 floors planned, the layout is approved fees charged for all 6 floors, with the permission to construct 2 or 3 floors. After the construction of 3 floors, a fresh application has to be put into seek permission for building the remaining floors.

[19]183 out of 211 respondents.

households surveyed in slums work in the informal sector with no paid leave or job security; leaving their job to go house-hunting would not only result in loss of income, but it might also even mean losing their job.

The builders were of the opinion that the difficulties with house hunting are due to the absence of a formal affordable housing market. Most builders said they would advertise and operate booking offices in the slums that are open in late evenings to service their clients, and even organise transport for site viewings; ensuring that their potential customers are aware of their supply and have a chance to view it.

The government facilitators had varying opinions. There were some who said that EWS/LIG living in slums, like everyone else looking for a house, will have to make time and effort to secure a home that meets their needs. Others mentioned that it would not be a daunting task for government agencies building homes to run advertisements in slums or even a bus service; high demand for affordable housing currently warrants no such need. The constraint was stated as an effect of not having enough housing stock, as scarcity increases the time required for the search.

2.4 Getting Approval to Build

Transaction cost with regard to real estate development was analysed in terms of the time taken to get the approvals for building construction. A timeline of the approval process was charted, starting with the registration as the first step.

The total time, as estimated by each builder interviewed, was 18–26 months. The consensus was that the builders who were politically connected, or had more resources to spend on bribes, could get the approvals in about 18–20 months, while those lacking such resources could only get the approvals in about 24–26 months.

The builders clearly view the delays as a constraint. Some[20] believe that corruption significantly exacerbates delays, others,[21] while accepting corruption as a problem, consider the delays to be caused largely by a complex of issues such as bureaucratic hurdles, resistance to change, red tape, stockpiling of rules and regulations, too many departments controlling housing, and most importantly an inefficient and inadequate workforce in government. The builders perceive neither the current regulations as fair/justified nor the imposing authority legitimate. Their perception of the government authorities is that of a rent-seeking, corrupt and inefficient system that lacks clarity of purpose and coordination among its various departments. There is considerable trust deficit between the private builders and the government [bureaucrats and politicians]. This was especially evident in the reluctance of builders to deal with the government. When asked if they would prefer that the government could act, perhaps, as an intermediary, buying the houses and selling them to the families under some guarantee, the standard view

[20]7/30 builders (23.3%).

[21]11/30 builders (36.6%).

was that it would be good to have a guarantee, but they would rather not deal with the government.

The government facilitators, accepting the timeline as being realistic, defend the procedures as necessary, and delays as unavoidable. They are of the opinion that the procedures are required to check, process and control private interests. Mahadevia et al. (2009) highlight similar issues in the supply of land for government agencies in India, where, in most cases, clearance for land acquisition is hard to obtain because the land is under litigation. By the time the clearance certificate is available, the costs of construction would have increased, and the rates on which the tender was awarded would be outdated.

Delay in approvals acts as a constraint because it gets translated into cost for the final buyer. This cost can be in terms of the interest accrued on the loans taken out to cover the costs of land purchase or construction, bribes and fees involved in actually getting the approval, or the hours and manpower involved in office visits and waiting time in the lobbies (opportunity costs). While this cost can be borne by MIG and HIG housing sectors, it can render LIG/EWS housing non-viable.

2.5 *Buying the Completed Building*

Corruption increases the transaction cost incurred when buying and registering the sale of the house. The EWS/LIG households[22] mentioned the registration of property as expensive, largely due to bribes. While most people had never attempted to register a property, their perception is not baseless. Studies on corruption and bribery faced by slum dwellers in India suggest that the problem[23] is acute, rampant and worsening (Paul and Shah 1997; CMS Transparency 2012; Hugi 2012; Panchu and Rastogi 2013).

Property owners in India often resort to strategies, such as, evading registration or using long-term leases, transfers under court decrees, and cooperative housing, to avoid property tax. Because of such practices, approximately 90% of the total time spent on registering property in India[24] is spent in verifying that the property is free of dispute. Moreover, according to the report, for the remaining 10% (approximately) of the time, one would have to spend 55 days and 10.6% of the property value, and complete five procedures to register (transfer) the property under one's name. The report mentions "backlogged caseloads" and "lack of staff" as the

[22]165 out of 211 households.

[23]The CMS study (2012), found that three out of every four slum dwellers claimed they were asked to pay a bribe to receive at least one of the following three public services: distribution of food rations or free kerosene; healthcare; and municipal services such as public sanitation and waste removal in the 12 months prior to the survey. About 35% of slum dwellers reported that they have been denied services at least once because they could not pay a bribe.

[24]Average for the cities sampled by the study.

leading causes of delay which pushes the prices up. The costs[25] include stamp duties accounting on average for 70% of all costs incurred,[26] registration and legal fees, and payments to the brokers (World Bank 2009). As mentioned earlier, registering the land is only the first of several steps to be taken before the builder gets the building permission.

With the global interest focusing on emerging markets, the World Bank had started rating the developing countries on the ease of doing business in the country. The rating depends on the number of steps involved, and days it takes to complete processes, such as starting a business, dealing with construction permits, registering property, getting credit, paying taxes, enforcing contracts. In 2014, India was ranked 134 among a list of 189 countries, which indicates that the transaction cost regarding the time and resources spent to get through the bureaucratic steps is considerable. After corruption and bribery (which have not been accounted for in the WB report) are factored in, the system is simply not feasible for the urban poor.

2.6 The Building Industry—Taxation Regulations

The recommendations of the Working Group on Construction Sector (2011) are that high taxation at both the input stage (construction material, equipment and land and services) and at the process stage (work contract tax), along with the sectoral classification and definition of construction industry as 'Industry' as well as 'Service' for taxation purposes, are supply constraints and need to be addressed. This is in agreement with the findings of this study. The working group recommendations have not been implemented yet.

Property owners and builders resort to strategies to avoid property taxes, such as evading registration or using long-term leases, transfers under court decrees, and cooperative housing. Such practices, while legal, contribute further to the already muddled land administration and cadastral system in India.

2.7 Credit for the Builders

The construction industry's lack of easy access to institutional sources of finance serves as a major supply constraint. The Working Group on Construction Sector for Planning Commission for 2012–17 reported that small contractors who lack a

[25]Does not include the time taken; time taken was separately calculated as number of days.

[26]The stamp-duty varies from 12.5% of the property value (Kochi) to as low as 3% (New Delhi). It is 4.8% in Mexico.

Fig. 1 Loan outstanding in real estate sector in India (2012–13)

strong financial base and access to any institutional support execute over 90% of all construction works. A majority of these contractors employ their own funds or borrow money from the market, at the rate of 30% p.a. or higher, leading to higher project costs and therefore higher costs of production (2011).

The issue described by the builders as 'high-interest rate' is related to the under-lending. Both factors are mutually reinforcing, which makes it difficult to identify the primary cause (if any). For example, high-interest rates deter builders from taking bank loans. This results in under-lending. Under-lending, along with high Non Performing Assets (NPA),[27] lead to banks having high operating costs, which they cover by setting high-interest rates. This leads to further under-lending by these banks. To take another example, banks with a large existing stock of NPA naturally attract more public scrutiny. This makes their loan officers adopt a more conservative stance, leading to under-lending (Banerjee et al. 2003).

Banerjee et al. (2003) further found results that provide "definite evidence of very substantial under-lending with some firms clearly having the capacity to absorb much more capital at high rates of return". While their study considered firms in various sectors, the RBI's data estimates that the credit deployment by banks to the construction sector in India has been 2.3% of the total industry credit deployment during 2012–13, and has been in the range of 2.5–3.5% in the last five years. This study cannot assess what the portion of credit deployment for construction and real estate sector should be in India. However, in comparison to other countries, India's credit deployment (or loan outstanding) to the real estate sector is well below 9% (see Fig. 1) (Cushman and Wakefield 2014).

[27]A non-performing loan is a loan that is in default or close to being in default. Many loans become non-performing after being in default for 90 days, but this can depend on the contract terms.

2.8 Government Supply Affecting the Housing Market

Currently, government agencies provide subsidised housing to EWS/LIG.[28] This poses a risk for the builders, who wonder if there would be enough demand for similar property at the regular market price. Mostly, the facilitators agreed that the government provision depresses the 'regular' market price, reducing the return to private builders. However, the facilitators consider this to be serving as a check for the private sector "greed". Some were "surprised" it be seen as a check, given the government provision serves only a fraction of the demand.

Some academic studies support this view. Sengupta and Tipple (2007) refute the assumption that public sector interventions hold back the private housing sector. They are of the opinion that housing need in cities of developing countries is so enormous that the private housing market is neither threatened nor undermined by investments in public housing. Giving a corollary to their argument, they state, that the housing market's predominant actor has been, and will remain, the private (both formal and informal) developers and that the issue of 'control' over housing market does not arise. Giving the example of Kolkata, they state that a large market to house the city's over 15 million people is needed. This certainly points towards the enormous potential for both private and public housing providers to operate in the market without threatening each other's existence and continuation.

2.9 Restrictions on Selling the Dwellings

Under current arrangements, if the builders are to construct EWS dwellings on 15% of their land that is reserved for the purpose, an additional constraint is that they are not allowed to sell them on the open market. The allotment process through the collector's office is another source of delay. While the facilitators agree that the system of checks is not perfect, they still feel that the check needs to be in place when the housing stock is so low.

There were also cases reported by the facilitators, where the builders were given the permission to sell the LIG houses in the open market by accepting an affidavit from the buyer regarding their income levels. The requirements of the house were based on minimum criteria, in terms of area (500 $ft.^2$) and basic amenities. The government assumed that the builders would follow the bare minimum requirements and that no one other than the slum dwellers would be interested in living in such small homes. The government did not fix the sale price in this case. The builders instead built high-class studio apartments following the area requirements

[28]Sengupta and Tipple (2007) have documented a similar story of the public housing agencies in Kolkata which seem to be operating on market principles; even where they are not involved with private partners, the public housing agencies are in the market to make profits (even if they don't call it profits), like any other real estate developers, rather than building for low-income people.

and sold them to students from wealthy families. The students would sign an affidavit of earning within the specified limits.

2.10 Accumulation of Regulations

The lawmakers are constantly trying to plug the loopholes with small amendments, and this results in the accumulation of regulations which are beyond the capacity of the government to monitor and enforce. Low levels of monitoring and enforcement mean builders see these laws as challenges to be surmounted rather than rules that need to be followed. Some government officials reported that it is the same with the slum dweller who, being aware of the low monitoring capacity, tries to maximise the benefit he gets from the government. The rules tend to be followed on a selective basis, specifically where chances of getting caught are high, and the penalty is higher than the cost of following the regulation. For example, a builder might not dare to start a construction project without due approvals even if it takes two years to get the approval, but having acquired the approvals he changes the plans internally with the hope that it goes un-noticed.

Complicated accumulated regulations in an environment of insecure property rights and low overall enforcement increases the transaction cost for both the builders and the government (in terms of resources needed to police, monitor and implement the system), rendering the affordable housing market too costly to operate.

3 The Cyclical Interaction of Constraints: Institutions (Regulations), Property Rights and Transaction Costs

This study has identified several institutional constraints to the demand for and supply of affordable housing in Raipur, and some of these such as access to land and credit, as well as lengthy approval process, are mentioned in industry and government reports on affordable housing in India (see Table 1).

However, in contrast to what the above studies say or imply, these constraints cannot be addressed in isolation as they are not independent of each other. There are many instances of interdependence. Credit is a demand constraint; however, it leads to a supply constraint of ineffective demand. Another example is of public provision of housing lowering the market price of such housing. Lack of access to credit among the EWS/LIG households in slums, who can afford to pay for housing, leads to a vibrant informal land market. Moreover, being cheated in informal land markets can lead to low confidence in the real estate sector in general.

Table 1 Institutional constraints as listed in other reports

S. No.	Title	Published by	Year	Constraints identified
1	Housing: The Game Changer—Leading to double digit GDP growth	Cushman and Wakefield Research Publication	January 2014	Tedious and prolonged regulatory processes, land, banking and funding problems, manpower and technology problems
2	Housing Microfinance in India: Benchmarking the status	Access-Assist Research Publication	December 2013	Credit and housing finance
3	State of Low-income Housing Market: Encouraging Progress and Opportunity to Realise Dreams of Millions	Monitor-Deloitte Consulting	July 2013	Credit, land, lengthy approval process, rising construction costs, project delays due to labour issues, insufficient transparency on maintenance charges later
4	Task Force Report on Promoting Affordable Housing	Ministry of Housing and Urban Poverty Alleviation, GoI	November 2012	High taxation, lengthy approval process, land, credit, funding for builders
5	Affordable Housing in India: An Inclusive Approach to Sheltering the Bottom of the Pyramid	Jones Lang LaSalle	October 2012	Identification documents for slum dwellers, credit and flexible mortgages, land, density measures, dispute redressal mechanisms
6	Affordable Housing in India: Needs and Emerging Solutions	Escale Responsible	December 2010	Land, credit, lack of profit under current circumstances
7	Making affordable housing work in India	RICS and UK Department of Trade and Investment	November 2010	Inconsistent and fragmented government support, land, infrastructure, need for increasing the density measures
8	Micro-mortgages: A macro opportunity in low-income housing finance	Monitor Inclusive Markets	October 2010	Credit and housing finance
9	Building Home, Financing Homes: India's rapidly growing housing and housing finance markets for the low-income customer		July 2010	
10	Special Residential Zones: A viable and compelling solution to India's affordable housing crisis	CREDAI	August 2009	Land, lengthy approval process, high taxation, lack of infrastructure
11	Market-Based Experiences in Low-income housing in India	Monitor Group	May 2009	Construction Finance for builders

Discussing the constraints using the theoretical concepts of—institutions (regulations), property rights, and transaction costs, the study indentified the following institutional constraints (on both supply and demand sides) to an AH market

1. Insecure property rights affect the ability of the EWS/LIG living in slums to secure credit for buying the house due to lack of proof of address. Also, it lowers their trust in real estate dealings and makes house-hunting difficult due to insecure employment.
2. Insecure property rights increase transaction costs because of the time needed to verify that the property is free from dispute. High transaction costs facing builders/developers are also the result of the lengthy approval process, bribes and high taxation policy as well as complex regulations that cause avoidable delays.
3. Accumulated complex regulations reduce the enforcement capacity of the government. This combination of complexity and uncertainty of enforcement further feeds the cycle of insecure property rights that increase the transaction cost.

The point that needs to be highlighted is that the constraints are not isolated, but interact with and influence other constraints. As shown in Fig. 2, the influence is multidirectional which makes it hard to establish a cause-effect relationship in designing public policies to tackle the causes. Such an interaction reinforces the

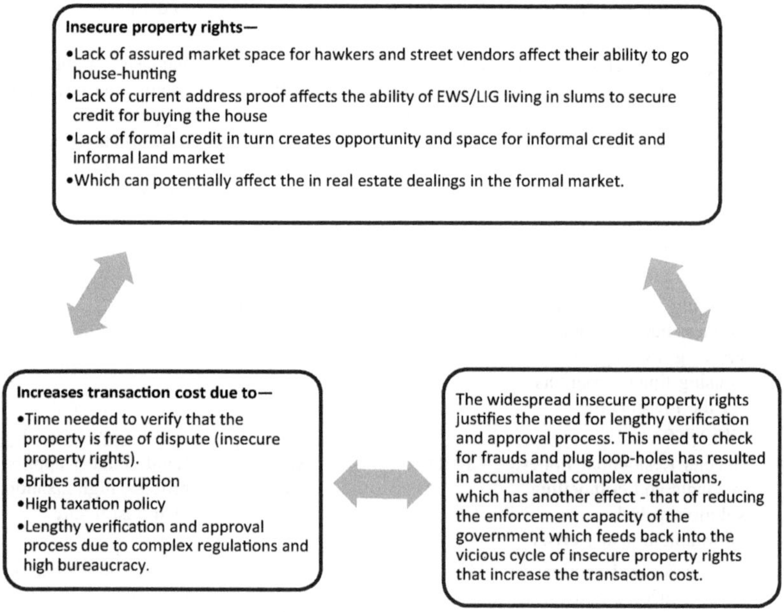

Fig. 2 Cyclical interaction of the constraints

status-quo. These constraints are part of the social structure in which the market operates. Therefore, while there are some constraints which are more binding than the others, they cannot be addressed in isolation.

4 Conclusion: Challenges for Public Policy on Affordable Housing

The above discussion on the institutional constraints has argued that high transaction cost, insecure property rights and complex regulations contribute considerably towards making formal affordable housing inaccessible to the urban poor and unviable for builders. They could not build the housing at a cost which would make it affordable, not because of costs of construction and land, but because of institutional constraints, government agencies who build AH and sell them below market prices thus affecting the market; high interest rates on loans (forward financing); fear of ineffective demand due to EWS/LIG households not being able to access credit. Apart from these, high transaction costs because of lengthy approval process, dual taxation, bribes and corruption raise the cost of building AH. Lack of secure property rights adds to the time taken to verify that the property is free of dispute. Regulations call for allotment (not sale) of EWS dwellings and limit the density of housing, which further fuels the scarcity of developed land. Therefore, it is argued that *existing institutional arrangements act to prevent the emergence of AH market in Raipur.*

These constraints are often the result of complex institutional arrangements; therefore, solutions which would work in a different institutional context might not work here. For example, the issue of credit cannot be resolved just by setting up institutions which supply loans at low-interest rates. In the case of the slum survey in Raipur, the monthly instalments for the mortgage were based on current (2012) market rate of 12%, and many households could afford to buy at that interest rate. Slum households who could afford to buy did not need interest subsidy. They were, however, unable to access loans because they did not have proof of identity and address. The constraints are not just related to each other; they are connected to the other components of the system. For example: while lowering taxes is desired to facilitate an affordable housing market, it would affect the government's revenue stream. Such decisions, therefore, need to be taken after making a comprehensive socio-economic cost-benefit analysis.

Any policy on creating an affordable housing market has to take into account (a) that existing institutional structure is constraining the affordable housing market in many ways, some more binding than others, and (b) that the constraints are interrelated. Because these institutions are connected to each other in complex ways, it is both difficult and inappropriate to isolate the institutions. Unlike other studies which focus on individual key constraints as being critical, it is vital to understand the relationship between the institutional constraints.

References

Agarwal A, Jain V, Karamchandani A (2013) State of the low income housing market: encouraging progress & opportunity to realize dreams of millions. In: Monitor Inclusive Markets, India. Deloitte Touche Tohmatsu India Private Limited (2013)

Allen DW (2000) Transaction costs. In: Bouckaert B, De Geest G (eds) Encyclopedia of law and economic, vol 1: The history and methodology of law and economics. Edward Elgar Publishing Limited, Cheltenham, pp 893–926

Banerjee, A.V., Cole, S., & Duflo, E.: Bank financing in India. A tale of two giants: India's and China's experience with reform and growth. International Monetary Fund and the National Council of Applied Economic Research (India), New Delhi (2003)

Berner E (2000) Informal developers, patrons, and the state: institutions and regulatory mechanisms in popular housing. In: ESF/N-AERUS Workshop 'Coping with Informality and Illegality in Human Settlements in Developing Cities'. Leuven

Berner E (2001) Learning from informal markets: innovative approaches to land and housing provision. Dev Pract 14(1)

Boudreaux K (2005) The role of property rights as an institution: implications for development policy. Mercatus Center at George Mason University

CGHB (2007) Housing revolution in Chhattisgarh: 3 years of Chhattisgarh Housing Board. Chhattisgarh Housing Board, Raipur

CMS Transparency (2012) Press Release 7 Dec 2012—CMS-India corruption study 2012: expanding slums & growing corruption. Retrieved 21 May 2014, from CMS India: http://www.cmsindia.org/PressReleaseCMS_ICS_2012.pdf

Cushman & Wakefield. (2014). *Housing: The Game Changer leading to double-digit GDP growth.* Cushman & Wakefield Research Publication

De Soto H (2000) The mystery of capital. Black Swan, London

Deb A, Karamchandani A, Singh R (2010) Building houses, financing homes: India's rapidly growing housing and housing finance market for the low income customer. Funded by First Initiative and Supported by the World Bank, A study commissioned by the National Housing Bank, India. Monitor Inclusive Markets

Demsetz H (1967) Toward a theory of property rights. Am Econ Rev 57(2):347–359

Eggertsson T (1990) Economic behavior and institutions. Cambridge University Press, New York

Ensminger J (1997) Changing property rights: reconciling formal and informal rights to land in Africa. In: Drobak JN, Nye JV (eds) The frontiers of new institutional economics. Academic Press, San Diego, pp 165–196

Ensminger J (1996) Making a market: the institutional transformation of an African Society. Cambridge University Press, Melbourne

Greif A (2006) Institutions and the path to the modern economy: lessons from medieval trade. Cambridge University Press, New York

GTZ ASEM (2010) Slum Profile [Raipur]. Alchemy Urban Systems (P) Ltd. (Alchemy), Bangalore Consortium for DEWATS Dissemination (CDD Society) Bangalore, CEPT Research & Development Unit (CRDU), Ahmedabad. Report commissioned by GTZ for RMC, Raipur

Hårsman B, Quigley JM (1991) Housing markets and housing institutions in a comparative context. In: Housing markets and housing institutions: an international comparison, pp. 1–29. Springer, Netherlands

Hugi A (2012) Transitions—India: Fighting graft at the grassroots, Sept 13. Retrieved 21 May 2014, from Foreign Policy: http://transitions.foreignpolicy.com/posts/2012/09/13/india_fighting_graft_at_the_grassroots_0http://transitions.foreignpolicy.com/posts/2012/09/13/india_fighting_graft_at_the_grassroots_0

Knight J (1992) Institutions and social conflict. Cambridge Univeristy Press, Cambridge

Mahadevia D, Joshi R, Sharma R (2009) Working paper 2: approaches to the lands for the urban poor. Centre for Urban Equity

North D (1990) Institutions and a transaction-cost theory of exchange. In: Alt JE, Shepsle KA (eds) Perspectives on positive political economy (Chap. 7). Cambridge University Press, Cambridge, pp. 182–94

North D (1986) The New institutional economics. J Instit Theoret Econ (JITE) 142(1):230–237

Panchu S, Rastogi A (2013) The battle between corruption and governance in India: strategies for tipping the scale. In: Cisse H, Menon NM, Segger MC, Nmehielle V (eds) The world bank legal review, vol 5: fostering development through opportunity, inclusion, and equity. The World Bank Group, pp 381–398

Paul S, Shah M (1997) Corruption in public service delivery. In: Guhan S, Samuel P (eds) Corruption in India: agenda for action. Public Affairs Centre, New Delhi, pp 144–163

Pellissery S, Chakradhar A, Iyer DK, Lahiri M, Ram N, Mallick N, Kumar N, Harish P (2016) Regulation in crony capitalist state: the case of planning laws in Bangalore (21 June 2016). Der öffentliche Sektor (The Public Sector): planning, land, and property: framing spatial politics in another age of austerity, vol 42, No. 1, pp 110, 2016. Available at SSRN: http://ssrn.com/abstract=2798748

Ram P, Needham B (2016) The provision of affordable housing in India: are commercial developers interested? Habitat Int 55(July):100–108

Ram P, Needham B (2016a) Why is public policy for affordable housing in India changing so slowly: explaining Institutional Inertia, environment and urbanisation, Asia, Special Issue "Towards HABITAT III: Housing and Sustainable Urban Development", 7(2):177–195

Sengupta U, Tipple AG (2007) The performance of public-sector housing in Kolkata, India, in the post-reform Milieu. Urban Stud 44(10):2009–2027

WIEGO (n.d.) Street vendors in India. Retrieved 18 Feb 2014, from women in informal employment: globalizing and organizing (WIEGO): http://wiego.org/informal_economy_law/street-vendors-india

Working group on Construction Sector for Planning Commission (2012–17) (2011) Report of the working group on construction for the 11th five year plan (2012–2017). Government of India, New Delhi

World Bank (2009) Doing business in india. World Bank and the International Finance Corporation, Washington, D.C.

City in Crossfire—The Environment Versus Development Debate in Navi Mumbai

Aparna Vedula and Sarika Bodhankar

Abbreviations

CIDCO	City and Industrial Development Corporation of Maharashtra limited
CRZ	Coastal Regulatory Zone
CZMP	Coastal Zone Management Plan
HTL	High Tide Line
LTL	Low Tide Line
MCZMA	Maharashtra Coastal Zone Management Authority
MIDC	Maharashtra Industrial Development Corporation
MoEF	Ministry of Environment and Forests
MR&TP Act	Maharashtra Regional and Town Planning Act
MRSAC	Maharashtra Remote Sensing Application Centre
NTDA	New Town Development Authority
NDZ	No development Zone
NMDP	Navi Mumbai Development Plan
NMMC	Navi Mumbai Municipal Corporation
PIL	Public Interest Litigation
PWD	Public Works Department
RPZ	Regional Park Zone
SPV	Special Purpose Vehicle
NCZMA	National Coastal Zone Management Authority
SRA	Slum Rehabilitation Authority

A. Vedula (✉) · S. Bodhankar
City & Industrial Development Corporation of Maharashtra (CIDCO) Ltd., CBD Belapur, Navi Mumbai, India
e-mail: aparnaown@gmail.com

S. Bodhankar
e-mail: sarikabodhankar@gmail.com

S. Pellissery et al. (eds.), *Land Policies in India*, India Studies in Business and Economics, DOI 10.1007/978-981-10-4208-9_9

1 Introduction

Triggered by the Bhopal gas tragedy, environmental protection discourse in India was channelized into the articulation of an overall protective legal instrument. Protection of air, water, land and other elements which surround human life became the foremost priority and the law enabled separate instruments to protect these elements. However, when put to practice these instruments often idolize the "environment" as an absolute entity in need of in toto preservation while the perspective of conservation is ignored. India has seen a steadily increasing growth of urbanization leading to the twenty-first century, when, in its history the highest percentage of its population is living in its cities. Provision of housing, urban services and a balanced built up in the environment is perhaps a higher challenge than protecting the environment. Moreover, the "environment" in need of protection being an absolute entity often exceeds the gamut of the natural environment. This coupled with the fact that many cities have started their journey prior to the promulgation of the environmental law, leaves them struggling to strike a balance between environment protection and urban development. In this paper, an effort is made to understand the deadlock between two sets of legal instruments, pro-environment and pro-development and how it is about to dismantle a city.

2 Environmental Protection Act, 1986

The Environment Protection Act of 1986 is a landmark legislation which brought together the environmental concerns of the country into a coherent whole and flagged off active protection and improvement of the natural environment. It was the first enabling legal aegis formed to take appropriate steps for protection and improvement of the natural environment in its living elements including human beings, plants, animals and other living organisms as well as the non-living elements which are crucibles of ecosystems, like water, land and air. Enabling provisions to prevent damage and destruction to the environment, to prevent from pollution are the cornerstone of the Act.

In the very first chapter, the Act defined the pollutants and the "Hazardous Substance" and its "Handling". Hazardous substance means any substance by reason of its physic-chemical properties or its handling, is liable to cause harm to living creatures, plants, microorganisms, human beings and the environment. The general and particular tenor of the definitions indicates that pollutants are products of industrial activity and hazardous substances thus generated are to be handled in an appropriate manner as set forth in the Act. Also, the term "occupier" is defined as that of industrial premises.

True to its raison d'être, the Act enabled execution of the nationwide programme for prevention, control and abatement of environmental pollution, laying down standards for the quality of the environment, standards for emission or discharge of environmental pollutants. More importantly, it facilitated the setting up of National and State-level mechanism/bodies for controlling the air, land and water pollution, in the manner of pollution control boards. The Act further spawned rules for maximum allowable limits of concentration of various environmental pollutants including noise, the procedures and safeguards for the handling of hazardous substances and importantly, the prohibition and restrictions on locations of industries and carrying on of processes and operations. The Act made provision to take samples of air, water, soil and other substances from the factory premises for the purpose of analysis. It also specifies remedial measures if the discharge of any environmental pollutant is in excess of the prescribed standards. It enabled the installation of adequate infrastructure for analysis of samples, the formation of the report and punitive actions towards contraventions of its provisions. But the overarching orientation of the act, as is evident is the ***protection of the environment from industrial operations, activity, effluents, discharge of waste***.

3 CRZ Notification, 1991

The stated purpose of promulgation of the Coastal Zone Regulations (CRZ) 1991, was the identification of Coastal Stretches and imposing restrictions on industries (location), operations and processes in the CRZ.

The Notification declared the coastal stretches of seas, bays, estuaries, creeks, rivers and backwaters which are influenced by tidal action (on the landward side) up to 500 m from the High Tide Line (HTL) and the land between the Low Tide Line (LTL) and the HTL as Coastal Regulation Zone.

The notification defines and enabled demarcation of the dividing line between land and water which is the High tide line which is defined as the line on the land up to which the highest water line reaches during the spring tide. The notification emphasized uniform demarcation of HTL in all parts of the country. It classified the CRZ into four categories in the following manner.

3.1 Category-I (CRZ-I)

(i) Areas that are ecologically sensitive and important, such as national parks/marine parks, sanctuaries, reserve forests, wildlife habitats, mangroves, corals/coral reefs, areas close to breeding and spawning grounds of fish and other marine life, areas of outstanding natural beauty/historical/heritage areas, areas rich in genetic diversity, areas likely to be inundated due to rise in sea level consequent upon global warming and such other areas as may be declared by the Central Government or the concerned authorities at the State/Union Territory level from time to time.

(ii) The area between the ***Low Tide Line and the High Tide Line***.

3.2 Category-II (CRZ-II)

The areas that have already been developed up to or close to the shoreline. For this purpose, "*developed area*" is referred to as that area within the municipal limits or in other legally designated urban areas which is already substantially built up and which has been provided with drainage and approach roads and other infrastructural facilities, such as water supply and sewerage mains.

3.3 Category-III (CRZ-III)

Areas that are relatively undisturbed and those which do not belong to either category-I or II. These will include the coastal zone in the rural areas (developed and undeveloped) and also areas within Municipal limits or in other legally designated urban areas which are not substantially built up.

3.4 Category-IV (CRZ-IV): Coastal Stretches in the Andaman and Nicobar, Lakshadweep

It emerges from the classifications that CRZ-I areas are part of the sea or tidal water body in constant inundation and CRZ-IV areas are specifically defined geographical locations, it being unclear whether it is land or water body or both. Noteworthy is that "*mangroves*" (without specifying the size or density of growth) were deemed CRZ-I, which means effectively that the land underneath is part of the water body, creek or unlike these two categories, CRZ-II and CRZ-III are clearly, areas on land along the coast and include and legally designated and defined extents of urban areas, some parts which are substantially developed (more than 50% of plots are developed) and other parts are waiting to be developed. While prohibiting activity on CRZ, the notification understandably prohibits new industries that are hazardous industries, dumping of untreated industrial or urban waste or effluent. While it prohibits these generically in the CRZ without specifying categories, it can be construed that it is actually according to highest protection via prohibition to the CRZ-I and IV categories. This is where it digresses from core spirit of protection from industrial pollution, but understandably pollution of coastal waters from urban untreated waste is a cause worthy of intervention. However, while describing the permitted activities, it intends to permit "construction" activities but only those which require foreshore or waterfront. Arguably, all activities in urban areas, e.g. residential, commercial, leisure would choose to be at the seafront though they may not "*require*" it. When seen in combination, the definition and permitted activities in CRZ-II and II (the "*land*" categories), make a crucial move to control urban development in the coastal land. In legally designated urban areas or cities, areas already developed are directed to freeze in time and adhere to the quality(land use) and quantity (buildability or FSI) of development as provided for in the Development Plan prevailing on the date of notification of the Regulations (February 1991). Moreover, it decrees that lands waiting to be developed are CRZ-II where only green spaces and temporary tourism structures can be constructed. In one stroke, this regulation overruled the legally approved instrument of the city development plan and eroded the power of mandated city development authorities to make a plan, update and upgrade plan according to changing needs of the city, have uniform policies in coastal and non-coastal parts of the city and develop cities in a phased manner. It completely looked away from the fact that some cities have made those plans or made investments on those lands prior to the CRZ Notification or its mother Act.

4 CRZ Notification 2011

When the CRZ 1991 notification was revised and upgraded in 2011, the objectives underwent a shift from the earlier preventive tenor of industrial location, operations and processes to the following:

- To ensure livelihood security to the fishing communities and other local communities living in the coastal areas;
- To conserve and protect coastal stretches and;
- To promote development in a sustainable manner based on scientific principles, taking into account the dangers of natural hazards in the coastal areas and sea level rise due to global warming.

Though sustainable development was introduced in the objective, there was no change in the prohibited or permitted activities, and these were made applicable to a generic concept of CRZ without specifying the "land" or "water" categories. There was a sea change in the definition of High Tide Line (HTL), which the notification stated: "will be governed by the distance up to which the tidal effects are experienced which shall be determined based on salinity concentration of 5 parts per thousand (ppt) measured during the driest period of the year". This new criterion swept aside the earlier concept of bund or site formation or a physical barrier being the dividing line between land and water and introduced a value of salinity coupled with tidal action to decide the line. This definition took the High Tide Line deep inland into lands wherever there have been man-made breach of bunds or other site formations which constituted the HTL 1991. The Same phenomenon was seen in man-made water bodies subject to tidal action being connected to the sea/creek, which was now to be considered as part of the natural water body.

As in the earlier one, the new notification considered land under mangroves in the category of CRZ-I, and in addition, stipulated that in case mangrove area is more than 1000 m^2, a buffer area of 50 m shall be provided. This was perhaps in deference to a High Court Order in 2005. Without any specification of density, it was not clear how a 1000 m^2 mangrove area was to be defined. If we imagine a scenario that four single mangrove plants are occupying four corners of a square-shaped land of 1000 m^2 area, would it entail a circle of 50 m radius around each of them as a No-development Zone or a buffer zone? Or a buffer of 50 m width is to be provided around the 1000 m^2 land? This movement of creek CRZ-I into the land due to the new definition. Also increased the length of the HTL and thereby put a much larger area under development frozen in the standards of February 1991. Also, land that has become saline due to man-made reason was deemed to be lost from development.

5 Hon. Bombay High Court Order (2005) on Protection of Mangroves

In 2004, two writ petitions took up the concerns of destruction of ecosystem along 720 km coastline of Maharashtra, They also mentioned that there is a considerable presence of mangroves in the creeks, which offer protection against not only the sea advancing into land but also natural disasters like tsunami. Understandably, mangroves played an important role in ecosystem and mangroves had to be preserved, and the petitioners made specific mention of certain stretches along the seafront in Mumbai. The Court then passed an order to prevent destruction and ensure conservation and rejuvenation of mangroves in the entire state of Maharashtra in the following lines:

(a) The State to map mangroves with the help of high-resolution satellite images and superimpose same on city survey maps. The state agency MRSAC to carry out such mapping.
(b) Destruction of mangroves will be a punishable offence and administrative/police officers of rank of collector/SP respectively shall act upon complaints from citizens in this regard.
(c) Dumping of debris/garbage on mangroves shall be prohibited.
(d) No development permission shall be issued in “area under mangroves”.
(e) All area under mangroves shall be declared as “forest” and governed under Forest Conservation Act 1980. Govt. owned land under mangroves shall be declared as ***protected forest*** and handed over to state Forest Department.
(f) All impediments towards the flow of seawater/creek water into mangrove area shall be removed.

This order prevented routine repair of bunds which separated developable land from creek water. This helped mangroves to grow inland and claim more land under “creek” every day. Also, the artificial water bodies, components of area drainage system, started losing their hydraulics capacity due to a vicious cycle of siltation and mangroves infiltration. Ponds could not be desilted due to fear of destruction of mangroves and now have almost lost their capacity. The Court issued further notifications in 2008 and 2010 and directed agencies involved in the development of infrastructure and city in general, to seek clearance through Notice of Motion. This pertained to "area under mangroves" and a 50 m NDZ around it. For any development in this area, seeking development permission from competent authority and leave of Court in this regard was stipulated.

One such case in point is in Dronagiri Township which has six holding ponds. CIDCO moved notice of motion (***PIL 87 of*** 2006, ***Bombay High court Order, 6th Oct.*** 2005) towards desilting. When the notice of motion was moved, the Court consistently involved the Petitioner of the original Writ petition of 2008 and directed that all developmental steps to be taken only upon mutual dialogue and consent. The petitioner/experts, however, took a staunch and clear stand that there was no physical need and legal base to clean holding ponds and cut mangroves therein. The Courts conceded that this was a mixed matter of law, implying that environment and development were at loggerheads. The matter was then referred to the MoEF and till date remains unresolved.

6 Mangroves, CRZ, Court Order and Dilution of Mandate

1. The Court order started from the CRZ notification which considered mangroves as a creek, even a single mangrove, and, in addition, accorded 50 m wide no development zone around it.
2. This was dissociated from the geographical/natural context of the mangroves. If the mangroves happened to grow on land, by accident, such land is to be considered creek or water. The mangroves being continuously growing and spreading entities have been bestowed with powers to "manufacture" environment.
3. The breach of bunds, due to human intervention, artificially induced creek water and mangroves into land in Navi Mumbai. The Court order furthered these interventions by stopping repairs of bunds so as not to impede the flow of water. This is a complete departure from the protection of a natural water body and a deviation from the very basis of the Environment Protection Law.
4. Allowing only the development that is found acceptable to the petitioners in disputed cases amounted to the dilution of the powers of the development authority while it remains saddled with its responsibility.

7 The Maharashtra Regional and Town Planning Act of 1966

Urban Development being a state subject respective states have promulgated suitable facilitative legislation in this regard. ***The Maharashtra Regional and Town Planning Act of*** 1966 ***(MR&TP Act)*** is a watershed legislation promulgated in Maharashtra a decade after attaining independent statehood, and about two decades after national independence. It was coterminous with the formation of Regional Planning Boards and has stratified planned urban development into three tiers. These are the Regional Plan (the regional context of a metropolis, predominantly economic plan with strategic infrastructure decisions), the Development Plan (for a metropolis or town, a predominantly physical plan with financial support framework) and the Area Plan (local area level detailed physical plan). This was a pioneer Act which was subsequently emulated by other States.

The Act facilitated a gamut of choices in the manner of urban development, with varying degrees of state intervention at varying tiers traversing the macro, the meso and the micro levels of plan. For example, New Towns, and Industrial Towns are maximum intervention models at the meso-level (Development Plan) while the Town Planning Schemes (Micro level, local area plan within the DP), promote a medium degree of intervention. The elaborate institutional framework supporting each tier and each model has been the hallmark of the Act.

In the mid-forties, the New town movement originated in England and spread to most parts of the world. This was a mode of development where the state by statute, compulsorily acquired land under the entire town or city as proposed in the plan, from private owners, to build the city. The development of the city was in itself a cause-célèbre and the entire city was considered a public purpose. This provided a wide canvas for generous provision of public infrastructure and offered more options for housing, industry or employment. Post-independence, the early industrial towns of India were built in the same model, a host of steel cities, Bhilai, Bokaro, Durgapur and Rourkela and a famous state capital, Chandigarh are examples. The movement continued into the sixties and seventies when few capital cities like Gandhinagar, Noida, were built.

In keeping with the spirit of movement, the MR&TP Act, 1966 dedicated one whole chapter to this maximum intervention model of city development, the New Town, detailing the institutional framework to plan and implement this almost sanctified entity. The whole being a public purpose reservation, the very day the extent of the city is notified to public, the New Town Development Authority empowered to plan and build the city, is also declared. Coterminous with declaration and delineation of a 344 km^2 site for Navi Mumbai, born out of strategic/regional/metropolitan planning decisions, City and Industrial Development Corporation (CIDCO) was formed as a special vehicle (under the Companies Act 1956) as its New Town Development Authority. The Act compelled the Govt. to acquire all the land and vest unto the NTDA, CIDCO, and also vest it with intricate powers to take all technical and administrative decisions to build the city.

By 1992 about 108 km^2 area within this was developed and handed over to the Navi Mumbai Municipal Corporation (NMMC) formed under the Bombay Provincial Municipal Corporation Act, 1949 (Act LIX of 1949). Apart this and certain area under MIDC, and the Municipal Council Boundaries of Panvel and Uran, CIDCO is responsible for planning, development and maintenance of physical infrastructure like roads storm water drain, water and sewage treatment and other systems. It is also responsible for planning development and disposal of plots of social infrastructure like schools, colleges, hospitals, community facility and other plots of residential and non-residential uses. However, it still continues its NTDA function in 108 km^2 of municipal area wherever there is vacant land.

8 Navi Mumbai—A New Coastal Town

In the year 1970, the Govt. of Maharashtra decided to create a counter magnet across the Thane creek to decongest Mumbai and address many of its urban problems through the facilitation of better livable urbanscape in terms of housing, social and engineering infrastructure. This city, created and developed through the complete acquisition of land was suitably named as New Bombay or Navi Mumbai. Land under 95 villages was notified and acquired in phases. Navi Mumbai, planned as a conglomeration of 14 nodes or townships with a present population of nearly 2 million, in keeping with its core objective has become an alternative metropolis to Mumbai. It has successfully grown into a destination providing planned and livable built-up environment free from the usual urban stress resulting from scarce resources and ever-mounting population figures.

8.1 The People's New Town—Public Investment

The entire 344 km^2 designated area was declared as a public purpose or a "reservation" and the Government intended to acquire all private lands within city limits. Value addition to raw land through infrastructure provision, the sale of developed land and investment of sale proceeds into further infrastructure development was the approach adopted by this fully self-financed city. The self-financed development model, which has been able to tap the market potential through the sale of a portion of the plots through tender, has been able to create a large plethora of public facilities including a large stock of affordable public housing (Fig. 1).

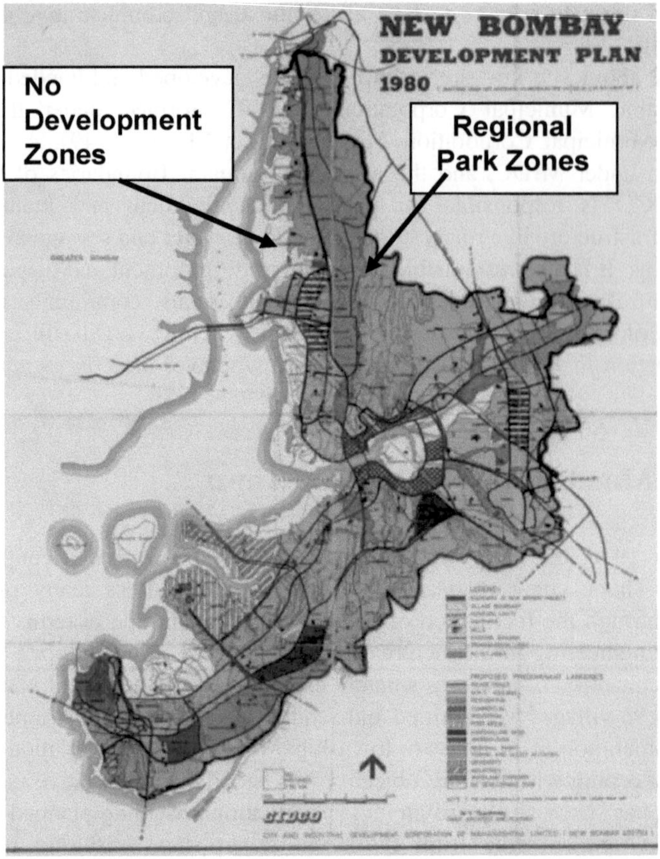

Fig. 1 Navi Mumbai Development Plan, 1980

8.2 Pro-environment, Before Time

There were two key environmentally sensitive features in this city, the creeks and the hills. In 1975 when the Navi Mumbai Development Plan (NMDP) was submitted to the state Govt. for sanction, it not only identified two crucial aspects of the environment, but also made provision within the development plan for much-needed protection of these features. The hills were designated as Regional Park Zone with sparse and predominantly green development and the creek front was designated as No Development Zone (NDZ), with no development permitted thereupon. This proactive articulation of environmental concern in the NMDP preceded the Environment (Protection) Act 1986 and Coastal Regulation Zone notification 1991 by 10 and 15 years respectively. The NDZ of NMDP delineated based on existing bunds, is akin to CRZ-I of 1991. A total 32% of the gross area of the city is dedicated to low intensity and green use of land. The NMDP was accorded sanction by the State Government in 1979 (CIDCO 1979)

8.3 *The Vulnerable Creek*

Out of 344 km^2 gross area, nearly 10%, i.e. 36 km^2 comprising of Intertidal land was kept aside as "No development Zone" (NDZ) in 1975. About 5 km^2 was added in terms of CRZ-I when the Chief Hydrographer of India delineated the High Tide Line (HTL) for the city under the 1991 notification based on existing bunds. Today the NDZ area stands at 36 km^2 nearly half of which, i.e. about 15 km^2 consisting of natural coastal mangroves is handed over to State Forest department for protection. Moreover, being a planned city, all effluent, sewage or solid waste generated from the phased development are treated and managed in a scientific manner. Therefore, the creek and its ecosystem are effectively immune from the development in the city.

9 The Unique Geomorphology—Navi Mumbai

Navi Mumbai notified area land is positioned lower than the creek level at high tide and was traditionally separated from the creek by indigenous bunds and gates which were created and operated by villagers who carried on agriculture, salt cultivation and shallow water fishing on the landward side. To bring the level of this landmass to a level higher than the creek at high tide would have required a high quantum of the landfill which would have entailed cutting of hills and excavation of earth on a large scale. Instead, the Dutch method of reclamation was adopted by CIDCO, where the design level of the landfill is lesser than the creek level, and storm water is drained through an elaborate system of detention ponds, diversion channels and holding ponds, while retaining and strengthening most of the indigenous bunds which separate creek from land (Fig. 2).

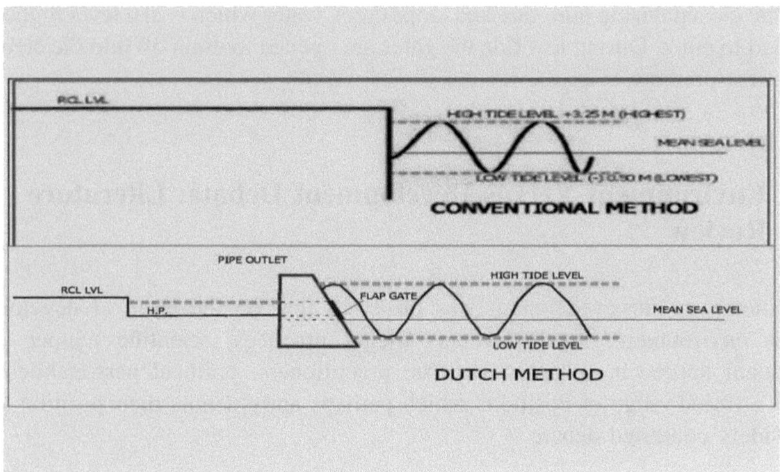

Fig. 2 Schematic section: methods of reclamation

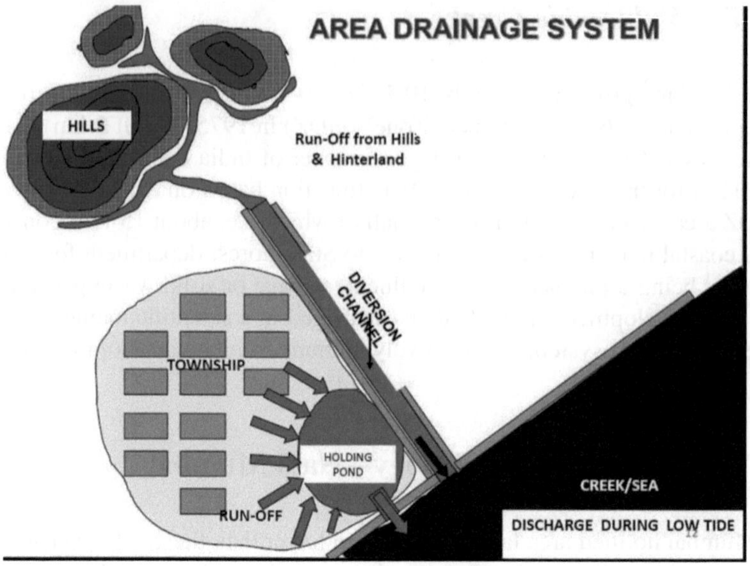

Fig. 3 Navi Mumbai drainage system: a concept

The creek at high tide has a level of 3.25 m whereas the average level opted for in Navi Mumbai is 2.25 m. For draining storm water two simultaneous systems are used in Navi Mumbai. The runoff from the hills is detained in ***detention ponds*** at foothills and the overflow diverted directly into the creek through ***diversion channels***. For surface drainage of the urban area, artificial channels carry storm water into holding ponds which drain into the creek through flap gates. The holding ponds are designed to hold water for four hours during such times when high tide and storm prevail together. The Flap Gates are designed as one-way valves so that they are closed during high tide and stops creek water which is at a level higher than the land to enter. During low tide the gates are opened to drain off into the creek due to reverse pressure (Fig. 3).

10 Environment Versus Development Debate: Literature Review

Literature was surveyed and it was observed that on the issue of development versus environment, legality versus illegal practices, scientific temper versus emotional approach, scholars, experts, practitioners, political personalities have taken a varied range of positions which perhaps aptly denote their position within the widely contested debate.

The World Commission on Environment and Development (WCED) (UNEP, Environment for Development,) recognized many years ago that the environment, economic and social issues are interlinked. It recommended that the three be integrated into development decision-making. In defining sustainable development, the Commission acknowledged the need for both intra- and intergenerational equity —development that meets not only today's human needs but also those of more people in the future. It also factored in that, changing drivers, such as population growth, economic activities and consumption patterns, have placed increasing pressure on the environment and that serious and persistent barriers to sustainable development remain. Environmental degradation is therefore undermining development and threatens future development progress. While it accepted development as a process that enables people to better their well-being, it felt that long-term development can only be achieved through sustainable management of various assets: financial, material, human, social and natural. Non-sustainable use of natural resources, including land, water, forests and fisheries, can threaten individual livelihoods as well as local, national and international economies. The WCED is of the view that alternative development paths that protect the environment are available. Human ingenuity, resilience and capacity to adapt are powerful forces from which to draw to effect change, and reconcile the debate between environment and development. The core belief which emerged from this position is the need to balance between environment and development.

The sustainable development goals (SDG) that emerged from the UN conference in 2012 at Rio is an ambitious set of goals that emerged from UN conference in 2012 at Rio is an ambitious set of goals with balance at its core. Climate action, life below water, life on land, sustainable cities and communities, sustainable consumption and production are five among a total of 17 Goals which pledges to uphold the balance between natural and built-up environment, to take cognizance of the natural systems on land and under water and essentially strike balance between the two. This position too, is that the balance between development and environment is the key to our survival.

In an analysis of the sustainable development goals, Le Blanc (2015) argues that the goals are interconnected and should be seen as a network and the strength of the network will be the key to achieve the right balance between economic growth and the environment protection. In his view, a science–policy interface is essential for this balance and attempts at policy integration in various areas will have to be based on studies of the bio physical, social and economic systems. This view advocates the interface between science and policy to attain the balance between development and environment.

Beder (2002) has argued that in the environment versus development debate, time has come to take an informed stand. He puts forth that the market economic growth or development per se cannot resolve environmental problems and that there is need to find the solution that embraces the ethical dimension of environmental protection in the sustainable development debate. He points out that the Limit To

Growth concept of the 1960–1970s expounded the need to curtail economic growth because this was exhausting the limited resources of the Planet and precipitating a crisis. He iterates that the 1980s saw a new concept surging through namely Sustainable Development, which upheld economic growth while maintaining integrity of ecology. This offered a scope for reconciliation and harmony among the two opposite camps in the environment versus development debate and work towards common goals. He concludes that both the approaches have neglected the ethical dimension and remedy lies in ensuring that the fruits of development are more evenly distributed within population and move away from the notion that any development that provides a net monetary benefit to the nation is justified. This position essentially upholds the quest for a balance along with social equity.

Alexander (2010) upholds the concept of Justice to Mother Earth or Earth Jurisprudence. He argues that existing legal system treat nature as resource to be exploited for human gratification and in the widely accepted "growth" model of progress; economic growth enjoys an unchallengeable consensus. This process of growth is unsustainable and has led to consumption to the point of obliteration of Natural capital. His contention is that when an economy has grown so large that it exceeds regenerative and absorptive earth's ecosystems. Then lawmakers ought to initiate a "degrowth" process. He upholds nature in its pristine glory as priceless and therefore to be kept above the domain of a consumerist society which would like to consume nature as any other commodity. This position is predisposed towards protection of environment in its pristine glory.

India's minister of state minister for environment and forest from 2009 to 2011 Jairam Ramesh (2010) provides an overview of the debate when he talks about "two cultures" and a continuing tension between those who espouse growth and those who call for environment protection. He advocates "balance" between the two where economic growth is propagated under strict caveats from the environment protection perspective while critiquing the ambient practice of the private sector to blatantly violet or bypass the legal template which is often tacitly supported by government, he calls for the need for a much sharply formulated scientific approach which can classify and measure the impact on development on the environment and provide transparent cognizable and calibrated mitigation measures. This position again is one for balance and for a scientific approach towards resolution of contentious issues.

Mumbai-based architect Anita Shyam (2016) takes up a GIS-based study of mangroves along Greater Mumbai coastline and identifies the areas which have undergone deterioration. She also identifies areas under maximum potential threat, she calls for stringent measures for protection of mangroves without addressing the concern that mangroves may have grown into what was land earmarked for development. She calls for strict enforcement of CRZ regulations while lamenting Government apathy, without addressing those aspects of the prevailing legal framework which are not based on science. This position is one inclined towards protection of "environment" per se.

Environmental activists Goenka and Patel (2010) contend that a recent flagship project with Mumbai Metropolitan region moved away from the shared vision of a legal regional plan towards site location and development of the said project based on indulging financial project consideration. He argues that the site selection was done through a non-transparent manner with no environment considerations with disregard to environmentally vulnerable coastal and hill Ecology. He criticizes the methodology adopted in environment Impact assessment study for the project as fundamental criteria for study have been diluted in comparison to international standards. This position laments the lack of balance between the two opposite perspectives.

In his article in a local Mumbai newspaper, Kulkarni (2015) Environmental Expert raises the banner in favour of planned urban development, where the plan has assimilated environment protection as a key concern. He thereafter upholds livable built-up environment as a subordinate concern. He espouses the cause of natural environment to be seen in appropriate context against the development template of planned urban area. This is a position which accords higher priority to development but through a plan discourse.

From the literature survey, it is observed that in the intense debate between environment and development the latter has been almost non-existent in terms of articulation. This necessitates that cases which illustrate this perspective, uphold the complications that arise in the path of legally mandated development due to lack of scientific approach in the formulation of the legal templates in environmental protection, needs to be highlighted. This article tries to illustrate this aspect by means of a live case experience.

11 Environment and Development at Loggerheads

The MR & TP Act, 1966 provides for elaborate institutional framework while implementing a new town. The planning authority or its Board of directors are empowered to decide the technical and administrative approaches and policies to implement a plan approved by the State Government and dispose of land as per govt. approved policy. The Environment Protection Act facilitates the protection of natural environment from the hazardous effects of industry, which in the strict sense of the term does not include general urban development though it may include individual buildings development as a part of real estate industry. The CRZ Notification 1991, rightly defined the high tide line as a bund or physical formation separating land from sea or creek or another water body under natural tidal action. It went ahead and equated such naturally inundated water body, with or without the presence of mangroves, to CRZ-I, which deserved protection in the manner of preservation and conservation. However, on the landward side, it restricted development to 1991 standards in already developed parts of the city as CRZ-II, and in the relatively undeveloped parts waiting for its phase of development as per prevailing legal city development plan; it decreed only green spaces and temporary structure for tourists. It was an act of overriding of the rights of the city authorities to carry out their mandate, to execute an already approved plan under appropriate legislations. It also overruled the citizens' right to articulate their evolving aspirations through the legal instrument of the development plan, to revise and mould it according to the future needs of the city. At this juncture, the right to protect the environment is overarching on the right to develop urban areas in a planned manner. The Notification was perhaps a minor digression from the core spirit of the Environment Protection Act 1986 in the sense that the main aim was to protect from hazards of industrial location, processes and operations.

Navi Mumbai continued in this path of development, by undertaking routine repairs of the bunds defining the HTL 1991 protecting them from frequent breach by villagers. The cycle of breach and repair continued.

At the genesis of the Bombay High Court's order on mangrove preservation in 2005, was the rampant destruction of natural coastal mangroves along the Mumbai coast. This order, followed by other subsequent orders, brought a sea change to the CRZ/mangrove discourse by equating a mangrove with a forest. The mere presence of a mangrove deemed the land underneath as Forest land and necessitated preservation under Forest Protection Act, 1980. This was dissociated from the geographical context and failed to pay heed to whether the land underneath was a creek, affected by the tidal action or purely terrestrial. This dissociation was coupled with a dictum that stoppage of flow of water to the mangroves would be a punishable offence. This is meaningful in case of natural coastal mangroves which are in danger of being bunded and destroyed by reclamation into the water body. But in case of mangroves which have entered the landward side of bund/HTL due to man-made accidental breach, which are thriving on such artificial incursion of creek into the developable land, which is nothing but weeds, this became a curse for development. The Same ban effectively stopped the authority from repairing the flap gates and desilting and removing the mangroves in artificial channels and holding ponds. The holding ponds are silting up every day and inching towards total loss of capacity which would lead to citywide floods. This was a direct assault on the powers of the authority to carry on its legally assigned mandate. Since the mangroves now could grow unabated into the land, the incursion of the creek into land continued and the legal development plan lost a little bit of its jurisdiction every day. These orders were lacking in legal base because the CRZ notification did not equate mangrove with forest land in dissociation from tidally active context. Also, the MoEF allowed context-based departure from provisions of the FC Act, 1980 by allowing the states to continue to implement The Maharashtra (Urban Areas) Protection and Preservation of Trees Act, 1975 and The Maharashtra Felling of Trees (Regulation) Act, 1964, to choose to cut mangroves and suitably manage trees which grew on land kept aside for infrastructure.

The CRZ Notification of 2011 legalized the results of this Order by equating tidal action plus salinity factor and presence of mangroves to a water body which needed protection. The lands lost under artificial ingress were now legally part of creek, as were the components of storm water drainage and a 50 m No development zone around them. The jurisdiction of the city shrunk in size, where right to protect the environment has infringed upon the right to shelter, education, healthcare and inter alia other urban services. The destabilization of the storm water drainage system has made way for infringement into right to life because of the imminent danger of floods in the city. Moreover, now that the HTL has moved inland a much larger area is forced to be developed as per lower standards were frozen in 1991. The population affected thereby, are not only those who are already citizens, who have been successfully brought into the planned New town by the authority in compliance with its mandate, but also the future population who are would come to live, work and enjoy leisure in the city towards which investments have been made.

In combination, the Court Order and the CRZ 2011 Notification have successfully created artificial "environment" by forcing into areas earmarked for urban development and now forcing the city to take its development elsewhere by destabilizing one of its vital infrastructure systems, to protect such "environment". Moreover, the Court has incorporated related petitioners into the decision-making process in this regard, who have no share of the responsibility towards the provision of urban services or development, undermining the powers of the authority mandated under appropriate legislation to carry on development in a manner approved under the same legislation.

12 Balance and Imbalance

In 1996, the MoEF approved the coastal zone management plan (CZMP) of Navi Mumbai which honored the bunds along the creek as the high tide line, in other words, the line dividing land and water, development and nature. The creek was designated as CRZ-I and adjoining land as CRZ-II with restricted development. This helped to strike the balance between environment and development and both charted their simultaneous paths in harmony. This balance was disturbed in 2005 due to the court order and suffered as a major blow in 2011 due to the new CRZ notification.

Navi Mumbai showcases a very interesting case of Environment protection law having moved beyond the geographical extent of the natural environment into the city and usurping rights to development, which is not benefitting the natural environment in any way. Caught in the crossfire between environment protection and development rights, the city is inching towards a standstill, raising a major concern about the fate of planned urban development in coastal areas (Fig. 4).

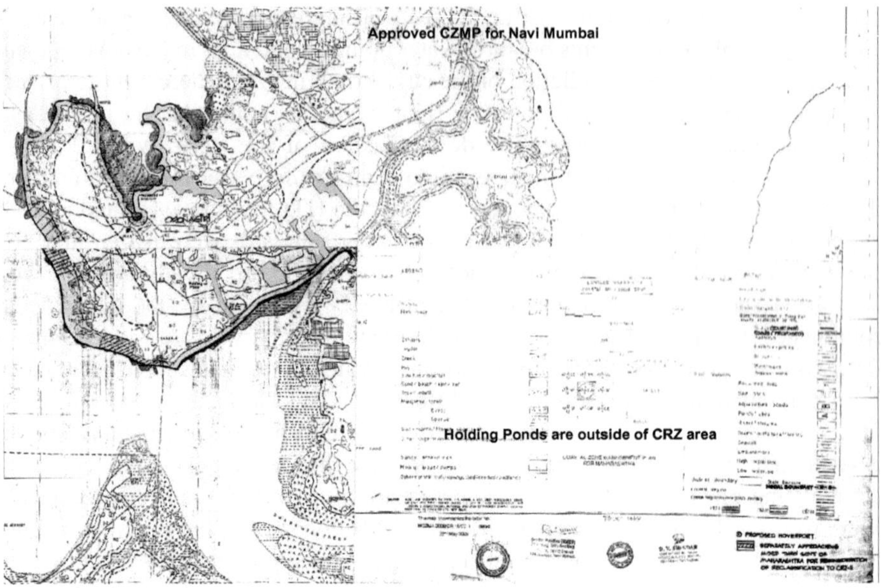

Fig. 4 Approved CZMP 1996: holding ponds are outside CRZ

13 Impact of the Imbalance—Destabilization of Storm Water Drainage System

The storm water drainage system in Navi Mumbai as described earlier is a complex hydraulic system designed to avoid excessive filling of land lower than incumbent creek level at high tide. Ironically most of the components of this system, i.e. the holding ponds and channels have been excavated out of firm land. They do not fall in CRZ-I as per the 1991 definition of HTL, i.e. they are not a part of the creek, while some of them fall in CRZ-II.

There is ingress of saline water in the artificial channels and holding ponds which have an interface of sweet water and saline water. Over the years, due to malfunctioning of Flap Gates, which require routine maintenance, the mangrove seeds made their way into these artificial water bodies and proliferated due to siltation process. Due to the freeze on destruction and cutting of mangroves, the flap gates could not be repaired and desiltation and removal of mangroves could be taken up since 2005 (Fig. 5).

Subsequently, the CRZ Notification 2011 with its new definition of HTL, has decreed that these areas are CRZ-I or part of the creek on count of salinity and presence of mangroves.

Therefore, mangroves cannot be removed; moreover, no development zone of 50 m should be kept around the mangroves. As a result, 675 ha. of artificial water bodies are suffering a loss of capacity up to 80% at present, which may grow to

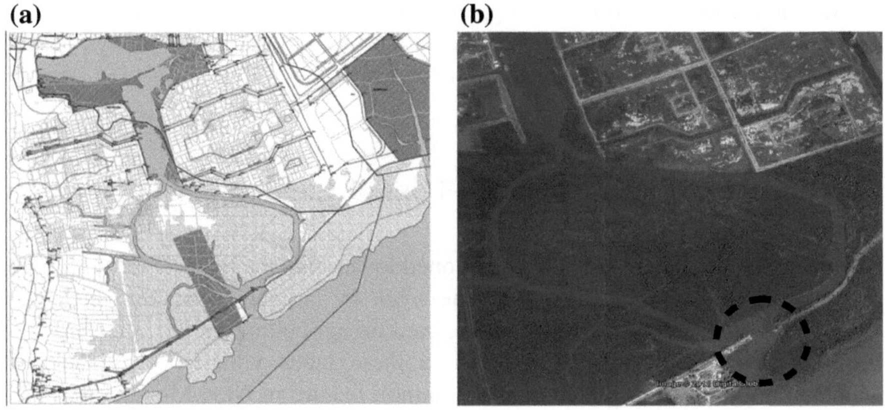

Fig. 5 **a, b** Ingress of saline water into holding ponds and channel-GIS and Google Earth Image

Fig. 6 **a** Malfunctioning of flap gates **b** Flooding in villages

100% since mangroves are an ever-growing entity. This is leading to flooding of surrounding areas (Fig. 6).

Taking the legal recourse offered by the High Court Order of 2005, as mentioned earlier, (***PIL 87 of 2006***) CIDCO had taken out a Notice of Motion to obtain permission to desilt and maintain the holding ponds of Panvel, Kalamboli and Dronagiri townships. Permission for desilting, without mentioning specifically the cutting of mangroves was granted in 2008 for holding ponds at Panvel and Kalamboli, but neither desilting nor of mangroves was allowed in case of Dronagiri holding ponds (High Court order dated: 28/7/2008). For the latter, CIDCO again approached Hon. High Court and in 2013, the Court directed MCZMA and MOEF to decide whether these holding ponds and channels fall in CRZ (implying perhaps CRZ-I of 1991 or CRZ-IV of 2011). The MCZMA submitted their report to MOEF, which is yet to conclude on the issue but is considering that matter under the definition of CRZ-IV in Notification 2011, and looking for five times compensation of such mangroves. Removal of mangroves and restoration of capacity in Dronagiri Holding Ponds are also being opposed by Writ Petitions on the basis of a provision in the notification of 2011. It is apparent that the 50 m buffer zone around the mangroves in these artificial ponds, which are protected and contained by retaining wall would fail to serve any meaningful purpose.

14 Impact of the Imbalance—Loss of Land

Navi Mumbai notified area land is positioned lower than the creek level at high tide and was traditionally separated from the creek by indigenous bunds which were created and operated by villagers who carried on agriculture on the landward side. But when subsequently CIDCO acquired these lands villagers lost interest in maintaining the bunds. Instead, it is a common feature in Navi Mumbai that local villagers puncture bunds and drive creek water inland for shallow water fishing and this resulted in saline water along with mangrove seeds entering in the plotted areas. The routine maintenance of bunds had to be completely stopped due to Court Order which directed not to take any steps that would stop the ingress of water into "areas with mangroves". This effectively stopped CIDCO from repairing of any bunds and propagation of mangroves on land continued unabated. On counts of salinity and presence of mangroves which grow every day, these areas are now considered as CRZ-I or part of the Creek. Navi Mumbai is facing a loss of about 1240 Ha of land. These are lands for which compensation money has been paid while acquiring and developed plots allotted to the projected affected under land-for-land scheme. Navi Mumbai project is unique in its self-sustaining approach to development, wherein sale proceeds from developed land are channelized into further infrastructure and city development. This is a huge loss of public investment considering that in mid-seventies and mid-eighties, land in bulk has been acquired, planned and commitments made in one go, in terms of an integrated physical-cum-economic plan. The loss of land affects CIDCO's commitments to the various land-for-land schemes designed for the project affected, the provision of engineering and social infrastructure as well as its affordable housing programs. On the other hand, loss of land (which is otherwise saleable) is leading to a conservatively estimated financial loss of Rs 37,200 Crores and rendering the development of this self-financed city unsustainable. Effectively, it is leading to the dismantling of the city systems and debilitation of the economics of the city developments.

15 Mangroves: A Sacred Entity?

15.1 Mangroves on Land, Not Creek

The mangroves discussed in the above paragraphs are mangroves are on land. Some of them occupying and growing on land waiting to be developed in the right phase.

Some of them are occupying and rendering dysfunctional the artificial components of storm water drainage, which are carved out from land. It is important to note that all of them are on the landward side of HTL 1991. There is a need, therefore, to distinguish between natural coastal mangroves and the artificially inducted inland mangroves which are unique to the city of Navi Mumbai. CIDCO has already handed about 1471 ha. Of intertidal land with natural coastal mangroves in its possession to the state Forest Department in compliance to the High Court Order to be managed as protected forest under the Forest Conservation Act, 1980, vide ***Notification issued by the Commissioner, Konkan Division, Navi Mumbai, 12th Jan 2007.***

15.2 Legal Provisions Judging the Context of a Forest

While looking into an appropriate approach to manage inland mangroves, it is important to consider the tract of a land on which mangrove plants are found to be growing. On terrestrial areas, trees of species like Tectona grandis (Teak), Terminala tomentosa (Ain), Pterocarpus marsupium (Bija), Adina cordifolia (Haldu), Ougenia dalbergioides (Tiwas), Terminalia chebula (Hirda), Acacia catechu (Khair) are found growing in forests as well as on private non-forest lands. These trees, though belonging to forest species, when existing on non-forest areas, are governed by the provisions under The Maharashtra Felling of Trees (Regulation) Act, 1964, which extends to the whole of the state of Maharashtra excluding urban area. Mangroves have been added to the list (serial no. 16) in the Schedule appended to this Act in 1987. This provision illustrates that merely the presence of a species on a geographic location does not automatically deem the location into a Forest. For urban areas, there is a similar and separate statute named as The Maharashtra (Urban Areas) Protection and Preservation of Trees Act, 1975. Under this Act, a Tree is defined as any perennial woody plant whether in the seedling or sapling stage and includes shrubs whose branches spring from the ground level. The MoEF has clarified in the set of guidelines for the purpose of application of the Forest (Conservation) Act, 1980 (under Chap. 2 titled as submission of proposals under para 2.5) that the land which had been acquired by The Govt. Dept. like railway, irrigation, PWD, etc., for the specific purpose like laying roads, railway lines, canals and the vacant area was planted with trees and those lands were not yet notified as protected forest, will not attract the provision of Forest (Conservation) Act, 1980 for the purpose of widening, expansion or realignment. This provision illustrates that trees of the forest species or otherwise can be managed with due heed to the geographical context where they are growing, the use of land for urban infrastructure and related purposes would supersede the conservation rights of the tree as part of the forest.

The inland mangroves of Navi Mumbai, i.e. those on the landward side of the HTL 1991, are of similar nature as these are plants on lands acquired for public purpose and are not notified as any category of forests.

However, management of these mangroves under trees act may not be practically feasible in urban areas, because complimentary plantation would require intertidal land which may not be available in the required proportions in coastal cities.

16 Way Forward

It is important that balance be restored between the opposite forces of law in the coastal city of Navi Mumbai in particular and all coastal urban areas in general. The following steps are recommended in order to restore such balance:

16.1 The natural physical barriers or bunds or roads, i.e. existing dividing line between the creek and land as per the first CRZ notifications should be considered as the final and sacrosanct division between the domains of natural environment and urban development.

16.2 Tidally affected water bodies to the seaward/creek ward side of the above sacrosanct line, already designated as CRZ-I should be protected from any manner of development. There should be a complete ban on untreated effluent being discharged into CRZ-I from the urban areas. Similar treatment should be given to CRZ-IV areas.

16.3 CRZ-II is by definition developed urban land along the coast. Such land needs to be developed to its full potential considering the changing requirement of the city and its populace, and increase in buildability/FSI on such lands in keeping with rising population growth. It is necessary to rescind all restrictions in CRZ-II with strict enforcement of treatment of effluents going into CRZ-I.

16.4 In the CRZ notification, Zone the CRZ-II area is defined as "area within the existing municipal limits or in other existing legally designated urban areas which are substantially built up and has been provided with drainage and approach roads and other infrastructural facilities, such as water supply and sewerage mains". By this definition pockets of coastal urban land earmarked for future development within the approved city plan are designated as CRZ-III and cannot be developed to their full potential. Moreover, new areas along the coast cannot be opened up for development, i.e. coastal cities cannot extend their boundaries despite tremendous pressure on the existing designated city limits. It is therefore proposed that CRZ-III be abolished.

16.5 Appropriate differentiation between inland and coastal mangroves and separate treatment of the entities are a necessary step. The prevailing order of the courts needs to be vacated upon appropriate policy revision by the MoEF. The inland mangroves once designated should be allowed to be treated as weeds.

16.6 The urban authorities constituted under appropriate legislations should be set free to develop the city as per legal mandate.

16.7 Given the incumbent pressure on large cities, "protected" coastal lands which are pockets of "manufactured" environment cannot be adequately protected and are likely to end up the worst affected with unplanned/unauthorized development. The balance between cause of environment and planned urban development can be restored in this manner.

16.8 The above measures would go a long way to duly protect the natural environment and allow planned urban development to take its legally validated course.

References

Alexander S (2010) Earth jurisprudence and the ecological case for degrowth. J Jurisprud. http://www.jurisprudence.com.au/juris6/alexander.pdf. Accessed 4 July 2016

Beder S (2002) Economy and environment: competitors or partners? Pac Ecol. http://www.herinst.org/sbeder/envpolitics/pacific2.html#.WSrLQtJEmM8. Accessed 5 July 2016

Bombay Environment Action Group (BEAG) vs. The State of Maharashtra & Others (2006) Public Interest Litigation no. 87 of 2006 order dated 12/7/2016. http://bombayhighcourt.nic.in/generatenewauth.php?auth=cGF0aD0uL2RhdGEvb3JpZ2luYWwvMjAxNS8mZm5hbWU9V1AzMjQ2MDQxNTA3MTUucGRmJnNtZmxhZz1OJnJqdWRkYXRlPSZ1cGxvYWRkdD0xNy8wNy8yMDE1JnNwYXNzcGhyYXNlPTI4MDcxNjE0MDk0OA. Accessed 12 July 2016

Bombay Provincial Municipal Corporations Act 1949. (Act LIX of 1949) www.mumbaisuburban.gov.in/borivali/pdf/mmc.pdf. Accessed 15 July 2016

City and Industrial Development Corporation of Maharashtra limited-CIDCO (1979) Report of the Navi Mumbai Development Plan sanctioned 1979 by the State Government of Maharashtra. http://www.cidco.maharashtra.gov.in/NM_Developmentplan. Accessed 2 June 2015

Environmental Protection Act (1986) http://www.moef.nic.in/sites/default/files/eprotect_act_1986.pdf. Accessed 15 Nov 2015

Forest Conservation Act (1980) http://www.moef.nic.in/sites/default/files/Forest.pdf. Accessed 15 Nov 2015

Goenka D, Patel G (2010) The plane truth. Econ Polit Wkly. http://environmentportal.in/files/The%20Plane%20Truth.pdf. Accessed 10 July 2016

High Court of Bombay (2005) Order dated 6th Oct 2005 on Protection on Mangroves. http://bombayhighcourt.nic.in/casequery_action.php. Accessed 19 July 2016

Indian Companies Act (1956) www.mca.gov.in/Ministry/pdf/Companies_Act_1956_13jun2011.pdf. Accessed 10 July 2016

Kulkarni V (2015) Khaarfuti laa Vinaakaaran Daivatwa (Deification of mangroves without reason) Panel discussion organized by newspaper Loksatta, with Hon. Minister of Forests, Maharshtra State, 1 July 2015, Mumbai. Published in the same newspaper

Le Blanc D (2015) Towards integration at last? The sustainable development goals as a network of targets. Working Paper No. 141 ST/ESA/2015/DWP/141 at the United Nations Department of Economic and Social Affairs, UN DESA. http://www.un.org/esa/desa/papers/2015/wp141_2015.pdf. Accessed 3 July 2016

Maharashtra Felling of Trees (Regulation) Act (1964) http://www.bombayhighcourt.nic.in/libweb/acts/1964.34.PDF. Accessed 3 July 2016

Maharashtra Regional and Town Planning Act (MR & TPA) (1966). https://mahadma.maharashtra.gov.in/DmaCmsHomepages/publicdownload/eHg%3D. Accessed 3 July 2016

Ministry of Environment & Forests Govt. of India (1991) Coastal Regulation Zone Notification dated 19th Feb 1991. http://envfor.nic.in/legis/crz/crznew.html. Accessed 2 June 2016

Ministry of Environment & Forests Govt. of India (2011) Coastal Regulation Zone Notification dated 6th Jan 2011. http://www.moef.nic.in/downloads/public-information/CRZ-Notification-2011.pdf Accessed 2 June 2016
Ramesh J (2010) The Two Cultures Revisited: The Environment-Development Debate in India. Econ Polit Wkly. http://www.epw.in/journal/2010/42/commentary/two-cultures-revisited-environment-development-debate-india.html. Accessed 9 July 2016
Shyam A (2016) Impact of development on the mangrove cover in the Mumbai metropolitan region. Architect Time Space People 16(5) (Indian Council of Architecture, New Delhi)
United Nations Development Program (2012) Sustainable development goals Rio 2012. http://www.in.undp.org/content/india/en/home/post-2015/sdg-overview.html Accessed 7 July 2016
World Commission on Environment and Development (WCED) http://www.unep.org/geo/geo4/report/01_Environment_for_Development.pdf. Accessed 7 July 2016

Property Regimes in India: A Study of Political Determinants of Structural Factors

Deepa Kylasam Iyer

1 Introduction

At the heart of land policy in India is a contradiction—the attempt to ensure welfare through land reform and the strategy to promote development through land acquisition. Land is a 'state subject' in India that gives considerable autonomy to sub-national governments to pursue land policies, depending on the historicity, social, economic, geographic and political compulsions. After independence from the British colonial rule in 1947, a national reform objective on land was enunciated in the 1950s.[1] The primary objectives of this framework were extensive land reform that would redistribute land to the tiller, abolish the intermediaries and give the peasants tenancy rights.

Meanwhile land acquisition was governed by a Union law of colonial vintage, the Land Acquisition Act 1894. It was in 2014, that a new legislation called the Right to Fair Compensation and Transparency in Land Acquisition, Rehabilitation and Resettlement Act (RFCTLARR) that overthrew the previous law, came into effect. The stated objective of this law was to meet farmer welfare and economic development through industrialisation. With this law coming to force, the revival of land redistribution, which was the original promise of Indian freedom struggle, remains a bleak possibility. On the other hand, land acquisition which also had a nationalist rationale of 'nation building through publicly owned enterprises' has undergone transformation. The new land acquisition act attempts to accommodate the need of private capital to fuel economic development in a neo-liberal paradigm.

[1]The land policy objective centering on land redistribution was a product of two events: The Karachi Resolution of 1931 and 1936 during the Indian freedom struggle and the recommendations of the JC Kumarappa Committee that looked into agrarian relations in 1949.

D.K. Iyer (✉)
National Law School of India University, Bengaluru 560072, India
e-mail: deepakylasamiyer@gmail.com

S. Pellissery et al. (eds.), *Land Policies in India*, India Studies in Business and Economics, DOI 10.1007/978-981-10-4208-9_10

In this context, it is apposite to look into the original land reform agenda, how it fared in different sub-national units in India and what the political arguments were, that supported it. Such an analysis could explain in parts, why after two rounds of land reform till the 1980s, redistribution still remains incomplete and is not likely to revive as a credible land policy option in India.

Since land reform was left to the sub-national units with only a national framework as directive, there were two related consequences. Primarily, 'reform' was understood differently in different regions of India based on their historicity and political expediency. Consequently, the particulars of reform such as ceiling limit, and conditions and degree of tenure security were widely different in different regions. Some interesting questions emerge from observing what went on during the land reform years in different states of India. For instance, what were the different kinds of land reform responses that emerged out of the Indian sub-national units and what caused them? This paper argues that land reform was largely a product of structural features of political regime, especially its social base. By analysing the structural features of political regimes, there are possibly four types of property regimes that came out of India during this period.

Two qualifiers seem to be in order here. The first is the rationale for studying 'regime' as opposed to any other political unit, which is dealt with in the next section of this paper. The second point is that historicity of property institutions also played a role in determining the implementation of land reform[2] (see Banerjee and Iyer 2005, 2008). My argument is that while historicity determined the *nature* of land institutions in both the erstwhile princely states and colonial presidencies, social base of political regime explained *why* land reform took different forms in two regions with same historical institutions of land. For example, a largely benevolent princely state of Travancore in southern Kerala had already facilitated land reform laws in the region by the turn of twentieth century that encouraged reform-based thinking in the state after it became part of independent India. But the nature of design and implementation of land reform in the state was the product of political variable because political regimes had an acute interest in ordering the rights in a property regime, determined by which social classes were successfully transferring their proximity to power into property rights. Unlike the colonial regime whose interest in land was revenue generation with minimum protest from the natives, the democratically elected regimes had the additional responsibility of welfare of voting classes and Constitutional commitments[3] to adhere to. This made the emergence of property regimes a turf of political negotiation, between organised groups of social classes and castes.

---

[2]For a comparative perspective from other regions, refer Engerman and Sokoloff (2005), Porta et al. (1998), and Açemoglu et al. (2001).

[3]Initially, the right to property was a fundamental right in the Indian constitution under article 31. Many sub-national governments faced contentious litigation from large land owners while they tried to appropriate land for redistribution because of this clause. Eventually, this right was transferred to article 396 as a mere legal right but not fundamental right, i.e., the violation of this right could not be justiciable in a court of law.

This paper attempts to trace this evolution of property regimes in four subsequent parts. The first part deals with the idea of regimes and property in theory and why political regimes have an interest in ordering property regimes. The second and third part analyses the Indian sub-national context with four typical types of political regimes in order to examine the types of property regimes that evolved from them. The last part summarises the findings and conclusions.

2 Why Do Regimes Order Property Rights?

The idea of 'property' has some interesting interpretations in literature. This paper borrows from the idea of property regime used by Daniel Bromley as a 'stream of benefits or income' (Bromley 1989). Bromley defined property right as 'a claim to a benefit stream that is usually guaranteed to be protected by an authority like the state or any other legitimate unit of coercion, by assigning duty to others who may covet or interfere with the benefit stream through adverse claims' (Bromley 1989, p. 2). Defined in this sense, property is not an object but a *social relation* that defines property holder with respect to something of value (benefit stream) and against all other adverse claims.

In this study, property is considered in the context of a regime. Regimes are human artefacts that are instrumental in origin, i.e. specific regimes are created for specific purposes (Ibid.). Regimes perform their function by virtue of commonly held perceptions regarding what is scarce as well as valuable by protecting them with rights. In a property regime, there are bundle of rights on property that constitute the benefit stream. These bundle of rights can be classified based on the types of rights, i.e. physical or social as shown in Table 1.

This brings us to the question: why are political regimes interested in ordering property rights? Primarily, property conceived and claimed is allied to the other institutions that subsist within the jurisdiction of political regime. Property regimes are thus 'embedded institutions' (Bromley 1989). They are structural attributes of a political regime that gives its agents a domain to exercise their choice. Property regimes have a pre-allocative function because a political regime in which it has been decided who has control over the scarce economic resources and property relations, can determine the terms of trading and contracts. A political regime has incentive to determine property regime by setting these constraints and choices.

Table 1 Types of bundle of rights (Maine 1861)

Physical rights	Social rights
Air	Control of access
Water	Use
Soil	Sale
Tree	Lease
Animal	Gift
Mineral	–

It must be noted here that political regimes as referred to in this paper, denotes the structures of the political system and not specific governments. Political regimes determine the allocative and legitimate use of power. They can be used to indicate how political elites deal with public interest, in this case, vis-à-vis, property relations.

Then again, how does the regime perform this regulatory function of ordering property rights? The establishment and evolution of standard norms in property that constitute a property regime is often through dialogue between legislature that makes new law and the courts that interpret the legislations. This collaborative process has been described by Carol Rose as that of 'crystal and mud' formation (Rose 2002). What is inserted as crystalline clauses in laws are interpreted with flexibility and latitude by courts of law. This is again contested by private orderings and further modified leading to judicial 'fuzzying' or 'muddying'. Standardization and plurality of property, in other words, 'facilitates the regulation of particular problems in property in a more targeted manner than regulating on a system-wide basis' (Merrill and Smith 2000).

In India, comparative work on land reform implementation has been done within the axis of land ownership from a class and caste perspective with interesting results. PS Appu's review of regulation on tenurial status in India in his paper 'Tenancy Reform in India' (1975) sheds light on the way uniform tenancy reforms were initiated in different states of India despite historical differences in land tenure systems like zamindari, ryotwari and mahalwari systems. Land tenancy reforms in India have aimed at three rights—giving tenancy rights, permanent user rights and ownership rights to tenants. However, different states have interpreted and implemented tenancy reforms with varying results.

Following this, state-specific studies were conducted on specific land policies in Gujarat, Karnataka, Andhra Pradesh and Kerala. Pani (1983) has worked on land reform, transfers and tenancy policy in the state of Karnataka, Kumar (2005) has mapped the changing priorities of land use policy in Kerala and Sud (2007) has worked on Gujarat-specific land policy. While these state-specific land studies bring out the nuances of context, research on structural reasons as to why different states pursue different land policy approaches to land use is missing. This study attempts to fill this research gap.

In a comparison of Indian states on implementation of land reforms, Sharma (1994) identified how the land ownership in both owned and operated land holdings has been affected by the land reform policies in India. He pointed out that the level of hierarchy at which reshuffling of land ownership happens as a result of land reform is at the lower landholdings.

Pellissery (2016) has analysed land alienation that has resulted from unsuccessful policies from a 'mode of production' point of view. Viewing land inequality through ownership holdings, his inference is that the lower castes like Dalits, Adivasis and Other Backward Classes have ended up in the lower strata with the least land holding. From the survey of literature, path dependency and social composition of political regime emerge as the two variables that determine the property regime in sub-national states of India. While the former determines the

Table 2 Type of data used (author)

Legislation	Policy documents	Case laws	Plan documents	FDI agreements	Economic data
Land reform	Record of rights	Writ petition	Plan development	Reports of land grab	Economic surveys
Land acquisition	Land grants	Public interest litigation	Plan infrastructure	Revoked agreements FDI	Directorate of economics and statistics
Land revenue	Conversion of land use or tenure	Case law	Perspective plan		
	Land ceiling and tenancy				

strength of continuity, the latter introduces the degree of change. These studies emphasise the degree of importance social base has in influencing political regimes.

Another interesting question is how a political regime considers ordering property regime through land policies. Usually, it is assumed that the relative costs involved in each land policy option is considered by the political regime while selecting land policy as shown in Table 2. Comparative analysis of Indian states based on typology studies gives us an insight over and above 'cost benefits approach' about the political regimes operating in the states. This paper begins with the typology framework given by Atul Kohli that categorises political regimes based on the success or failure of redistributive programs in the poverty reform agenda. Using variables like political leadership, social base of the political party, organisational style of the political party and frequency of anti-incumbency, Kohli charts out three types of regimes (Kohli 2009). The first type is a state where there is a well-organised left-of-centre regime that is able to push through distributional reforms like that of Kerala and to a limited extent, West Bengal. The second type is a state that has a regime being co-opted by the propertied class as in the case of Gujarat. The third type is an in-between state that has been able to push through limited reforms through a populist leader as in the case of Karnataka.

This paper begins with these type states and examines land reform policy as the political regimes implemented them. The assumption is that different kinds of political regimes (as they have been classified based on distributional aspect) would lead to different kinds of property regimes based on land reform agenda pursued. Table 2 shows a comprehensive list of type of data used in this study.

3 The Type States in India

3.1 Gujarat

The original land reform program that the Union Government launched post independence was as a result of the agrarian land reform program of the 1931 and

1936 sessions of the Indian National Congress that tried to cater to diverse interests like social justice, economic efficiency and abolishment of landed intermediaries. There were two kinds of forces operating to make land reform policies work in the opposite direction. On the one hand, there was the early government machinery of the 1960s with elaborate land institutional structures comprising Agricultural Land Tribunal Officers and Tenancy Deputy Collectors who worked to make land reform a success.

At the same time, there were parts of the State in which land reform failed, due to the failure of the state to take possession of declared surplus land or redistribute it. This too was the result of the institutional structure for entirely the opposite reason. Many of the land revenue officials belonged to the same caste as that of the owner cultivators. Often land was not acquired under the law, or acquired only on paper, while the owner continued to till and reap benefits from the land. For instance, Saurashtra and Kachchh saw 21.4 million hectares of land transferred from former princes and large landowners to tenant tillers since these areas had Rajput princes as the intermediaries and the distributed land was predominantly given to Kanbi and Patidar castes, comprising 12% of the total state's population. In mainland Gujarat, surplus land had to be taken from the same upper and middle castes comprising Brahmin, Baniya and Kanbi Patidar castes and given to the Scheduled Castes (SCs), Scheduled Tribes (STs) and Other Backward Classes (OBCs). Thus the same regime promoted 'social justice' in one part of the state and remained status quoits in another depending on the constituents of the landed class.

The land reform laws was revived in the early 1980s when a regime change brought lower and backward castes, Muslims and Adivasi groups from within the Congress party to power in the state. The leaders of these groups used existing land reform laws to redirect land to the tiller. This was followed by a pendulum swing of ideas. In 1988, under the Chief Minister Amarsinh Chaudhary, a law was passed disallowing the 'eight kilometre rule' (section 2(6) of Bombay Tenancy and Agricultural Land Rules 1956). This was a reversal of the prohibition of buying or selling of agricultural land beyond eight kilometre limit in order to keep the transferred land in the hands of the new tenants. By revoking this provision, the state was opening a speculative market in land. Further in 1995, section 65 of the Bombay Revenue Act 1969 was amended to revoke the necessity of permission for conversion of land use from agricultural to non-agricultural purposes, to ten hectares.

The Union Government allowed the initial Land Acquisition, Rehabilitation and Resettlement Bill[4] to lapse and asked the state governments to pass their own laws. Subsequently, the Gujarat State Government made amendments to four existing land laws in August 2015 namely The Gujarat Agricultural Lands Ceiling Act, 1960, The Gujarat Tenancy and Agricultural Lands Act, 1948, The Saurashtra

[4]This bill introduced in 2010 by the Congress majority Union government was the first attempt to amend the 1894 land acquisition law. This law exempted five categories including industries to seek consent while acquiring farm land. Many controversial clauses in the bill made it impossible for it to sail through the Parliament.

Gharkhed, Tenancy Settlement and Agricultural Lands Ordinance, 1949 and The Gujarat Tenancy and Agricultural Lands (Vidarbha Region and Kachchh Area) Act, 1958.

3.2 Kerala

The present-day state of Kerala comprises the erstwhile Travancore kingdom, Cochin and Malabar regions. By the beginning of twentieth century, there were major land policy changes already taking place in Kerala. In the north, the Malabar region was under the British rule. Here, a system of survey and settlement had led to land tax imposition with high rent. In the Travancore region, the Pattom Declaration (1865) gave ownership rights to tenants in *Pandaravaka* land (land owned by the king) on payment of revenue. Further the Nayar Regulation Act 1925 allowed breaking of the matrilineal lines into lineages (*thaivazhi*) to enable inheritance of land along family lines. Meanwhile, the Cochin Tenancy Act 1914 and 1938 enabled tenancy at will as well as sharecropping possible in the Cochin region. Only in Malabar region, the old land tenure system clashed with the British revenue system.

After independence, the land reform agenda was brought to Kerala with five objectives—abolition of land lords, tenancy reforms including ceilings of ownership, consolidation of land holdings, redistribution of surplus lands and reorganisation of agrarian economy. The Agrarian Relations Bill 1957 that was passed in 1959 by the first-elected communist government in Kerala gave a number of provisions. The government also launched into direct action, procuring land from land lords that led to the imposition of President's Rule in 1959.

Subsequently, the Congress government came to power and introduced the Kerala Agricultural Relations Act 1960. This Act provided for new exemption categories but left the major provisions of the old act intact. While attempting to implement this act, the High Court of Kerala stayed many orders of land reform as ultravires the Constitution under article 31 (Right to Property). Consequently, Kerala Land Reforms Act (KLRA) 1963 was passed and inserted the law in the ninth schedule of the Constitution in order to prevent judicial review.

The delayed KLRA received a new lease of life with the Communist government coming to power again in 1969 and amending the act to include certain important provisions. The burden of proof of tenancy was shifted to the landlords and not the tenants as before. However, there was a provision to accommodate 'deemed tenants' who according to the law 'honestly believed themselves to be tenants and took the risk of the cultivator'.

The peasant unions in the 1970s ensured successful registration of tenancy applications. However, the ceiling provisions were not implemented uniformly across the state. Furthermore, the land reform laws did not touch certain marginalised groups like the indigenous people. As a result, land reform was implemented to some extent, however, intermediaries and informal leasing continued to persist.

Land Reform has grabbed the attention of policy makers once again in the 2000s. This was triggered by agrarian protests. In the bill proposed by the Congress government in 2005, it is explicitly mentioned that ceiling exemptions for new crops over and above plantation crops are 'considered necessary to grant exemption to lands planted with cashew, medicinal plants and vanilla from the ceiling provision' since 'they will not get exemption from ceiling limits if the land is used for non-plantation purposes'.

There has also been a move to introduce contract farming as a measure to solve agrarian crisis with the state Agriculture Produce Marketing (Development and Regulation) Act that hoped that those enterprises that are 'capital-starved and cannot make major investments in technological inputs would find this a big help. Contract farming agreements would provide them with quality inputs, technical guidance, credit and management skills'. These proposed bills have elicited protests with fears of reverse tenancy where big farmers may lease out land from small agriculturalists (Kuriakose and Iyer 2015).[5]

Development projects have also clashed with land-related conservation agenda in the state. For instance, the Left Democratic Front government in 2008 brought out the Conservation of Paddy and Wetland Act 2008 that prevented filling of paddy fields and wetlands in Kerala. A proposed amendment in 2015 changes two important provisions. One is to permit filling of paddy lands under certain conditions. Another provision that has been inserted is a section that gives title deeds to land in *puramboke* (state-owned land) areas.

3.3 *Karnataka*

At the time of independence, land in the Mysore State was mostly held by three communities—Brahmins, Lingayats and Vokkaligas. Brahmins held most of the Inam lands[6] and were absentee landlords. The Lingayats and Vokkaligas were owners as well as tenant cultivators in Inam lands. Soon after independence, there were two strong grassroots movement in Karnataka—the Communist movement that promised radical land reform as well as anti-Brahmin movement. The ruling Congress Party reacted to this development by passing a number of laws to abolish Inamdars since they were a minority land-owning community that had aroused opposition through social movements. There was a delay in land reform implementation since the implementation of laws vested on the bureaucracy that was populated by Brahmins.

After the reorganisation of erstwhile Mysore State into the present-day Karnataka State, the Lingayat community was in power for 15 years.

[5]In their draft discussion paper, the argument put forth by the authors is that the same instruments like land legislations and policies have been increasingly used as instruments to reverse tenancy in Kerala. The relation between absence of adequate agrarian reforms and subsequent problems with land reform is discussed in Kuriakose and Iyer (2012).

[6]Inam lands were given in the British revenue system to the priestly classes.

Land Reforms Committee was formed in 1957 that submitted its recommendation; a bill was drafted in 1960 and came into effect by 1965. The domination of landed communities in the legislature was an important reason in delaying the implementation of land reforms as well as tinkering with some of its cardinal provisions.

There were two major ways in which land reforms were impeded by the design of the legislation. The first one was through the provision of high ceiling on land holdings as high as 27 standard acres for a family of five that was much more than the 10–18 acres suggested by the Planning Commission. In matters of tenancy rights, a number of tenants were evicted based on the provision of 'self cultivation' as given in the 1960 Act. Due to a split in the then-ruling Congress Party, a new coalition was formed mainly consisting of backward castes and Muslims in 1969. A new bill for land reforms was formed and enacted in 1974 that took the recommendations of the fourth Five-Year Plans seriously. The number of tenancy declarations arose considerably in the following years and steeply declined after 1977.

The post-1980 period saw further changes in the way land policy was perceived and implemented. It was felt that due to the heavy burden of application, an appellate authority over and above Land Tribunals was required under section 48. However, the decision to have appellate authorities was revoked in 1990 and the decision of the Tribunal was final.

In its vision 2020 and the 12 point formula devised by the State planning board, 'job oriented growth, vibrant knowledge society and rural prosperity through agriculture and allied activities' were highlighted as the top three priorities. Consequently, the land policy focus changed from reform to regulations through Transfer of Development Rights (TDRs)[7] and Regularisation of illegalities through *Akrama Sakrama* law.

This facilitation of land for industrialisation continued with new amendments proposed to land laws in 2015. There were two significant changes to the legislation proposed. The law was supposed to 'enhance the annual income limit from two lakhs to twenty-five lakhs from sources other than agricultural lands to acquire any land taking into consideration the revision of rupee value since 1995; (2) to empower Deputy Commissioner instead of Assistant Commissioner to grant permission for non agriculturist to purchase agriculture land under section 80'. The law was expected to 'regularise land' and free it up for free market transactions.

3.4 *Tamil Nadu*

The Tamil Nadu land reform Act was enacted in 1961 having provisions that contravened the proposed sections in the National Policy. The ideal rent was fixed

---

[7]Bangalore was one of the first Indian cities to have implemented TDRs. But the scheme landed in controversy when the Office of the Vigilance Cell in BBMP found a scam involving nearly 9 lakh sq km land in the city.

between 20 and 25% of the produce. There was to be an earnest attempt to give ownership rights to tenants as well as bring sharecroppers on records. The importance of recording tenancy was to both claim tenurial status thereafter and have access to facilities like credit institutions. The maximum area of land captured under tenancy under the Land Reform Law was about 10% of the total land. There were no ownership rights provisions for tenants in the Land Reform Law of 1961. The fear of ejection was very high since in many districts the land-owning class also belonged to the upper or middle Hindu castes like Vellalars where as tenant belonged to lower castes like Pallas.

There were three important restrictions that were placed on possession clauses of land by tenants. The tenant could not claim land if (i) he had worked on wet land exceeding about 6 acres, or (ii) whether the owner was self-cultivating and, (iii) his claim was made within 30 days from the commencement of the Act. The third provision was especially unfair on the tenants as sufficient publicity was not given to the law, and many claimants could not rest their case in time for possession rights.

The Tamil Nadu (Panchayats) Act 1994 conferred special powers to Panchayat for transfer of *inam* land, *puramboke* lands as well as communal lands. There was to be a three-tier structure with a Panchayat union council vested with powers of review, monitoring and assessment of land reforms activities. These powers were suggested by the State Planning Commission. For instance, village Panchayats were entrusted with maintenance of land records, tenancy and distribution of surplus land. The district office could supervise the legal proceedings concerning land reform measures. The Panchayats could compile data on the ceiling limits placed in the Panchayat Union region and assist in securing tenancy rights by identifying families who were in need of surplus land.

Tamil Nadu had passed their land acquisition law in 1999. The act had allowed the residents to voice their grievances after the state expressed its intent of acquiring land. The state government subsequently made its policy priority of developing infrastructure and industry clear, through its vision and plan documents.

Tamil Nadu follows nodal mode of investment in which it has selected five districts of Kanchipuram, Tiruvannamalai, Tirunelveli, Tuticorin and Krishnagiri, mostly non-agricultural districts for industrial projects. The characteristics of Tamil Nadu while negotiating land for industrial projects are that (a) the government has identified five non-agricultural districts to predominantly house industries (b) the government negotiates with the land owners directly rather than use acquisition laws through by the State Industries Promotion Corporation of Tamil Nadu (Sipcot) and (c) the state has been successful in utilising wasteland for its industrial projects.

The thrust on infrastructure development has been clear from the plan and vision documents of the state since 2005. The Tamil Nadu vision 2023 document prepared in 2011–12 has pushed energy, industry, transport and infrastructure above agricultural activities as a policy priority. There is also a strategy given to develop the state-based industries through growth of nodal cities.

4 Basis of Building Typology

Based on the state-wise study, this paper has attempted to assess how power could wield through the structures of property to create regimes from the analysis of the type states. One of the ways power acts in the case of property regimes is in the area of access to property. The outcomes of land policy implementation (through access to property) and land policy design (ideational influence) are indicative of the power distribution of the structures of political regimes.

4.1 Access Mapping

Access mapping was done to understand the way land policies gave rise to access to property. The question asked was whether implementation of land policy gave access to the variables in question to the landless. The high or low access to each of these resources would determine the distribution of power in favour of the beneficiaries of land reform. The intended beneficiaries of land reform wherever it was unsuccessful, have been of the lower classes and castes (Table 3).

Gujarat as a state has followed a land policy that has favoured formation of land markets by making land mortgage worthy and saleable. This was done through the registration program of title deeds as well as jantri rates (state index rate for property in a circle). The state also had a land acquisition policy that gave ongoing benefits from the land sold through land pooling and zoning the regions. Culturally, the spirit of entrepreneurship that the dominant community of Patidars (who are also the land owners) are known for, helped to make negotiations easier. The political regime in Gujarat has been favouring the industrial class through market intervention based land policies with fairly easy negotiation with the public opinion on this issue. The property regime developing in the state has been a market-oriented land acquisition based transactional model.

Kerala on the other hand has given land reform a predominance that is historically related to grassroots peasant struggles as well as institutional land policies that favoured tenancy from pre-colonial times. Hence, over the period, land tenancy has been successful with the state directly mediating between land owners and tenants.

Table 3 Access mapping through land reform policies (author)

Particulars	Gujarat	Kerala	Karnataka	Tamil Nadu
Capital	High	Low	Low	Low
Labour opportunities	Medium	Low	Low	High
Land markets	High	Low	High	High
Technology	High	High	High	Medium
Authority	Low	High	Medium	High
Social identity	Low	High	Low	Low

However, the enforcement costs of registering tenancy applications as well as ceiling limits with the judiciary reversing several reform based policies has made the monitoring and enforcement costly and land reform to fizzle out in later years. Land acquisition has been difficult and the most recent amendments to land reform bill as well as wetland conservation bill have met with opposition based on grounds of land grab and corruption. Limited access to state or market created labour opportunities and the agrarian crisis of 1998 has created a unique situation. The political regime in Kerala when colluding with landed interest has tried to tinker with land reform by exempting new types of land that produce cash crops, from redistribution. It has also attempted to dilute environmental conservation laws in an attempt to build infrastructure and industry. But the property regime developing as a result of the manoeuvres of political regime is an oppositional kind that hopes to marry equity concerns of social justice with those of environment justice.

The third type of state is Karnataka which has a history of failed land reform primarily because the political regime had colluded with upper caste landed class except for a brief period. They have also failed in their attempt to provide state-given infrastructure and housing. As a result illegal markets for land and property developed especially in city zones. Here, access to land had been state facilitated for digitisation of land records through e-bhoomi project and through state index rate of land prices. Regularisation of irregularities and acquisition with regulation are the main land policies used. The intended beneficiaries of land reform remain without access to land and with reinforced social identity bias. The negotiation with the urban population has been constantly made through new land policies and judicial intervention and therefore access to authority has been present to some extent. The political regime has favoured regulation with less negotiation with stakeholders and the property regime formed has been a regularisation-based model that recognises titling and ownership through market-based transactions.

Tamil Nadu, the fourth type of state, also failed in land reform due to the landed interest playing a part in political regime. However, the state did not abandon the lingo of reform by incorporating these interests through decentralisation in 1994, about the same time it welcomed industrialisation as a major policy. With a substantial vote bank comprising agrarian class and with progressive social movements, a dual strategy was adopted. There were a large number of welfare policies announced for the small and the marginal land holder. At the same time, a growth-based industrial and infrastructural policy was selected for five urban nodes. Thus the political regime favoured a substitution of land reform with welfare and inviting land acquisition through well-directed state policies. The property regime that has formed is a dual regime that has land reform component and acquisition component in practice.

Based on the mappings done above, four types of property regimes are proposed. They are Acquisitive State, Redistributive State, Facilitative State and Substitutive State.

Acquisitive state like Gujarat is the first type that has a development discourse hinged on industry-based growth. As a result, a lot of policy making is around attracting investment and providing land to industries at reduced rate. Land acquisition is the most preferred land policy used to acquire vast tracts of land, along with land pooling. The central policy value is efficiency and liberty. The tools used here are digitisation of records and transparent record of rights. The bundle of rights emphasised is the ownership right of individuals. Historical and cultural factors like business acumen of the people help in communicating the market-based approach of land policy successfully to the public. Conflicts of land issues that capture public attention involve government grant of land to industries, at concessional rates.

Redistributive state like Kerala that comes in the second category is historically inclined toward land redistribution through ceiling and tenancy laws. The central policy value is welfare and security. A strong left movement along with social movements of women and the environment has impacted the land policy formulation through a rights-based approach. The tools used are government acquisition of land through ceiling laws and transferring of land through land banks. The state is seen as a welfare institution that protects land rights, manages natural resources of the people and imparts skill and training to the people to have meaningful employment opportunities. Civil society organisations are more active in ensuring land rights and opposing large industrial projects that involve land acquisition. The most important conflict that captures public attention is corruption in land deals involving politician–bureaucrat nexus.

The third category is the Facilitative state like Karnataka that focuses on revenue from land as a major policy priority. The central policy value is efficiency and security. Hence registration of land through titling is taken on large scale and innovative land regulation policies like TDRs and regularisation are extensively used. It is interesting that attempts to correct historical wrongs failed through land reforms and hence the policy focus has shifted to regularisation. There is emphasis on attracting investment in large projects involving vast tracts of land. Conflicts in land ownership and corruption in land deals are resolved by petitioning the judiciary and through positive judicial intervention. The government is seen as a facilitator of land transfers.

The fourth category is the Substitutive state like Tamil Nadu which began with one land policy discourse like reform and transformed its policy goals to another end such as acquisition. This dramatic volte-face happens even when the political regime remains the same over the years. The state is seen as patronising the interest class of farmers with subsidies while acquiring land for industrialisation. This dual character makes the state both a facilitator and a welfare provider. Interest group organisations are active and enunciate their class interest clearly. This is responded to, by the political regime, depending on the political power they wield. Conflicts around land are politicised and are usually resolved through policy and vision documents.

5 Summary and Conclusions

The study set out to find out how political regime in a state affects the property regime. The questions were whether property regime evolved in a linear manner or went back and forth. The primary finding of the study is that political regime does affect the property regime in a state. The composition of the political regime determines what kind of property regime is likely to develop in a state. A political regime composed of backward class, agrarian group and lower caste groups is likely to favour a reform-based property regime. A political regime with landed gentry as one of its classes tends to support land revenue based system. A political regime with predominantly trading classes may favour land acquisition and industrial growth as in Gujarat. A regime with mixed interest group of farmers and traders may have a property regime where reform was reattempted through decentralisation as in Tamil Nadu. It is also clear that the four types are not discrete set of property regimes mutually exclusive from one another. Instead one type of property regime is in continuum with another.

References

Açemoglu D, Johnson S, Robinson JA (2001) The colonial origins of comparative development: an empirical investigation. Am Econ Rev 91(5):1369–1401
Appu PS (1975) Tenancy reform in India. Econ Polit Wkly 10(33/35):1339–1375
Banerjee A, Iyer L (2005) History, institutions and economic performance: the legacy of colonial land tenure systems in India. Am Econ Rev 95(4):1190–1213
Banerjee A, Iyer L (2008) Colonial land tenure, electoral competition and public goods in India. Harvard University Working Paper 08-062
Bromley D (1989) Property relations and economic development: the other land reform. World Dev 17(6):867–877
Engerman SL, Sokoloff KL (2005) Colonialism, Inequality and the Long-run Paths to Development. NBER working paper no. 11057
Kohli A (2009) Democracy and development in India: from socialism to pro business. Oxford India Paperbacks, New Delhi
Kumar BM (2005) Land use in Kerala: changing scenarios and shifting paradigms. J. Trop Agric 42(1–2):1–12
Kuriakose F, Iyer DK (2012) Land use policy and agrarian relations in India. In: Mandal RK (ed) Management and policy issues. Discovery Publishing House, New Delhi
Kuriakose F, Iyer DK (2015) The promised land: analysing land distribution policy through the typology of political regimes. Paper presented at the 1st south asian regional conference of international academic association on planning, law, and property rights, National Law School of India University, Bangalore, 1 Sept 2015
LaPorta R, de Silanes FL, Shleifer A, Vishny R (1998) Law and finance. J Polit Econ 106(6): 1113–1155
Maine H (1861) Ancient law. Crayon 8(4):77–80
Merrill TW, Smith HE (2000) Optimal standardization in the law of property: the numerus clausus principle. Yale Law J 110(1):1–70
Pani N (1983) Reforms to pre-empt change: land reform in Karnataka. Concept Publishing House, New Delhi
Pellissery S (2016) Land alienation infused poverty in India. In: Wright GC, Braathen E, Julian M, Ulriksen M (eds) Poverty and inequality in middle income countries: policy achievements and political objectives. Zed books, London

Rose CM (2002) Common property, regulatory property, and environmental protection: comparing community-based management to tradable environmental allowances. Drama Commons 233:250–253

Sharma HR (1994) Distribution of landholdings in rural India, 1953–54 to 1981–82: implications for land reforms. Econ Polit Wkly 29(13):A12–A25

Sud N (2007) From land to the tiller to land liberalisation: the political economy of Gujarat's shifting land policy. Mod Asian Stud 41(03):603–637

Property in India: Global Perspectives, National Issues

Sony Pellissery and Harvey M. Jacobs

Property—who should own and who control land—has been a central and contentious issue throughout Indian history. The long-standing tensions within Indian society were further sharpened during the time of British colonization, and then from the time of Indian independence in 1947 to the present took on strong symbolic, political, and practical content. Some of this is because of the traditional population distribution within India, with large numbers of people who continue to engage in agriculture and thus depend directly on land for sustenance. But much of it is also cultural, as it is in so many other parts of the world, where the ownership and control of land is linked to conceptions of independence of the individual and family.

As politics is changing in India the discourse about property is also changing. Most recently this has taken the form of heated public debate about proposed revisions to the national law on expropriation. Several changes have been made and proposed over the last several years and what these changes do is evidence to an underlying tension between those who view land as a necessary element of economic development (land as a commodity) and those who view land primarily from the perspective of the user and owner (land as a resource).

In this final chapter, we do two things. In section one, we put current debates in India into a long-standing and current global theoretical perspective. Here we are seeking to ground the Indian policy debate about property into a global discourse about property's future, in a world which is urbanizing and where environmental conditions are changing, and thus where land holds a different role than it did over

S. Pellissery (✉)
National Law School of India University, Bengaluru, Karnataka, India
e-mail: sonyp@nls.ac.in

H.M. Jacobs
Department of Urban and Regional Planning, University of Wisconsin-Madison, Madison, WI, USA
e-mail: hmjacobs@wisc.edu

S. Pellissery et al. (eds.), *Land Policies in India*, India Studies in Business and Economics, DOI 10.1007/978-981-10-4208-9_11

the last several centuries. In section two, we focus specifically on what is to be learned from the contributions to this volume, and the conference at which many of these authors first presented their work. We are interested in the very specific ways in which policy as an importantly cultural discourse about land and property is likely to evolve in India in the immediate future.

1 A Classical View That Emerges in the Eighteenth Century

As noted in this book's introduction, the social and legal form of property and property rights is central to the ways land is managed. The way property is configured establishes realms of what comes to be considered private action, and thus solely within the purview of the resource "owner" (whether that owner is an individual, a family, a tribe, a community, or some other unit which can claim an exclusive right to a resource) and public action, where the state may set rules and standards which shape private decision-making over resources. Much of the time in law, planning and resource management property systems seem to function as stage settings—the focus of the viewer is on the more immediate play which is occurring on the stage, the words and movements of the actors. But, in fact, just as in theater or film the setting is immensely influential to the perception of the actors; so it is with property systems and resource management.

The theory which gives rise to the contemporary form of property in the western world—and especially the idea of private property rights—came into being in the eighteenth century, post the American and French revolutions. It reflected the influence of the political philosophers John Locke (most prominently influential on American founders) and Jean-Jacques Rousseau (most prominently influential on the French founders), and the political economist Adam Smith (see Jacobs 2016 and 2010 for a more specific discussion of this history). These three were writing in a world quite different from the world of today. Most people lived rurally; at the time of the American Revolution (1776) Philadelphia, Pennsylvania was the country's largest city and its population was only about 20,000. Yet the world of today was beginning to emerge, a world of urbanization and industrialization.

Questions which bound these thinkers together had to do with what today we refer to as human rights, and whether the political and economic systems then current were appropriate for the emerging world. Relative to property, the European world of the 1700s was one where most land was still owned and controlled by an aristocracy. These thinkers, among others, brought forth an argument about how to create and realize democratic governance structures and market economies. Central to their thinking was the need for a strong and enforceable set of privately owned property. It was land ownership which would allow people to have political freedom and it was land ownership which would allow people to make innovative and creative (and individually and socially beneficial) decisions about land use. In fact

Ely (1992) argues that contrary to widespread popular understanding, it was in fact conflict over property that was the central matter of contention in the American revolutionary war (not matters related to religious freedom, freedom of speech, etc.).

What was the form of property that was coming into being? It was one in which the natural world is conceptualized as a bundle of rights—where what is in actuality a whole can be treated as fragmentable. An owner owns the soil, trees, air, water, minerals, as well as the right to control access and use, and transfer land through gift (inheritance), lease or sale. The rights to use or transfer apply to land as whole as well as individual rights within the bundle. This is the basis of the idea that there are water rights, air rights, mineral rights, etc., and that these rights can be separated from the bundle. This is what gives rise to the ability to create conservation easements, carbon trading markets, water quantity markets, payments for ecological services, and so on.

The idea of the natural world and the urban world as property is widely understood as contributing to the economic, social, political, and technological transformation—the progress—of the west from the eighteenth century to the world of the twenty-first century (see, e.g., Bethell 1998). Yet, the world of today is not the world of the eighteenth century—it is a world which is predominately urban, and expected to become ever more so in the next decades, and where two billion people are expected to live in slums in these cities by 2030. And in this world the evidence of climate change and its consequences are ever-more apparent. Melting glaciers in Greenland, island nations in the Pacific literally disappearing, severe storms impacting major coastal cities, and vanishing species are but some of the phenomena which challenge long-standing social, economic, political, cultural systems. A question that needs to be posed is how and whether the form of property invented in the eighteenth century, a social and legal invention which facilitated the creation of the modern world, remains appropriate for the twenty-first century or whether it needs to change.

Skepticism about eighteenth-century property arose within a century of its invention. In the mid- to late nineteenth century, during the periods of rapidly evolving social ferment, leading thinkers, primarily on the left, questioned the social and legal institution of property. So, for example, in 1840 Pierre-Joseph Proudhon, the French anarchist, famously declared "property is theft!" in his book *What is Property? Or, an Inquiry into the Principle of Right and Government.* A few years later, in 1844, Karl Marx published *On the Jewish Question* and in it began what became a series of comments about private property central to his theory of social construction and change: "The right of property, is, … the right to enjoy one's fortunes … without regard for other men and independently of society… It leads every man to see in other men … the limitation of his own liberty." Several decades later in 1880 Pyotry (Peter) Kropotkin, the Russian prince, anarchist and geographer, argued in *The Spirit of Revolt* "Society … clamors loudly for a complete remodeling of the system of property ownership." All of these social commentators, who could also be referred to as social critics and social reformers, saw severe limitations to the system of private property.

In the same period as Kropotkin, but from a very different perspective, Henry George, the American tax reformer, published his book *Progress and Poverty* (1879). His question—the book's title (which over a century later remains a very contemporary question in India and globally)—poses the quandary of how there can be so much progress and so much poverty co-existing? George's answer—it is about who owns the land! So while George was a committed capitalist, in contrast to Proudhon, Marx, and Kropotkin, with regard to land he held a view consonant with these radical-left theorists: "We must make land common property."

The impact of these ideas has been significant. During the twentieth century, Marx's ideas in particular formed a component of the rationale for the Russian Revolution and the rise of the Soviet Union and its member states, the Chinese Revolution, the Cuban Revolution, and other socialist-communist states globally. In all these places, private property in land was, to a greater or lesser extent, diminished, if not eliminated altogether. Likewise, though quite differently, George's ideas for a differential tax system directed at breaking up large land holdings had significant influence throughout the British colonies and as well as limited influence in the U.S.

But these ideas about land and private property also became entangled in a century-plus debate about fundamental political ideology—an east-west debate—about capitalism versus communism, about democracy versus socialism, about the rights of the individual versus the rights of the community (the state). And so for much of the last century-plus notions of non-private property seemed to many to suggest a rejection of capitalism, democracy, and individual human rights.

Beginning in the late twentieth century, a new set of perspectives emerged around this question. In his famous article "The Tragedy of the Commons" (1968) Garrett Hardin, a population biologist, brought the issue of property rights back into academic and policy discourse from a different perspective. The article examines the case of what he refers to as the commons—property resources owned by none but used by all. Examples of the commons include the atmosphere and the oceans. Hardin argued that in the case of open access commons, where there are no assignable property rights, what resulted was what he deemed a tragedy. Why was this true? Because—and this was his insight—individual rational decision-making relative to natural resources use did not result in socially rational outcomes. Individuals had motivations to exploit resources for their benefit without considering the cumulative effect of their own and others actions. In order to solve this problem, Hardin's solution was a further extension of the eighteenth century concept of property. If commons resources were privatized they would be better—i.e., more sustainability—managed: "The tragedy of the commons … is averted by private property" (p. 1245).

As noted by Sinden (2007) and others, Hardin's metaphor has become ubiquitous. There is perhaps no environmental issue or problem that has come to attention since 1968 which has not been described by someone somewhere as a tragedy of the commons. This is true even when the issue or problem does not strictly meet Hardin's description of a commons, and in fact can even be resources which are owned. The key lesson many take from Hardin's article is not about the commons per se, but about the mismatch of individual logic and social outcomes. And even though the veracity of Hardin's central story and his logic has been subject to wide-ranging and widely legitimated criticism (see, for example, Ostrom 1990 and related works) his metaphor holds sway, as does his proposed solution. This is especially true as it fits in with and is supported by a broader economic literature drawing on the work of Coase (1960), and which has come to be known as free market environmentalism (e.g. Anderson and Leal 1991; Anderson and Libecap 2014).

In 2000 this "rediscovery" of property rights was extended to the rapidly growing mega-cities of the developing world. Hernando De Soto examined the problem of poverty in urban slums in these cities and argued that the slums, but more importantly the poverty of the people living in these slums, was solvable through the creation and distribution of the eighteenth-century form of property rights. In his words

> The poor. .. have things, but they lack the process to represent their property and create capital.. .. It is the unavailability of these essential representations that explains why people who have adapted every other Western invention. .. have not been able to produce sufficient capital to make domestic capitalism work (pp. 6-7). Property. .. is. .. a mediating device that captures and stores most of the stuff required to make a market economy run.. .. The connection between capital and modern money runs through property. (p. 63)

For Garrett Hardin and Hernando De Soto (and others) eighteenth-century property is relevant, appropriate and necessary. For these analysts, in this century of mega-city urbanization and climate change, the solution to our urban and environmental problems is more private property! They see problems through a lens akin to classical economics. For them, these are primarily problems of scarcity and management. When they pose the question about "what to do," privatization of natural resources offers itself as a reasonable and even logical solution. Why? Privatization—a robust set of private property rights—over a diverse set of natural resources should, they believe, lead the owners of the resources to manage them for long-term sustainability, including wanting to avoid instances of liability for misuse or abuse of the resource. In addition, a robust set of private property rights allows for a set of owners to bargain over the composition and use of a set of resources, which should lead to a situation of positive outcomes for both individuals and society. So even a set of radical urban and environmental conditions—e.g., rising sea levels which threaten the very existence of major coastal cities globally or Pacific island nations themselves—does not, *prima facie*, negate the utility of property rights as a potential solution.

Hardin's and De Soto's ideas have been particularly influential with institutions like the World Bank, and serve as the bases for proposals for property rights reform in developing and transition countries globally. But whether Hardin and De Soto are actually correct is hotly debated (as noted, Ostrom 1990 vis-a-vis Hardin, and Gilbert 2002 vis-a-vis De Soto). And yet the idea of private property as a solution continues, and in the last decade-plus another strand has been added to these arguments: a suggestion that private property may be (should be?) part of a core realization of human rights in the twenty-first century (Jacobs 2013, Davy within this volume).

2 An Alternate Twentieth-Century View

Yet throughout the twentieth century a very different, counter-narrative emerged. Eventually partially drawing from Hardin, and his insight about the mismatch between the rationality of individual decision-making and the social outcomes of these decisions, a set of institutional economists, ecologists, environmental ethicists, legal scholars, policy analysts, planners and others, began to wonder if the eighteenth-century property rights scheme was truly functional for long-term urban and environmental sustainability. Multiple proposals have been offered forth in this counter-narrative; only a limited treatment of this literature is addressed here.

As noted, a pointed critique of private property emerged by the mid-nineteenth century, largely, though not solely from those on the political left. By the late nineteenth and early twentieth centuries another strand got woven into this critique, though this time, a decidedly nonpolitical one. Also as noted, Henry George, an American tax reformer, took up the issue of property from a non-left perspective, and his work was extremely influential in its time. By the early twentieth century new economic thought—institutional economics—emerged drawing from the pioneering work of Thorsten Veblen, Richard T. Ely, John R. Commons and others. Their emphasis, like those of Locke and Rousseau, was the centrality of land ownership to citizenship, and like George they were concerned with land concentration. But as scholars (and scholar-activists) they emphasized the social construction of property, how property is what it is because of social agreement, and how property can, does and should change to reflect changing social and technological circumstances. Using this perspective they engaged in wide-ranging explorations of land use, and also developed some of the intellectual foundations for the emergence of public sector land policy (e.g., zoning and related land-use regulations) in this period.

But it was in the middle of the twentieth century that the current form of counter-narrative began really to take form in a way that broadly resonated with scholars and activists. Aldo Leopold was a University of Wisconsin professor of wildlife management (the country's first such professor) and a preeminent twentieth century environmentalist. His most famous work is *A Sand County Almanac* (1968 [1949]) which continues to inspire students and environmentalists. In this book (published posthumously after an untimely death) his most famous essay is titled "The Land Ethic." Here he argues

> There is as yet no ethic dealing with man's relation to land and the animals and plants which grow upon it. Land, like Odysseus' slave-girls, is still property. The land relation is still strictly economic, entailing privileges but not obligations. (Leopold 1968[1949], p. 203)

What is his proposed alternative?

> The land ethic. .. enlarges the boundaries of the community to include soils, waters, plants, and animals, or collectively: the land.
>
> A land ethic. .. affirms. .. [the] right [of resources] to continued existence, and, at least in spots, their continued existence in a natural state.
>
> .. . a land ethic changes the role of Homo sapiens from conqueror of the land-community to plain member and citizen of it. (Leopold 1968[1949], p. 204)

Leopold came to writing about land use and land ethics after decades of working on land management, initially in the American west. There he came to a conclusion that would later be drawn upon by Hardin, that what is logical to the individual is not always logical for society. In Leopold's case, he concluded that private ownership of land (private property) was a problem, because the owner did not understand what should be done to properly manage land and the economic system sent out signals relative to land use which encouraged an owner to use land to the point of over use. The problem was clear, but what was the answer? For Leopold, at least in his formal writings, this was not so obvious. (However, Freyfogle (2003) has spent considerable effort working with Leopold's many works to derive what he believes to be a way to formally and legally realize the land ethic.)

Decades later Leopold's concerns and his sense of a new direction appeared to be ready to take form. In 1970 Americans celebrated the first Earth Day. A new environmental consciousness had appeared and it seemed to be growing rapidly and with its growth there seemed new possibilities for rethinking the very nature of private property. A seminal legal case provided one basis for these new ideas.

In the 1960s, the state of Wisconsin, Leopold's home state, developed environmental rules which were to implemented by local governments for the use of privately owned property that abutted lakes. Marinette County in northern Wisconsin adopted such a regulation, including rules for any proposed changes to privately owned wetlands. A landowner who believed these regulations to be inappropriate proceeded to drain a wetland he owned and built without permission. The issue ended up before the Wisconsin Supreme Court which ultimately decided in favor of the government requiring a permit for land-use change. But the real significance of the case was in the rationale the Court articulated in legitimizing governmental action. In a ringing opinion the Court argued that landownership was only of land in its natural state

> An owner of land has no absolute and unlimited right to change the essential natural character of his land so as to use it for a purpose for which it was unsuited in its natural state and which injures the rights of others.

In other words, as it has come to be characterized,—"you bought a wetland, you own a wetland." Any changes had to be asked for and given (see Large 1973 for a discussion of this case and its apparent implications). Here was Leopold's land ethic in operation. At the time the environmental community hoped that those who opposed the decision of the Wisconsin Supreme Court would appeal the decision and that the U.S. Supreme Court would review and affirm the State Court's finding. The U.S. Supreme Court chose not to review the case. If the nation's highest court had reviewed and affirmed the State's decision it would have resulted in a fundamental change to the core notion of private property rights in the United States.

In this same period Dr. Seuss, the children's author, published *The Lorax*, a fable about environmental management and destruction with the themed message "who speaks for the trees?" Christopher Stone, a law professor and environmental ethicist, posed the same question but in a slightly different way (Seuss 1971). Stone asked why nature only had rights as filtered through its ownership by humans (Stone 1972). Should nature, and aspects of nature—landscapes, forests, etc—have rights in and of itself? Asked this way the question struck many as silly, even outrageous. But Stone pointed out that the very concept of ownership has evolved significantly (the point made by the institutional economists). In the early twentieth century parents owned their children, husbands their wives, people their domestic animals. And in all cases owners could do as they wished with their possessions (husbands could beat their wives, parents could send their children to the mines or the mills, people could abuse their animals). And the law expressly recognized this. Property was defined in law as one's land, spouse, children, and animals. This changed. The Society for the Prevention of Cruelty to Animals pioneered the idea that animals had rights. Children came to have rights independent of their parents (to go to school, to be well cared for), women to expect full human dignity. All of these changes were not without significant social struggle, but all came to be. Stone's work asks: isn't it time for a similar change with regard to nature?

As the rate of urbanization and environmental change has accelerated the ideas put forward by Leopold and Stone, and articulated in the Just case, have been revisited, revised, and further elaborated. Drawing from the core conception of western property—land as a bundle of sticks (rights)—and both preserving it but also seeking a modification in line with a perception of necessary change sympathetic to environmental concerns, one scholar has pondered how society might add "green wood to the bundle of sticks" (Goldstein 2004). Others note that the long-standing frame for property in the west (private versus public) is too narrow and does not capture the reality of property ownership and management forms. Geisler and Daneker (2000), for example, wonder if there are alternate, more nuanced property forms. Still others emphasize that all forms of property have always been and continue to be "polyrational" and that management structures for it need to understand this and incorporate a necessarily messy reality (e.g., Davy 2012). And there are others who vigorously join into this debate offering a range of theoretical and strategic ideas (e.g., Gray 1991; Chrisman 1994; Frazier 1995; Krueckeberg 1995; Steinberg 1995; Meyer 2009). Regardless of their particular position, though, together they share a perspective—eighteenth-century property is a problem, alternate property systems must be developed, property can be designed (should be redesigned) to serve current needs, social and political systems have in the past and can in the future recreate private property ownership systems.

3 Private Property for the Future?

So the facts are largely not in dispute—the planet is undergoing rapid urban and environmental change. Exactly how resources are owned and managed is an important element of the possibility of successfully managing through this period. But what this means exactly is in great dispute. Broadly there are two positions, and within those positions important nuances of difference. Drawing from Hardin, De Soto and the free market environmentalists is an argument that success will be a function of further embracing eighteenth-century property. From their perspective, the fundamental arguments of Locke, Rousseau and Smith are correct and governance, markets and sustainability will best come about through clearly defined and widely distributed private property. Drawing from the radical-left critics of the mid-nineteenth century, the institutional economists of the early twentieth century, and the mid- and late twentieth century work of Leopold, Hardin, Stone and others is an argument that the form of property created in the eighteenth century was functional for many aspects of social and cultural development, but changed conditions require changed property.

What set of ideas are correct? What form of property is the right form for sustainability, for the twenty-first century? An answer is not obvious or clear. Advocates on all sides of this debate are passionate, and it can often seem that it is ideology more than anything else that drives discourse.

So one question to pose is: if the eighteenth-century form of property needs to change in line with the critiques of environmentalists, is such a change even possible? Yes it is. The institutional economists are correct. The form of property rights in the early twenty-first century is not what it was in the early twentieth century. In the early twentieth century an owner "owned" (possessed) his (and it was largely men who owned) children, his wife, his animals and his land and could (ab)use them as he saw fit. With regard to ownership many changes ensued. With regard to urban land since the early twentieth century forms of public regulation which reframe and redirect private ownership for use and control—via zoning, via environmental rules—have greatly expanded and in general been largely accepted, though they always came into being with significant social contention (see Wolf 2008 for a detailed discussion of the emergence of zoning in the U.S., see Jacobs 2010 for a discussion of the contemporary social conflict over proposals to shape individual decision making over privately owned land).

Globally, we have multiple examples of how urban and environmental resources can be owned, controlled and managed differently than the classic eighteenth century model would suggest, and perhaps more in line with the proposals of Earth Day-era reformers. And this is especially true in the developed world. In the U.K. in the mid-twentieth century (after the Second World War) the right to change the use of land—especially urban land—was taken away from all individual land owners and vested with the public to provide a broader perspective on what is in the best interests of the community as a whole (Haar 1951). Today, proposed land-use changes are negotiated between an owner and a public authority, and if the authority denies a proposed change, such a decision has, for decades, been largely accepted. Similarly the Netherlands has a multi-decade tradition and experience with the idea that property rights are shared between the private and public spheres, and the public interest must be afforded a significant voice in land-use decisions (Needham 2014). And throughout the globe, though originating in the developed world, there are active experiments with alternate property systems, many of which share ownership between a private and public owner with the express purpose of maximizing the benefits of each form of ownership (see, for example, Davis 2010 and Moore and McKee 2012). So alternate (more "green"?) notions exist and can be feasibly implemented.

What kind of property is right for this century with rising demand on environmental resources such as water, air and land for food production, where climate change is changing the very contour of land and water globally, and where rapid urbanization has created an emergent world of global mega-cities with an exploding population living in marginal conditions? Should there be continuity or disruption in the eighteenth-century property form which created the modern world? There is no clear answer to this question. But there is no doubt that this is a question which is central to creating a sustainable future globally and for our purposes most specifically in India.

4 Future of Land Policies in India

In this second section of this chapter, we make certain conjectures regarding the future of land policies in India. We present five tensions that are prominent around land in contemporary India. The papers in this volume have served as evidence for many of these conjectures. Our principal argument is that the direction in which the tensions presented here are resolved will shape land policies in near future.

5 Idea and Materiality of Land

"One group of people may defend an idea, others are defending their life and their livelihoods" (Rivera-Ferre et al. 2014, p. 316). This quote refers to the context of changing patterns of food intake and struggles against those changes, yet it seems to be equally true for the case of land policies in India. Policy making on land is facing two groups at loggerheads. Historically the question of absolute ownership of land was of muted importance (Neale 1979). Rather, how different people (artisans, village record keepers, cultivators, and intermediaries) shared rights on valued resources in land was the key concern until the twentieth century. Often, consolidation of local strength determined how multiple rights were distributed across different stakeholders over a piece of land (Embree 1979). The reasons for wanting to possess land went beyond that of production and livelihood. Land was and continues to be a critical symbolic instrument to exercise power, and to control labor.

At the time of independence land in India was in a few hands, since British colonial administration had created a property registration system whose primary focus was on an attempt to collect taxes.[1] Chapter "Postcolonial Evolution of Water Rights in India and the United States" in this volume discusses how the Indian case is not unique when property rights are transferred in the context of post-colonialism. After independence, attempts to take away the land from these "owners" were foiled (discussed in Chapter "Evolution of Property Rights in India" of this volume). The aim of the land reform, immediately after independence, was to produce an egalitarian politics based on equality of assets (Mehta 2010). However, inequality justified through ideational, philosophical, and religious precepts (Pellissery 2016), prevailed. Thus, land inequality is directly linked with the social inequality in India. As Table 1 shows, among different social groups, there are stark differences in the pattern of land ownership.

The material importance of land as a means of production has been considerably reduced in recent years. Yet, the imagination about land has become more diverse today rather than what it was in the past. A section of society imagines land as "social security" or last resort; another section of society imagines land as infinite resource for realizing the "good life" through a variety of investment opportunities. And yet another section associates their very identity with land. These different imaginations about the very idea of land—what land and property mean—has to be juxtaposed with the relationship of property and citizenship, a debate that was very important in the beginning of twentieth century globally (as shown in the first section of this chapter). The proposals of Thomas Paine in the eighteenth century, Henry George in the nineteenth century and others for progressive taxation on property have, in our opinion, great relevance for India today.[2]

As we show later in this chapter, due to diminishing agricultural productivity, there is eagerness to sell land and to invest in other forms of capital. In particular the urge is to invest in education where skills can be gained and used for upward mobility. However, since land is the primary means to exercise power in rural areas,

---

[1]The East India Company gained revenue collection rights (*Diwani*) from Mughal emperors (in 1765) though their primary interest was in trading. Eventually, they realized revenue from huge agrarian tracts was more profitable than income from trade. Subsequently, systems of property rights were created to suit this revenue collection system. Different systems were developed in different parts of the subcontinent (*Zamindari*—permanent settlement through intermediary for 100 years; *Ryotwari*—direct revenue collection from cultivators which necessitated identification of property and its registration). The question of property rights in independent India became entangled with these path dependent legacies. This issue of how modern India's property regimes has path dependency with colonial times is examined in Pellissery and Sattwick (2012).

[2]While some scholars (e.g. Trautman 2012) argue that ancient India had a system of land ownership and property sale as early as the 3rd century as documented in Arthshastra, public policy debates on progressive taxation on property as a tool for brining about equitable ownership of land have not taken place. Where the debates got closest was in the rights of tiller to own land in the context of land reforms (Appu 1996).

Table 1 Intersection of land and group inequality in rural India

	Upper Caste	OBCs	Scheduled Castes	Scheduled Tribes	All Groups
Proportion of population (total)	26[a]	49.2[a]	16.6	8.2	100
Mean household per capita consumption (Rs.)	1037	748	657	511	776
Proportion of households owning or cultivating land	74	65	44	62	60
Average area owned (high caste = 100)[b]	100	78	25	75	64

[a]The percent of upper caste and OBC are approximate, since Census do not collect data on caste systematically. Other religions such as Muslims and Christians are also divided into different castes

[b]Since this is estimation, other groups' landownership is estimated in proportion to High Caste

Source Compiled from Census of India (2011) and analysis (Borooah et al. 2014) of household survey data collected during 2004–2005 by the University of Maryland in collaboration with the National Council of Applied Economic Research (NCAER) from 41,554 households of 1504 villages and 971 urban areas across 33 states of India. This table presents data relevant for rural areas to show the relationship between landlessness and poverty with reference to social groups. Data from urban households shows poverty measured as per capita consumption is the same, i.e., highest in upper caste households and lowest among Scheduled Tribes

the idea of land is more important than the actual materiality of land. Thus, the aim is to hold on to land and to access education through special provisions. For the communities which have been historically deprived (Scheduled Castes and Scheduled Tribes) there are special provisions of "reservation" for admission to educational institutions. As the farming communities want entry to educational institutions, there is a competition for spaces. The violence against marginal communities by farming castes (Patels in Gujarat and Marathas in Maharashtra) as well as claims towards "deprived groups" in recent times is directly linked to changes to the valuation of land. Thus, land remains at the center of social contention.

6 Technology and Land

One of the biggest changes that took place in the second half of twentieth century in India was in the context of the Green Revolution. Agriculture, based on high-yield varieties required intense use of water. Thus, agrarian capitalism became closely connected to water capitalism. Three related technological developments added fuel to this new idea. First was the drilling technology for finding water. Traditional dependence on surface water gave way to drilling. The second development was the introduction of grid electricity to rural areas. As electricity was used to pump water through drilled wells, unsustainable land use began to occur. Due to the pressure to meet food security requirements the government provided subsidies both to use drilling technology and for electricity in the farming sector. Thus the policy environment facilitated an extractive behavior among farmers. Today, water drawn through borewells are estimated to be 3–8 times (considering the variations between different states) more than the recharges that occur through annual rainfall. As borewells run dry, digging down to beyond 1000 ft. to reach water has become common. The third technological development has to do with the use of pesticides. High-yield variety agriculture necessitated the use of fertilizers and pesticides which resulted in a degradation of land quality. This introduced a vicious circle where ever-more fertilizers and pesticides were used which further impacted (reduced) land quality.

While these changes are visible across the world, the impact of these technological changes is much higher because of the small land holding pattern in India. India has the highest rate of borewells drilled to land per hectare and water extracted in the world. This unsustainable agricultural practice led to structural transformations. Efficiency levels for agricultural growth have declined since 1997 (World Bank 2014, p. 66). For these and other reasons the contribution of the agricultural sector to the economy has declined from 54% of GDP in 1951 to 16% in 2013.

Yet, India did not make a transition from an agrarian economy to an industrialized economy. "Premature deindustrialisation" (Rodrik 2015) occurred through expansion of the service sector, which contributes 58% of GDP today. However, the service sector is facing tremendous challenges since the sector is increasingly becoming technology driven and a skilled work force is demanded. It is in this context that the economy transforms itself to become extractive. The extractive economy views property rights as a door to the treasure beneath the land.

India produces 89 minerals. Of these four are minerals, 11 metallic, 52 non-metallic, and 22 minor-minerals (TERI 2001). For some of the products (mica, coal, iron ore, bauxite) India is a leading producer ranking in the top 10 globally. With liberalization, as foreign investment was allowed in the sector, with limited home-grown technology for mining, a new trend emerged when foreign firms wanted to invest in India for extraction of minerals. In most of central and eastern India, where there is armed insurgency, there is tension between indigenous communities, whose culture and livelihoods are associated with the life on these mineral-rich regions (Padel 2011) and private (multi-national) companies (and the government) that view these minerals as sources to boost the economy.

As noted in the first section of this chapter, one of the ways extractive behavior on land has become checked globally is through the use of public policy tools such as zoning, as well as distinguishing use rights from ownership rights. In the Western world, the goals of the common good were advanced when the public authority exercised its duty in the public interest by negotiating with private property owners. However, in weak states, such as India, it is unclear that public authorities can act independently to make impartial decisions on issues of land use change through mechanisms such as zoning.

7 Livelihood Versus Growth

Though India has a huge agrarian sector it is, primarily made up of small land holding agriculturists. 31% of households are landless. 30% households own less than 0.4 ha of land and cumulatively accounts to 5.11% of total land. On the other extreme, 2% of households hold more than 5 hectares of land, and cumulatively this is 27% of total land (Pellissery 2016). Some scholars (Chand et al. 2011) have pointed out that this smallholding pattern was not as acute in the 1960s when only 62% of small holders existed. As the property gets further subdivided among family members, smallholding is bound to happen, and that is one of the directions of the land story, and it looks nearly irreversible. It is in this context of huge land inequality that the debate of livelihood versus growth has gained currency for future policy choices.

The school that emphasizes that land policies should primarily be for achieving growth often asserts that small land holdings are inefficient arrangements (Lipton 2006). Land acquisition for larger projects (both business development and infrastructure) is one of the answers to the problem of small holdings. Another possible solution is consolidation of small holdings through market processes. However, there is evidence to show that disadvantaged groups choose to use land for livelihood rather than to rent their land (World Bank 2007, p. 51).

The school that argues that the purpose of the land is for livelihood has debated the agrarian mode of production for decades (see Patnaik 1991 for a summary of these debates). They conclude that landless and small holding agriculturists were subservient to the large capitalist agrarian producers, and state policies primarily served rich agriculturists. The dominant political voice of the country is primarily from these farmer lobbies, with variant forms of mobilization in different states of India. Thus, political and economic rent is conflated when it comes to land policies. The school that demands adoption of the livelihood frame is seeking space for the historically neglected landless and small farmers who served as laborers in the capitalist farms.

These laboring communities were often neglected when land acquisition for large projects was adopted. Owners received compensation for property, while laborers lost a livelihood. The owners had the capital to reinvest in a new business or to acquire skills. The laboring class had neither. Thus, the livelihood framework argues that policy makers should treat economic and social rights as a single unit rather than separately. As Dreze (2004, p. 1729) points out: "The economic and social rights complement and reinforce each other. Taken in isolation, each of them has its limitations, and may not even be realizable within the present structure of property rights."

The livelihood versus growth debate has muted the environmental value of the land (refer to Leopold's view in the previous section). Unfortunately, in India, the environmental valuation has been restricted to common property resources (refer Chapter "Conflicting Interests and Intelligible Utilisation of Common Property Resources: A Study of a Tropical Wetland in South India" in this volume) and in limited ways in the urban private property holdings. This neglect has resulted in a situation of humanity sitting on a time bomb. The Food and Agricultural Organisation of the United Nations has estimated that 1.5 billion people, a fifth of the world's population, depend on land that is being degraded. Earlier in this chapter, we discussed how the use of technology can exasperate negative land policies if environmental values are neglected. In fact, environmental valuation may be a key to resolving the livelihood versus growth debates in land policies.

8 Rural Shrinkage and Urban Transformation

Mahatma Gandhi celebrated the rural face of India, with his oft-quoted statement —"India lives in her seven and a half lakhs of villages, and the cities live upon the villages" (1921). The majority of the Indian population still lives in rural areas (as per the Census of 2011, it is 68.5%) and more than 60% of the labor force depends on agriculture for their livelihoods. Yet, a much quicker transformation is taking place globally, and particularly in India. According to decadal census, the level of urbanization increased from 27% (in 2001) to 31% in 2011.

Two key aspects of the urban transformation have been discussed in detail in Chapter "The Cyclical Interaction of Institutional Constraints to Formal Affordable Housing Market in Raipur, India" (on the issues of housing and real estate sector) and Chapter "City in Crossfire—The Environment Versus Development Debate in Navi Mumbai" (on the issues of urban infrastructure) of this book. A third issue that is sandwiched between these two issues is that of informality. Informality in the urban environment arises in a variety of ways, including informal housing (slums), informal labor practices, informal planning, and informal care (Davy and Pellissery 2013). Informality is a fusion of traditional values, as emerging from people acquainted with agricultural and rural living, and modern values. Modern urban planning (born in the early twentieth century) is rooted in a modernist-rationalist intellectual tradition. It struggles with an informality born out of a fusion of values. Thus the global explosion of informality, and its particular from in India, poses a serious challenge to the assumptions, theories, and practices of urban planning. From the land-use policy perspective, some of the theoretical positions elaborated in the first part of this chapter, particularly that of Hardin's tragedy of the commons and Hernando DeSoto's solution of property titling, would appear to have particularly relevance to assessing and addressing the informality issue in India today. While these issues—housing, urban infrastructure, and informality—will continue to be great importance for land policy in the near future, it is the creation of urban areas through their expansion into rural areas, first peri-urban areas and then towns, that will assume the greatest significance for land policies into the future.

A city that has grown tremendously in the post-liberalization phase in India is Bangalore; it has become a hub of business around information technology. In 1981 Bangalore had an area of 365 km^2. In 2011, the city expanded to 741 km^2. Seven neighboring city municipal councils, one municipal town and 110 villages were merged into Bangalore in 2007. This pattern is not unique to Bangalore. Across India, villages are being engulfed by the new urban transformation. This urbanization has to be appreciated in the context of declining agricultural productivity, and the eagerness to sell land in villages to buy urban real estate properties, where legal titles are clear and appreciation for land value is quicker. This mode of financialization of urban land, with reference to its rural counterpart makes land a capital accumulation. Compared to the investment in productive capital in rural areas, the investment in urban land is motivated by speculative monetary gains.

This fusion of urban transformation with rural shrinkage creates new tensions in land-use patterns. Since the entrepreneurial class is buying and developing the fringe areas of metropolitan cities, the capital accumulation motifs shape the character of the city. In the context of a weak state of India, with limited institutional caliber to control the social forces (Migdal et al. 1994), the planning process becomes privatized. In the case of Bangalore, the planning laws, that were meant to guide the expansion of city, were hijacked by crony capitalists (Pellissery et al. 2016). As a result, the commons have been systematically destroyed. Bangalore which had 260 lakes in 1960 has had their number reduced to 17 lakes in 2012! Calamities similar to this could be preempted by efficient land-use regulations, effective implementation of existing planning laws, updating of the planning laws as required by the new requirements, and sequencing policy actions such as creating necessary infrastructure for urban growth rather than firefighting once city has grown.

In this context, it is important to take note of some of the major developments that are going to shape the urban character in India in near future. Of particular importance are the industrial corridors being planned in India. The first one of these is the Delhi–Mumbai Industrial Corridor that will stretch 1483 km. Similar projects are being planned connecting the cities of Bangalore–Mumbai, Amritsar–Kolkata, Chennai–Vizhag, and Chennai–Bangalore. The development of industrial corridors has to be juxtaposed with the new investment that government has committed to develop 109 smart cities across India. These smart cities are to have integrated plans for water, electricity, sustainability measures, urban transport, and IT connectivity. In order to be successfully realized these efforts will require new land policies and planning laws.

9 Legal Versus Policy Approaches

A recent national survey (Access to Justice Survey 2015) showed that land and property disputes dominate civil litigation across India. 66% of survey respondents reported land as the subject matter of the cases they are involved in the litigation. These large numbers of cases have to be considered along with a huge backlog of cases. On average, it takes 10 years for disposal of a civil case in India. Thus, very often, the apprehension about possible property disputes becomes a major hurdle for the land market, eventually leading to a halt of business development or any other investment where land is a critical factor. Sometimes, individuals and land developers venture into threat and crime to get property clearance. The Crime Records Bureau of India reports that property disputes are second only to personal vendettas as the reason for murder.

One of the key reasons for disputes on the matter of property right is the vagueness in property titles, particularly in rural areas. Since 1988 the central government has supported a programme to computerize land records (Saxena 2005). Different states of India are at different stages in the implementation of the computerization of land records. While south Indian state such as Tamilnadu, Karnataka, and Andhra Pradesh has achieved significant strides in this direction, most of the North Indian states are lagging. Another step in the direction of bringing clarity was the introduction of Property Titling legislation. However, a comprehensive bill that was prepared in 2010 has been sent to cold storage.

An institutionalized dispute on forest rights exists between traditional forest dwellers (adivasis) and the government forest department. The state forest officials claimed that the State owns natural resources such as forests. On the other hand, adivasis and environmentalists hold a position that through corrupt processes, forest officials destroy forest resources (rent seeking by illegally selling timber and other goods). Adivasis claimed that they lived with forests in a sustainable rather than exploitative manner. Very often this institutionalized dispute has led to a loss of livelihoods and lives of the poor sections of adivasi population. Fines and legal cases that state forest officials imposed on adivasi population created a wall of distrust between people and the state. The overtures of the State Forest Department were a breach of the old "five principles" that the first Prime Minister of India scripted to integrate adivasis with national life (Menon 2008). A major change to this long-standing dispute was brought through a policy reform in 2006 through the Forest Rights Act.

Another arena of conflict in the domain of land is around the issue of land acquisition. The taking of land by the state for official purposes is governed by a legislation that was scripted in 1840. This legislation was made by British colonizers with an aim to advantage the state over land owners. In the post-liberalization scenario (since 1991) as more and more land was required by investors for development, the state became actively engaged in acquiring land to give it to investors. As pointed out earlier, vagueness in property titles has limited the capacity for capitalists to make direct purchase from the landowners. This has led to violent struggles between people whose land was to be taken and state forces (see Chapters "Development or Disaster? Land Acquisition and Dispossession in the Mining Belts and Coastal Zones of Rural Odisha, India" and "The "Public Purpose" That Is Not Inclusive" in this volume).

In the east Indian state of West Bengal, the Communist party that ruled the state for more than three decades lost its power due to people's struggle when the state government attempted to acquire land for a car company—Tata Motors. The subsequent government that came to power, reversed the land acquisition and through legal processes returned the land to farmers. In the East Indian state of Orissa, indigenous communities fought hard to reverse the government's permission for forest clearance (of 664 ha) given to Vedanta, a bauxite mining international company in Niyamgiri. The political route that this struggle took influenced the Ministry of Forest and Environment, before the Supreme Court canceled the forest clearance permissions. Further the Court set a procedure of democratic voting in the communities before any further land acquisition is done. The case brought out how the environmental values (including cultural, social and religious rights) are to be determined by people rather than laws.

The three arenas of land conflicts—leading to crime and violence, conflicts around common property resource of forest, and around land acquisition—are clear instances of archaic laws unable to deal with new dynamic situations. How the state has responded to these situations is through policy initiatives. Policy initiatives require the state to specify a future vision. Legislative frameworks that depended on precedents and individual rights failed to provide solutions for such futuristic visions. However, policy initiatives are an intersection of political mandates and the aspirational nature of the society (Bromley 2006). Chapter "Property Regimes in India: A Study of Political Determinants of Structural Factors" in this volume deals with how different political regimes in different states of India determine these patterns of change.

10 Conclusion

India is undergoing fundamental changes. For example, spatially it is becoming more urban, with much of that urban ever-more informal; economically it is becoming ever-less dependent on agriculture and ever-more affluent; socially it is becoming more educated and grappling with challenges to millennial-long understandings of gender roles. Land and property have always been important within Indian society. As is true for so many other societies, peoples within India traditionally defined their very sense of self and their autonomy via their relationship to land.

For countries and societies in the west, the core relationship of people to land seemed to weaken with the process of urbanization in the twentieth century. As people move to cities, became educated, took up employment in the manufacturing and service sectors, realigned long-standing gender roles, and as government became a more dominant force in public life, land appeared to diminish in importance relative to other factors. Property became, instead of land, "the new property" (Reich 1964). That is there was still an interest in property but it was not about land per se but rather the benefits that one received and was entitled to as a citizen of a modern society (social benefits, health care benefits, educational benefits, etc.).

But as we make clear in this chapter, what appeared to be true in the west has not, from our perspective, been the way social discourse and policy has evolved. Land, as the physical property of the natural world, and property, as the social and legal institutions developed to manage land, have continued to be central for western society. And western societies and societies globally are currently involved in heated debates about exactly how land should be managed and what property should mean, to individuals, families, tribes, communities, and societies.

As true as this is for societies and countries in the west, it is equally true for India. And why this is the case is partially captured in comments by jurist K.K. Mathew. Reflecting sentiments that harken to those of Locke and Rousseau in the seventeenth and eighteenth centuries he noted

> People without property have a tendency to become slaves. They become the property of others as they have no property themselves. They will come to say: "Make us slaves, but feed us." Liberty, independence, self-respect, have their roots in property. To denigrate the institution of property is to shut one's eyes to the stark reality evidenced by the innate instinct and the steady object of pursuit of the vast majority of people. Protection of property. .. may quite fairly be deemed. .. an aspect of freedom. (Mathew 1978, p. 71)

What is needed is both clear headed understanding of the problems faced in formulating and implementing land and property policy in India, and a sense of direction for how solutions to these problems might be developed that are respectful of India's history and its cultural, religious, and geographic diversity. These are significant challenges, but ones we believe can be realized.

References

Access to Justice Survey (2015) Access to justice survey 2015–16. Bangalore, Daksh

Anderson TL, Leal DR (1991) Free market environmentalism. Westview Press, San Francisco

Anderson TL, Libecap GD (2014) Environmental markets: a property rights approach. Cambridge University Press, New York

Appu PS (1996) Land reforms in India: a survey of policy, legislation and implementation. Vikas Publishing House, New Delhi

Bethell T (1998) The noblest triumph: property and prosperity through the ages. St. Martin's Press, New York

Borooah VK, Diwakar D, Mishra VK, Naik AK, Sabharwal NS (2014) Caste, Inequality, and Poverty in India: a re-assessment. Dev Stud Res 1(1):279–294

Bromley DW (2006) Sufficient reason: volitional pragmatism and the meaning of economic institutions. Princeton University Press, Princeton

Chand R, Lakshmi Prasanna PA, Singh A (2011) Farm size and productivity: understanding the strengths of smallholders and improving their livelihoods. Econ Polit Wkly 46(26,27)

Christman J (1994) The myth of property: toward an Egalitarian theory of ownership. Oxford University Press, New York

Coase RH (1960) The problem of social cost. J Law Econ 3:1–44

Davis JE (ed) (2010) The community land trust reader. Lincoln Institute of Land Policy, Cambridge, MA

Davy B (2012) Land policy: planning and the spatial consequences of property. Ashgate, Burlington, VT

Davy B, Pellissery S (2013) The citizenship promise(un)fulfilled: the right to housing in informal settings. Int J Soc Welf 22(S1):S68–S84

De Soto H (2000) The mystery of capital: why capitalism triumphs in the west and fails everywhere else. Basic Books, New York

Dreze J (2004) Democracy and right to food. Econ Polit Wkly (April 24) 1723–1729

Ely JW Jr (1992) The guardian of every other right: a constitutional history of property rights. Oxford University Press, New York
Embree AT (1979) Landholding in India and British Institutions. In: Frykenberg RE (ed) Land control and social structure in Indian history. New Delhi, Manohar, pp 33–52
Frazier TW (1995) The green alternative to classical liberal property theory. Vermont Law Review 20(2):299–371
Freyfogle E (2003) The land we share: private property and the common good. Island Press, Washington, D.C
Geisler CC, Daneker G (eds) (2000) Property and values: alternatives to public and private ownership. Island Press, Washington, D.C
George H (1929 [1879]) Progress and poverty, an inquiry into the cause of industrial depressions and of increase of want with increase of wealth; the remedy. Robert Schalkenbach Foundation, New York
Gilbert A (2002) On the mystery of capital and the myths of Hernando de Soto. Int Dev Plann Rev 24(1):1–24
Goldstein RJ (2004) Ecology and environmental ethics: green wood in the bundle of sticks. Ashgate, Burlington, VT
Gray K (1991) Property in thin air. Camb Law J 50(2):252–307
Haar C (1951) Land planning law in a free society: a study of the british town and country planing act. Harvard University Press, Cambridge, MA
Hardin G (1968) The tragedy of the commons. Science 162(December):1243–1248
Jacobs HM (2010) Social conflict over property rights: the end, a new beginning or a continuing conversation? Hous Policy Debate 20(3):329–349
Jacobs HM (2013) Private property and human rights: a mismatch in the 21st century? Int J Soc Welfare 22(S1):S85–S101
Jacobs HM (2016) Private property in historical and global context and its lessons for planning. In: Smit A, Valiante M (eds) Public interest, private property: law and planning policy in Canada. University of British Columbia Press, Vancouver, BC, pp 37–58
Kropotkin P (1880) La Prochaine revolution. Le Révolté February 7
Krueckeberg DA (1995) The difficult character of property: to whom do things belong? J Am Plan Assoc 61(3):301–309
Large DW (1973) This land is whose land? changing concepts of land as property. Wis Law Rev 1973:1039–1083
Leopold A (1968[1949]) The land ethic. A sand county Almanac. Oxford University Press, New York, pp 201–226
Lipton M (2006) Can small farmers survive, prosper, or be the key channel to cut mass poverty. J Agric Dev Econ 3(1):58–85
Mathew KK (1978) K. K. Mathew on democracy, equality and freedom (Editor: Baxi U). Eastern Book Co., Lucknow
Marx K (1919 [1844]) Zur Judenfrage. Ernst Rowohlt Verlag, Berlin
Mehta PB (2010) The politics of social justice. Available at http://www.cprindia.org/sites/default/files/politics.pdf
Menon TM (2008) Tribal development and governance. In: Narayanan NC (ed) State, natural resource conflicts and challenges to governance. Academic Foundation, New Delhi, pp 145–164
Meyer JM (2009) The concept of private property and the limits of environmental imagination. Polit Theor 37(1):99–127
Migdal J, Kohli A, Shue V (1994) State power and social forces. Cambridge University Press, Cambridge
Moore T, McKee K (2012) Empowering local communities? An international review of community land trusts. Hous Stud 27(2):280–290
Neale WC (1979) Land is to rule. In: Frykenberg RE (ed) Land control and social structure in Indian history. New Delhi, Manohar, pp 3–16
Needham B (2014) Dutch land use planning: planning and managing land use in the Netherlands, the principles and the practice. Ashgate, Burlington, VT

Ostrom E (1990) Governing the commons: the evolution of institutions for collective action. Cambridge University Press, New York

Padel F (2011) Sacrificing people: invasions of a tribal landscape. Orient Blackswan, New Delhi

Patnaik U (1991) Agrarian relations and accumulations: mode of production debate in India. Oxford University Press, Delhi

Pellissery S (2016) Land alienation-infused poverty in India. In: Braathen E, May J, Wright G (eds) Poverty and Inequality in Middle-Income Countries. Zed Books, London

Pellissery S, Sattwick B (2012) Emerging property regimes in India. IRMA Working Paper No. 234

Pellissery S, Chakradhar A, Deepa KS, Lahiri M, Ram NS, Mallick N, Kumar N, Harish P (2016) Regulation in a crony capitalist state. Publ Sect 42(1):111–119

Proudhon P-J (1994 [1840]) What is property: an inquiry into the principle of right and government. Cambridge University Press, Cambridge

Reich C (1964) The new property. Yale Law J 73(5):733–787

Rivera-Ferre MG, Constance DH, Renard M (2014) Convergence and divergence in alternative agrifood movements. In: Alternative agrifood movements: patterns of convergence and divergence. Emerald, Canberra, pp 313–322

Rodrik D (2015) Premature industrialisation. NBER Working Paper 20935

Saxena NC (2005) Updating land records: is computerization sufficient? Econ Polit Wkly 40 (4):313–321

Seuss Dr (1971) The Lorax. Random House, New York

Sinden A (2007) The tragedy of the commons and the myth of a private property solution. Univ Colorado Law Rev 78(2):533–612

Steinberg T (1995) Slide mountain: or the folly of owning nature. University of California Press, Berkeley

Stone C (1972) Should trees have standing: toward legal rights for natural objects. South Calif Law Rev 45(2):450–501

The World Bank (2014) India—accelerating agricultural productivity growth. World Bank Group, Washington, DC

Trautmann T (2012) Arthashastra: the science of wealth. Penguin, New York

Wolf MA (2008) The zoning of America: Euclid v. Ambler. University of Kansas Press, Lawrence, KS

World Bank (2007) India land policies for growth and poverty reduction. World Bank, New Delhi

MIX
Papier aus verantwortungsvollen Quellen
Paper from responsible sources
FSC® C105338

If you have any concerns about our products,
you can contact us on
ProductSafety@springernature.com

In case Publisher is established outside the EU,
the EU authorized representative is:
Springer Nature Customer Service Center GmbH
Europaplatz 3, 69115 Heidelberg, Germany

Printed by Libri Plureos GmbH
in Hamburg, Germany